M000165341

Vladimir Kramnik:
The Inside Story of a Chess Genius

By

Carsten Hensel

Quality Chess
www.qualitychess.co.uk

First English edition 2018 by Quality Chess UK Ltd
Copyright © 2018 Carsten Hensel

VLADIMIR KRAMNIK: THE INSIDE STORY OF A CHESS GENIUS

Hardcover ISBN 978-1-78483-076-2

All sales or enquiries should be directed to Quality Chess UK Ltd,
Suite 247, Central Chambers, 11 Bothwell Street,
Glasgow G2 6LY, United Kingdom
Phone +44 141 204 2073
e-mail: info@qualitychess.co.uk
website: www.qualitychess.co.uk

Distributed in North and South America by National Book Network

Distributed in Rest of the World by Quality Chess UK Ltd through
Sunrise Handicrafts, ul. Szarugi 59, 21-002 Marysin, Poland

Published in German by Verlag Die Werkstatt as
Wladimir Kramnik, Aus dem Leben eines Schachgenies
Translated from German by Ian Adams
Edited by Jacob Aagaard & John Shaw
Typeset by Jacob Aagaard
Proofreading by Colin McNab & Andrew Greet

Cover design by Jason Mathis

Printed in Estonia by Tallinna Raamatutrükikoja LLC

Contents

Appendices

For Birgit and Marie-Laure, who were always there for us!

"The most talented of all the players here is Vladimir Kramnik. All the others are making moves, but Kramnik is playing chess!"

Garry Kasparov, 13th World Chess Champion

Prologue

13th of October 2006, 19:10, Elista, Federal Russian Republic of Kalmykia: the deathly hush in the over-filled playing hall is shattered by an outcry. On move 44 of the decisive fourth tiebreak game, Topalov has blundered and left his rook en prise. Kramnik's posture changes to bolt upright. Miguel Illescas pinches my leg and whispers: "We've done it, that loses!" On move 45 Kramnik places his rook on b7. Check! Topalov stares for a moment at the chess board, shakes his head and resigns. Kramnik's fist leaps upwards in a sign of triumph, just as it did after his epic World Championship victories over Garry Kasparov and Peter Leko. The insane tension I am feeling is released and the otherwise so-restrained spectators turn the auditorium of Kalmykia's government building into a madhouse. Cheering, stamping and staccato applause go on for minutes.

In the Kramnik team we hug each other. I cannot stay in my seat any longer. Vladimir is standing somewhat bemused by the playing table, trying to clip his pen into the inside pocket of his jacket. I rush onto the stage, giving vent to the pressure built up within me in tears of joy, and cannot resist brandishing my fist in the direction of Topalov's team.

This match for the World Chess Championship ended a thirteen-year division within the chess world and was the most dramatic of all time. Aside from the 1972 match between Boris Spassky and Bobby Fischer, no World Championship had ever attracted such powerful interest from the media. This was caused not mainly by the exciting course of the contest, but by "Toiletgate" – nothing less than a scandal.

All this was more than ten years ago.

This book is first and foremost about the person and the chess player, Vladimir Kramnik. Like the squares on the chess board, the stories are grouped into 64 sections, linked to my personal experiences and other events within the chess world, seen from time to time within the context of contemporary history. Kramnik's years as World Champion from 2000 to 2007 are considered the most difficult and conflicted in the history of chess politics. I stood by his side during this time and was perhaps able to some extent to contribute to him remaining on the chess throne for seven years under adverse conditions.

Chess world champions are encircled by legend; they have an aura of myth in the public imagination. In sport this title is considered one of the most important. As heavyweight boxing champions are seen as the greatest fighters, and the 100-metre sprint champion the fastest humans, the chess World Champion is considered to be among the most intelligent people on the planet – and frequently correctly so! In its long and varied history, the royal game has far produced 16 Classical World Champions. All were famous among chess lovers and their playing style influenced their generations.

Much has been written about Vladimir Kramnik. What I can add is an authentic first-hand impression of this extraordinary man and the most important events in his great career. Nobody else was as close to the great matches of the 14th World Chess Champion over such a long period of time. Our friendship began back in the 1990s and stays strong. And in the intense period from 2002 to 2009, I was his professional advisor.

During specific phases of his career, certain circles have tried to portray Kramnik as a boring, self-centred pragmatist. Even Garry Kasparov, his predecessor on the chess throne, joined in this criticism for a while. But those presenting such an image of Kramnik have either no idea of who or what they are talking about, or simply wished to create this image out of self-interest.

Kramnik, a positionally active and very creative player, has played some of the most beautiful games in chess history. And the way he plays chess is how he conducts himself away from the board: sometimes chaotic, sometimes emotional, sometimes brilliant – but consistently authentic. Few, if any, have enriched the development of this magnificent game as much as Vladimir.

We are setting out on a journey through four decades of the life of the 14th World Chess Champion. On the way we will experience many emotional moments and come into contact with the dark side of the chess world.

In 1992 Garry Kasparov won the super-tournament "Dortmund Chess Days", nowadays known as the Sparkassen Chess Meeting. On the floor below, in the public bar of the Westfalenhalle, 17-year old Vladimir Kramnik shared first in the accompanying Dortmund Open. He achieved this in great style, ahead of another 541 participants, including more than 100 international title holders. This success drew the attention of the chess media to the young Russian for the first time.

Garry Kasparov said: "The most talented of all the players here is Vladimir Kramnik. All the others are making moves, but Kramnik is playing chess!"

I had heard of Kramnik the year before, picked up in passing in conversation with the ex-world champion (1948-1963) Mikhail Botvinnik, but it was only at this moment I really paid attention. Vladimir and I got to know each other better and better during the 1990s. After the Dortmund tournament of 1992, Kramnik received invitations to all the top events. He quickly climbed into the top 10 of the world ranking list, a place he would not relinquish until November 2014 (at the time of printing, October 2018, Kramnik is ranked 7th).

In 1993, Kramnik was invited to the top group in Dortmund, a tournament which he won for the first time in 1995 and would go on to win a further nine times in his "Dortmund living room". His ten victories in such a high-level international competition represent a special record in the history of sport.

In the account which follows it is Vladimir Kramnik the man who is to be portrayed, while at the same time priority will be given to what happened during his time as World Chess Champion. It is the first biography to be published since he won the world championship title in a match in 2000 against Garry Kasparov.

Vladimir has contributed to this book quite considerably. My work was made easier by notes I had made during his great matches. Once years have passed, we tend to see things through a particular lens. For that reason, I have tried to present Kramnik's and my views from as close as possible to what was happening at the time. I was helped in this by a dozen folders of material, notes in my weekly planners, as well as interviews and comments made by Kramnik at the time.

At the end of each chapter Vladimir Kramnik himself reviews the most important games played at these key moments in his career. These annotations are not the usual deep analysis of possible variations we see in magazines and tournament chess; rather they describe what the 14th World Champion was feeling at these peaks of his career.

At the end of the book there is a detailed historical record. This includes, amongst others, all Kramnik's world championship games played between 2000 and 2008. There is also information about all previous world champions in the history of classical chess, based to a great extent on the opinions of Vladimir.

It would be a great satisfaction to Vladimir Kramnik and me if this book ignites in any reader of this book an interest in the most splendid of all games, chess. I hope you will read on and patiently study many wonderful games by the 14th World Chess Champion with a smile on your face.

Carsten Hensel
Dortmund, October 2018

Chess Geniuses and the Fine Arts

 1

Every person who really engages to some depth with the game of chess will at some point ponder the questions: What is special about chess? Why is this game so extraordinarily attractive and timeless? And: why won't it let go of me?

One person sees chess as a sport and is fulfilled by victory alone. Another prioritizes the analytical/scientific side of the game. A third loves the beauty and the sometimes unfathomable depths which can be found in the games played at the highest level. A considerable number of chess lovers are fascinated by the psychological side to the game. They examine how the great masters' play revealed their character. Quite a few see the game as a war between opposing armies and feel like generals during their games. While yet others define the strategic boardgame as the way an individual expresses their creativity, that is to say, chess as an artform. And then there is the large group of collectors whose interest lies in chess books, chess sets or even postage stamps with chess motifs.

It is in this variety we find the key to the success of chess. For those who have had only slight contact with chess, let me quote Stefan Zweig. Shortly before his suicide in 1942 the Austrian novelist wrote his final and most famous work, *The Royal Game* (*Schachnovelle* in German, English translation below by Nicholas Stephens, who used the less common title *Chess Story*). I consider these to be the most suitable words about the attraction of chess:

"I had not in my life so far had the opportunity of making the personal acquaintance of a chess master, and the more I tried to visualize the type, the more inconceivable a lifetime's mental activity purely centred on 64 black and white squares became. I well knew from my own experience the mysterious allure of the 'royal game' which, alone among the games devised by man, stands above the tyrannical vicissitudes of luck and awards its victory laurels solely on the basis of intellect, or rather a specific kind of intellectual endowment. But isn't one guilty of insultingly diminishing chess by even calling it a game? Isn't it also a science, an art form, floating between those categories as the coffin of Mohammed betwixt heaven and earth, a one-off union of all opposing forces; ancient and yet forever new, technical in its layout and yet only operable through

imagination, limited by a geometrically rigid space yet unlimited in its combinations, constantly evolving and yet lifeless, cogitation that leads to nothing, art without display, architecture without bricks and despite this, proven in its very being and existence to be more durable than all books and academic works; it is the only game that belongs to all races and all time, and nobody may know which heavenly power gave it to the world to slay boredom, sharpen the senses and capture the soul. Where is its beginning and where its end? Every child can grasp its basic principles, every dilettante can dabble at it, and yet it is capable within its fixed, tight square of producing a special species of master, bearing no comparison to others, people with a talent solely directed to chess, idiosyncratic geniuses in whom just as precise a proportion of vision, patience and technique is required as in a mathematician, a poet or a musician, merely in a different formula and combination."

Vladimir Borisovich Kramnik is such a genius, equipped with exceptional gifts of potential and talent. He has often been underestimated, including during his reign as world champion. Principally and deliberately by people who feared him because of his strength and wanted to do him harm. But those grandmasters who come to an objective assessment of his play and abilities count him among the most innovative and strongest champions of all time.

When that judgement is made, the modest Russian's indubitably great sporting successes are not always in the foreground. The focus when he is judging his own play is much more on the depth and beauty of the process itself. Hardly anyone before him played so many of the deepest and most beautiful games of all time. Kramnik's primary motivating force for playing chess is the creativity, the art which can arise from the game. As a rule, those who come to the game from this standpoint are not very successful. They may prefer to focus on creating chess studies, but are ineffective in competitive play.

Of course, Vladimir Kramnik is first and foremost a professional chess player. In his major duels he often, despite his nature being less results-driven, had to play unconditionally for a win. Whenever he had to do so, he was a powerful fighter. But in principle Vladimir's motivation is different. For him chess is not a sport first and foremost. It is not without reason his public image is of a bohemian and an artist.

This means that he does not always display the highest level of energy when playing. At least compared to such world champions as Bobby Fischer or Garry Kasparov. Vladimir also feels no need to market himself to the public. He is principled in what he does and expects this to help with the business in hand: the never-ending search for truth and beauty while playing chess.

Kramnik, for whom integrity and loyalty are the most important characteristics, does have a goodly portion of emotions; something one might not believe of the friendly and at first sight introverted-looking Russian. For him there have been only a few exceptional occasions, when his victories and the financial gain have been important. Fundamentally, he was always focused on immersing himself in the game.

Precisely because Kramnik was playing less for results, his great sporting achievements, with three successful world championships as the highlights, cannot be assessed highly enough. As far as his chess-playing abilities are concerned, he need not fear comparison with the other world champions.

Many top grandmasters who has trained with Vladimir Kramnik have been impressed and were all in agreement that none of them were able to "extract" as much out of a position as Kramnik. Peter Svidler, eight times Russian Champion, who was a second in Kramnik's team for the 2004 world championship against Leko, said: "The amount he can see in a position on the board is incredible. Sometimes too much. In specific situations in a match that can even be a disadvantage."

This unique ability, his pronounced feeling for the nuances of a chess position, has enabled Kramnik to make a considerable contribution to the theoretical development of numerous opening systems. During his career he has been a trendsetter. Professional players still follow his path in many opening systems, such as the Berlin Defence, the Catalan, the Sveshnikov Variation, the Semi-Slav and the Petroff Defence.

This "theft" could appear unfair to laypeople, but it is a part of the game. Those who contribute to the development of the game go down in history. No player has been more productive and innovative in the development of chess theory than Vladimir Kramnik.

When asked in 2004 whether he was a genius, Kramnik's answer to the German news magazine Der Spiegel was: "I am quite talented. Sometimes I think I have understood a position, but two years later I realize that I had not understood anything at all. That is what is mysterious about chess. Really fascinating. You have a small board with 64 squares, but things are sometimes so deep that not even ten Kramniks can know which move is best. Then you simply feel lost. You feel that things are so deep that there is absolutely no bottom which can be reached."

♔2

Vladimir Kramnik is well aware that failure is guaranteed in the eternal search for truth in chess. He can only try to plunge in so as to get somewhat closer to the "bottom". To paraphrase Confucius, he will follow this path throughout his life. This is his passion and his goal; it spurs him on and satisfies him at the same time.

Vladimir expressed it as follows: "Whenever I start to understand the incredible depth of a game of chess, I realize that some rules become blurred. I suddenly feel that I need to create a bit more space here and to attack there. But I do not really know why that is so. Play following the manuals is only enough to reach a certain level. Perhaps as far as international master, but not grandmaster. At that level you have to have a feeling for the game. It comes to you."

For Kramnik chess is a complex business. Everything has a part to play. This includes emotions. If he feels in harmony, then he is in a creative mood. If something is disturbing him or for some reason he is in a bad mood, it is difficult for him to be creative: this is his sensitive side, which can be a target for his opponents.

For a long time he managed to hide his emotions. However, nothing was further from reality than the image attributed to him for years as the "iceman" or the "rock". Some of his rivals eventually discovered Kramnik's very sensitive nature. At some of the world championship matches, attempts were made to take advantage of this side of his personality, to knock him off balance. This was quite effective as his sporting biography will show.

In an interview with Ugo Dossi, the famous German painter and object artist, he made very clear how he sees chess, what creativity, beauty and depth mean to him. During the conversation Kramnik gave convincing reasons why for him chess is first and foremost an art. Every great player has his style, just as every painter does. He was convinced that chess reflects the character of the player. If something like chess, music or painting defines the essence of an artist, then at the same time it defines the playing style of the person.

Kramnik said: "Take Kasparov as an example. He is like a tsunami, who keeps surging forward and tries to drown his opponent. My way is a different one and also different from that of Anand or of Karpov and cannot be compared to them either. An impatient person may start an attack which has not been thought through down to the most insignificant detail. But from a certain level upwards, it is really possible to recognize the personality of a player in the choices he makes. I see that as being similar to art."

Whenever Vladimir begins to speak about the beauty of the game his eyes light up. Of course, according to Kramnik, beauty is subjective. It can, for example, be found in very technical, mathematical play. That is the beauty of clarity. Beauty can equally well be found in precision. Neither fireworks nor brilliant imagination is required. And then there would be those games which are technically not perfect, but contain imagination which is full of beauty. Kramnik said: "I believe that every chess player feels the beauty when he acts against all rules and expectations and yet is master of the situation."

There are heaps of examples for Kramnik's thesis. Let's mention his blindfold game against Topalov in Monaco in 2003. When I collected him after the game, he was moved and kept on murmuring: "Such beauty, incredible beauty." The Indian superstar Viswanathan Anand felt exactly the same. Impressed, he sincerely congratulated: "Vladimir, you created a masterpiece."

This game saw the unfolding of a series of moves which were extraordinary, amazing and unorthodox. For example, in the middlegame the world champion's king wandered up the board; something which rarely happens. But in this situation the manoeuvre worked perfectly, and the king penetrated deep into the opponent's defences. Seen from a military point of view, it was as though the general was marching in the front rank against the foe with a levelled bayonet. Kramnik sacrificed, Topalov won material, and the threat from this attack could not yet be clearly seen. Nevertheless, in only two moves the attack developed its full force. Kramnik: "There was no way for him to stop it. He had the material, the space and the time, but was unable to defend himself any longer. It was an incredible situation on the board, unexpected and full of beauty."

Whenever beauty is concerned, in chess you are also dependent on your opponent, on his playing strength, precision and creativity. According to Kramnik, sometimes a game takes an unexpected course and beauty starts to arise. Therefore chess tolerates comparison to the art of dance. Playing against someone who is much weaker than oneself is unsatisfactory. One's own strength can only develop when faced with a strong opponent.

The following statement also reveals a great respect for his rivals and their performances. This recognition is a prominent character trait of the 14th World Chess Champion. It may be in stark contradiction to the way of thinking of the majority of other elite grandmasters, whose principal aim is to win. But Vladimir believes that all of them, consciously or subconsciously, would like to create beauty at the board. "I respect every top player. Each one of them resembles a universe. His whole personality, his charisma and the many years of concentrated preparation influence his play. His way of looking at the world, how he sees chess, all that comes together in his style. My style is my style, but millions of others can exist alongside it, all leading to the same result."

Kramnik goes further by including the spectators: "It is hard to put into words. Every single game is surrounded by a specific aura: the more important the game, the greater the tension and the stronger this aura. I remember my world championship match against Garry Kasparov. The decisive phase was dominated by enormous tension. In Russia we say: you could cut the atmosphere with a knife. There was not a sound, no loud breathing, no coughing. I had the same experience in the 14th (and final) game in the match against Leko, or in the tiebreak against Topalov. Normally I am so deeply immersed in these games that I do not notice anything else. But at those moments, when I relaxed slightly, I physically felt this hush. We were in a large playing hall and I felt this enormous tension everywhere, including and especially among the spectators. It was tangible. Something like that always happens when people are deeply moved. Even with hindsight, I can never say exactly when this aura was strongest during a game, but my people describe to me the same phenomenon: at such and such a moment you produced incredible tension. Precisely these moments represent for me a strong motivation to give my all. That does not always work. But when it does, then I create real beauty!"

So chess is definitely not war for Kramnik. What concerns him during play is the creation of beautiful and intense situations within the micro-structure of the game. The idea that two armies are facing each other on the board would probably tend to disturb him during a game. He is aware of the drama of the individual pieces before and after games, but never during play itself.

 3

Vladimir's style is linked to enjoying the game. He likes to play beautiful chess. For him beauty comes to life more in the depth of the process and less in some extraordinary event: "As a child I would have liked to become a painter and later I integrated this desire into my play. I like to be creative. In this way I can penetrate more deeply than usual into the subtleties of a position."

The public is another important factor for Kramnik. When hundreds of people stream into the playing hall and millions of chess fans follow his games on the internet, that is a great source of satisfaction. However, not all chess lovers can see all the nuances of the game. When we talk about depth and understanding, the analysis provided by a chess engine is often of little help. Kramnik does not find this so tragic: "The more people there are at a concert by a musician, the more intense the effect the performance will be on each individual. Whenever I am at a concert, I know that I can only reach a certain depth in my listening to the music. But feeling that perfection is to be found at a greater depth than my subjective experience has always fascinated me."

Vladimir Kramnik's favourite colour is blue, and he is particularly fond of desserts. He likes double espressos, from time to time a good glass of red wine, and also after particularly great efforts sometimes a small glass of single malt Scotch whisky. He can no longer tolerate much alcohol since in 2005 he was diagnosed with a rheumatic illness, which is chronic and demands almost total abstinence.

Kramnik is a lover of literature. His favourite works include *Siddharta* by Hermann Hesse, whose work he has discovered in recent years, *The Master and Margarita* by Mikhail Bulgakov, *Animal Farm* by George Orwell, and *Generation P* by Viktor Pelevin. He likes the movies directed by Stanley Kubrick and Miloš Forman, although in general he prefers reading. His favourite actors are Robert De Niro and Inna Churikova.

His musical interests are universal, though he is turning more and more to classical music. His favourite composer is Johann Sebastian Bach. Vladimir is good friends with several virtuosi, including Vadim Repin, about whom Yehudi Menuhin once said: "He is simply the best and most perfect violinist that I have ever had the privilege of listening to." In painting he feels an affinity to impressionism and loves the works of the Italian painter Amedeo Clemente Modigliani.

Karpov's Best Games was the chess book which had the greatest influence on him as a child. For one simple reason: in the Soviet Union it was for a long time the only chess book which was available to him. As for his favourite players, he names them in chronological order: Emanuel Lasker, Alexander Alekhine, Bobby Fischer and Garry Kasparov.

What Kramnik considers as the most important character trait in a person is integrity. Vladimir Kramnik is married to Marie-Laure Kramnik, née Germon. He got to know the former journalist at the major Paris newspaper *Le Figaro* during an interview in 2003. Marie-Laure and Vladimir married in 2007 in the Russian Orthodox church in Paris and are proud parents of two children: Daria and Vadim. The family lives in Geneva, Switzerland.

Vladimir Kramnik – Veselin Topalov

Monaco (blindfold) 2003

1.e4 c5 2.♘f3 e6 3.d4 cxd4 4.♘xd4 ♘c6 5.♘c3 d6 6.♗e3 ♘f6 7.f4 a6 8.♕f3 ♕c7 9.0–0–0 ♗d7 10.♘b3 ♖c8 11.♔b1 b5 12.♗d3 ♘b4 13.g4 ♗c6 14.g5 ♘d7 15.♕f2 g6

16.♖hf1 ♗g7 17.f5 ♘e5 18.♗b6 ♕d7 19.♗e2 ♕b7 20.♘a5 ♕b8 21.f6 ♗f8 22.a3

22...♘xc2 23.♔xc2 ♗xe4† 24.♔b3 ♗a8 25.♗a7 ♕c7 26.♕b6 ♕xb6 27.♗xb6 h6 28.♘xb5! ♔d7 29.♗d4 ♗d5† 30.♔a4 axb5† 31.♗xb5† ♗c6 32.♗xe5! ♗xb5† 33.♔xb5 ♖c5† 34.♔b6 ♖xe5 35.♖c1 ♖xa5

36.♖c7†! ♔d8 37.♖fc1 ♖c5 38.♖1xc5 dxc5 39.♔c6!! ♗d6 40.♔xd6 e5 41.♖a7 ♔c8 42.♖a8† ♔b7 43.♖xh8 1–0

Vladimir Kramnik:

"I very much like this game. The reader should know that we were playing blindfold and in rapid chess mode. Each player had only 25 minutes plus ten seconds increment per move for the entire game. That of course makes it much more difficult to calculate variations.

At that time Topalov played only the Sicilian against 1.e4 and was very successful with it. I had the initiative coming out of the opening, but in these sorts of positions it is easy to make bad decisions, not only in a blindfold game but also in classical chess. The first important moment was Topalov's knight sacrifice 22...♘xc2.

After 23.♔xc2 and 23...♗xe4† my king was vulnerable. Objectively White should have been better, but in fact the position is not so simple.

Black had a strong knight on e5, which was controlling the centre. He was wanting to activate his rook on the h-file. There was no direct way for White, and Black had potentially dangerous counterplay. I exchanged the queens, after which he played ...h6 in order to activate his rook. If he had succeeded in doing so, the position would have been very unclear. So I took on b5, a decision which I had calculated seriously during the game – as far as was possible in the short time available and with the fact we were playing blindfold. In doing so, I returned the extra material, however in return I got the initiative. After that we played interesting and strong moves: play on both sides was high-class.

Topalov began with the strong 28...♔d7, after which the game became unbelievably fierce.

After 29. ♗d4 ♗d5† I had to flee with my king to a4, the best defence. Topalov played 31...♗c6, a natural move, but would have done better to play 31...♘c6. Okay, White would still retain an advantage, but Black would have had considerably better chances to hold the game. And now I began to penetrate into his camp with my king: a quite astonishing motif. I was not able to calculate everything, but I felt that it would work. We were still in the middlegame and it is very rare for such a thing to happen in this phase of the game.

My king pushed forward onto the seventh and eighth ranks and in that way supported the attack.

35.♖c1 was a significant resource. Everything worked for White, simply springing from a single movement and with the advantage of a tempo. On move 36 it was very important not to recapture, but to play 36.♖c7†. That was something I had to see in advance, which I did. After 37.♖fc1 there were two nice motifs:

17

After 37...♖a8 I would have had 38.♔b7, which I like a lot. The king would have lured the rook into a trap; really outlandish and extraordinary business. But he played 37...♖c5, probably thinking that he could hold on to the piece.

But after 38.♖1xc5 dxc5 was played, the moment arrived when I really felt the beauty of it all and saw everything. My heart began to throb, to beat faster. It was so beautiful, so extraordinary that at first I could hardly believe it. I had only a little time on the clock, but it worked on account of the very accurate move 39.♔c6, with which I threatened mate in two.

It was madness, he was a piece up, my king was exposed, but there was nothing he could do against this threat.

It is always nice to win a game, however in this case the feeling was simply wonderful, as it is based on a study-like motif. When I later checked the game on the computer, I was surprised at how high a level we had both played. In rapid and blindfold chess it is often the case that one side bluffs. We had overlooked nothing, nor had we made any big blunders. And yet the outcome was like this. That shows how beautiful chess can be. From one moment everything flowed logically. If I had not had the resource of 35.♖c1, the pendulum would probably have swung in his favour. This inconspicuous move turned things around and made everything I had done before correct and good. At the end I had the feeling that I had created a symphony. Had there not been this finish, the whole picture would have remained incomplete and the symphony would have collapsed like a house of cards. That is the feeling one has on the completion of a masterpiece, and I was very happy."

The Pride of a Whole City

4

In 1975, the year Vladimir Kramnik was born, a very special event was to take place in Manila. The Filipinos really loosened the purse strings to persuade Robert James Fischer to defend his world championship title. Three years previously he had won it in Reykjavik in a legendary match against Boris Spassky, and in doing so had become the 11th World Chess Champion. The Marcos regime had guaranteed five million dollars sponsorship for this match. To this day, this (for chess) incredible prize fund has never been topped. The eccentric American, however, chose not to defend his title, even though most of his demands had been accepted by the world federation, FIDE. They thus named his challenger Anatoly Karpov the 12th World Champion by walkover. The decision was announced on the 3rd of April 1975 to the regret of millions of chess fans.

People's disappointment was understandable. Especially within the then Soviet Union the world championship match between Fischer and Karpov was awaited with feverish anticipation. In the middle of the Cold War there was total confidence that Karpov would be able to wipe out the shame that they had suffered. Whether, however, he would have had a different fate from that of Boris Spassky must remain a matter for speculation. Vladimir Kramnik sees things as follows: "It seems to me that Fischer would have had the better chances. However, he was a lone wolf working without a team. Preparing problems for him in the opening would have been Karpov's only chance."

Barely half a year later, nevertheless, the Philippines experienced a moment in the history of sport which has never been forgotten. Ferdinand Marcos and his regime absolutely wanted to move onto the world stage. Their efforts to get the chess world championship had failed because of Bobby Fischer, but then they got the nod for the match for the heavyweight boxing crown. On the 1st of October 1975 Muhammad Ali and Joe Frazier stood toe to toe in the "Thrilla in Manila". This was the third match between the two rivals and is today considered to be the hardest and possibly best boxing match of all time. So hard that Ali's doctor Ferdie Pacheco thought that in that humid hall both contestants were in mortal danger.

Besides this there was a lack of great international sporting events in 1975. Odd years, where there is no Olympic Games or football World Cups rarely go down in the annals of sport history. Even in world politics things were peaceful. West and East had long since adapted to the conditions of the Cold War. The Ostverträge (treaties regulating affairs between West Germany, East Germany and the Soviet Union), the Conference on Security and Cooperation in Europe process which produced the Helsinki Accords in 1975, and even the official end of the Vietnam War were the first signs of détente.

5

So when Vladimir Kramnik first saw the light of day, Bobby Fischer's great chess career was practically over. Born on the 25th of June 1975, he came from an artistic family from Tuapse – a sleepy little town on the Black Sea in the south of Russia. His father, Boris Petrovich, once a professor of art at the renowned Ukrainian University of Lviv, was working as a painter and sculptor. His mother, Irina Fedorovna, was a music teacher. His brother Yevgeny is today a successful businessman in the region of Krasnodar.

As far as conditions in the Soviet Union were concerned, the family of four were doing well. The father had a decent income and as an artist he was well thought of in the Soviet Union. The Kramniks were even allotted their own flat. At that time this was an extraordinary privilege, even if the two-room flat measured only 30 square metres. The parents shared one room, Yevgeny and Vladimir the other. There was a small toilet, a tiny kitchen and a balcony.

Vladimir made the most of the conditions. Already as a young boy he was quite creative in this respect. He often nested on the little balcony and was at peace there. Somehow his father had managed to separate a small corner and made it wind- and weather-proof. He often studied in his father's studio, in the middle of a bundle of Lenin sculptures, which were especially useful as nutcrackers.

Vladimir Kramnik has the star sign of Cancer and as such is traditionally considered to be endowed with sensitivity, as well as the capacity for great joy and love, as well as deep suffering. Male Cancers are supposed to be faithful, loyal and tougher than one might think. If such a man feels misunderstood and aggrieved, he can react emotionally. If he creeps into his shell, it is said to be difficult to extract him. Understandably these generalizations are not to everyone's taste. But it is amazing how accurate these descriptions are of Kramnik.

When Vladimir was four years old, his parents taught him to play chess. Then they quite deliberately left him alone with the board and pieces. Something about the game was magical to him and he required no further instruction. His interest had been awakened once and for all and Kramnik progressed quickly, as is usual for young children. At home he showed pleasure and persistence with the game and a natural feeling for the way the pieces work on the board. So, at age five he joined the chess section of the local pioneer palace.

Vladimir's example demonstrates how the former USSR encouraged talent. Children who enjoyed and showed abilities in a discipline in their early years found structures with people in charge and trainers responsible for their further development.

Vladimir Kramnik's talent for chess was of course recognizable at an early age. He developed at enormous speed. As a seven-year-old he was a first category player. And at eight, the dark-haired boy won the 1984 championship of Tuapse with the fabulous score of nine points from nine games. He never again managed a 100% score and to this day Kramnik says with a smile that this performance was the best result in his career.

Chess was the national sport in the former Soviet Union and played in almost every household. In a town with 60,000 inhabitants, winning the championship at eight – ahead of all the local stars – with a perfect score leaves one speechless even today. The news went round the little town like a shockwave. From then on, the child prodigy Vladimir Kramnik was a local celebrity and the inhabitants of Tuapse showed great pride in their young genius.

At this time the already tall boy (later he would grow to be a proud 1.95 metres) had above all not made many incursions into chess theory. In a few common systems he knew only the first five to eight moves. Nevertheless, his feeling for the positions allowed him to emerge from the opening well-developed. In Vladimir's small hands, the pieces worked well together.

Now and then clear plans could be seen in his games. These early-developed abilities were recognized by some experts in the area, even before his first success against a grandmaster, which however followed shortly. At the age of ten Kramnik defeated, to his opponent's consternation, local Grandmaster Alexander Panchenko, in a simultaneous exhibition.

The astonishment was followed by support. Vladimir was provided with access to two leading trainers, the International Masters Orest Averkin (who helped Spassky prepare for the match against Fischer in 1972) and Alexei Ossachuk. At the age of eleven Kramnik, a candidate master, was one of the leading players in the Krasnodar region, the home of more than five million people.

In 1986, still aged ten, he defeated Vadim Zaitsev, his first win over an International Master in a tournament game. Such a feat was rare for young players in Soviet chess, although wins against high-level opponents would no longer be uncommon for Vladimir.

6

Despite all the help from legendary trainers, the most important person for the development of Vladimir's talent up till his twelfth year was his father. But then it came to the point where Tuapse had played its part in nurturing his talent. The fact that Vladimir was able to progress without any delay was due to chance. Kramnik's father was working on a mural in the local post office building and got into conversation with the chief postmaster, Zahar Avetisian. They had a long conversation about Vladimir.

As the chief postmaster, Avetisian had access to all the telephone numbers in the country. Without Kramnik's father knowing about it, Avetisian called Mikhail Botvinnik in Moscow. The ex-world champion was a Soviet institution and ran the famous Botvinnik chess school, providing elite support for the biggest talents in the Soviet Union. Botvinnik and his colleagues received countless enquiries on a daily basis, but only the very best of the best got a chance. Avetisian, a passionate chess fan, must have been very convincing. It was agreed that he should send some of Kramnik's games to Botvinnik.

Botvinnik immediately recognized the unique potential of the young Kramnik. So, a few weeks after the call by the chief postmaster, an invitation from Moscow reached the family to six weeks of probationary training. Volodja or Vlad, as his friends called him, passed the test and was accepted into the Botvinnik chess school at the age of twelve in 1987.

There is no doubt that these events of 1987 were of decisive importance for the course of his future career. Still, when he thinks back to it with the reflection of having children of his own, Vladimir has mixed feelings: "It is nice to receive acknowledgement so early on and tremendously motivating. But I did not have a normal childhood. It was all about chess. I had no time for other things, like simply playing, as is normal for children. Every day I trained or studied for several hours. When there was no training I was travelling from tournament to tournament."

I met Mikhail Botvinnik at breakfast at the start of 1992 in Reggio Emilia, Italy. He was interested that we wanted to develop Dortmund Chess Days into a world-level tournament. We spoke a little about his chess school. Botvinnik, who well into the 1980s was still teaching his pupils himself, was very chatty about this subject. Of his protégés, he described Kramnik as the most talented. It was the first time that I had heard this name. Thereafter Jürgen Grastat, the then Dortmund tournament director, invited Kramnik to the A-Open in Dortmund Chess Days 1992. It was one of the strongest open tournaments of all time, and to everyone's surprise Kramnik shared first place.

At this time Botvinnik already had serious problems with his eyesight and hearing. He seemed to me a very modest man, who at the same time was keen for knowledge and in our half-hour's conversation he asked many questions. I never met him again; Mikhail Botvinnik died on the 5th of May 1995 in Moscow.

After the tournament in Reggio Emilia we hung out with the 23-year-old Indian super-grandmaster Viswanathan Anand, who was celebrating his overall victory. Anand was unmarried then and accompanied by Albert Toby, who supported him in many matters. In those days, things in professional chess were still casual and personal.

Jürgen Grastat and I went on to visit a discotheque in the centre of Reggio Emilia. Suddenly, the door was flung open and the dancefloor cleared by bodyguards. Grace Jones appeared in a furry outfit. The singer and actress was then at the peak of her career. She did two or three solo dances. Soon she no longer attracted much attention and left, visibly offended. The young Italians were allowed to continue dancing.

Earlier, in 1987, Vladimir had delivered further proof of his talent. At the age of eleven he won the U16 Championship of the USSR, held in Baku in Azerbaijan. In the penultimate round against Sergej Shilov, he found himself in a "must-win situation" and solved the problem brilliantly. His victory with Black came about through an impressive queen sacrifice. Even as a child Kramnik was able, in the decisive moments of a competition, to summon all his strength and deliver on command. He repeatedly deployed this strength in his career, which even allowed him to twice defend the world championship title, despite being up against the wall.

In 1989 one of his first trips abroad took him to Aguadilla (Puerto Rico) for the U14 World Championship. Kramnik took second place, behind Veselin Topalov.

At only 15 Kramnik was part of a four-way tie for first place in the 1990 Russian Championship in Kuybyshev. It was the year during which the present world champion, Magnus Carlsen from Norway, first saw the light of day. In 1991 Vladimir shared first place in a tournament for young Soviet masters in Kherson. In the same year he won the U18 World Championship in Guarapuava in Brazil with nine points out of eleven games. With seven wins and four draws he remained undefeated.

From the point of view of the chess world, the first years of Kramnik's life were dominated by the great world championship matches between Karpov and Kasparov, who fought out five great duels between 1984 and 1990.

7

In 1991 Kramnik was only 16 years old and at this extremely early age for a professional chess player, he was already on the brink of an international breakthrough. This year I first met the world champion Garry Kasparov, his predecessor Anatoly Karpov, and the three Polgar sisters and their lively father at the CEBIT (computer expo) in Hanover. The same year I experienced my first truly great chess event. The Candidates matches were organized in the Radisson SAS in Brussels by SWIFT manager Bessel Kok. There I witnessed the immortal game where Artur Yusupov, a world-class player who at that time was representing Russia, defeated Vassily Ivanchuk (Ukraine) with the black pieces. I also met Dr Helmut Pfleger, a grandmaster and well-known TV presenter, and many other leading lights of the chess scene.

While we in Brussels were occupied with the organization of a press conference, at the same time in Kramnik's then hometown of Moscow, a putsch against Mikhail Gorbachev took place. In August 1991 tanks appeared in Red Square. The coup by several powerful functionaries of the Communist Party failed after a few days, and sounded the rapidly-approaching end of the Soviet Union. On the 25th December 1991, Gorbachev resigned and the USSR was dissolved. Its legal successor was the Russian Federation, led by Boris Yeltsin.

To convey the situation in Russia at the start of the 1990s, the history of the aforementioned grandmaster Artur Yusupov may be an extreme but appropriate example. The Iron Curtain had fallen. In the West we were euphoric at having survived the Cold War. But the bill was paid by the people in the East, especially Russia. The collapse of the powerful Soviet monopoly that had been the Russian state could be felt in the capital on a day-to-day basis. Consequently, might was now the only right. State protection from criminal wheeling and dealing was practically non-existent.

Everyone was reliant on his own resources. During this period I travelled several times to Moscow. Without help from locals, this was a dangerous undertaking. Alexander Bakh, then director of the Russian Chess Federation, conscientiously looked after my safety, since people from the West with US dollars or German marks in their pockets were in mortal danger. During my visits, two businesspeople lost their lives in muggings in front of the Belgrad and Cosmos hotels.

At that time there was a ring at the door of the flat of Artur Yusupov. He had just returned from a tournament in Munich with prizemoney in his pocket. When he opened the door, young men were displaying police identification. Then they produced knives and a pistol. They stormed past Artur into the flat. He was shot in the stomach and tied up. His prizemoney, 50% of which he was due to hand over to the sports committee, was lying on the kitchen table. They took it and also several pieces of electronic equipment. Artur's wound was life-threatening and he was simply left lying on the floor. The culprits were never caught. Fortunately, this great player and human being survived. After his recovery he emigrated to Germany, where he could feel safe. He was not the only one to emigrate. More than 20 grandmasters from the former Soviet Union played in the German Chess Bundesliga in the 1991/92 season.

Alexander Licew – Vladimir Kramnik

Tuapse 1985

1.e4 c5 2.♘f3 e6 3.d4 cxd4 4.♘xd4 ♘c6 5.♗e2 ♘f6 6.♘c3 d6 7.♗e3 ♗e7
8.0–0 0–0 9.♕d2 a6 10.f4 ♕c7 11.a4 ♖d8 12.♔h1 ♘a5 13.g4 ♘c4 14.♕c1 ♘xe3
15.♕xe3 ♕c5 16.g5 ♘e8 17.♕d2 ♕b4 18.♘b3

18...d5 19.e5 d4 20.♘e4 ♕xd2 21.♘bxd2 ♗d7 22.♗d3 ♗c6 23.♔g1 ♘c7 24.♘b3
b6 25.♖f3 ♖ac8 26.♖h3

26...♘d5 27.♖h4 ♘b4 28.♘bd2 ♘xd3 29.cxd3 ♗d5 30.♖b1 ♖c2 31.b3 ♗b4
32.♘c4 ♗xe4 33.dxe4 d3 34.♔f1 ♖d4 35.♖h3 d2 36.♖d1 ♖xe4 37.♘e3 ♖c3
38.♔e2 ♗c5 0–1

Vladimir Kramnik:

*"I played this game when I was nine years old. My opponent set about things rather naively,
but of course you have to consider that we were still children. I find that for my age I played
quite well: a logical plan with control of the centre. Naturally White did not play perfectly,
but in a positional sense my play was rather accurate.*

*This is the first presentation of my chess style. It is classical. A player's style never really
changes. The fact is that for more or less the whole of your life you play the way you did
when you were ten years old. The games which I am showcasing in this chapter represent my
trademark active positional style. I play in a classical way, yet rather actively. I do not defend
too much, but my attacks are based on a solid positional foundation."*

Handszar Odeev – Vladimir Kramnik

USSR U18 Championship, Ukraine 1988

1.e4 c5 2.♘f3 e6 3.b3 ♘c6 4.♗b5 ♘f6 5.e5 ♘d5 6.0–0 ♗e7 7.c4 ♘c7 8.♗xc6 bxc6 9.d4 cxd4 10.♕xd4 c5 11.♕g4 0–0 12.♘c3 f6 13.♗f4 ♗b7 14.♕g3 ♘e8 15.♘e1 fxe5 16.♗xe5 d6 17.♗f4

17...♗f6 18.♖c1 ♗h4 19.♕h3 ♖xf4 20.g3 ♖d4 21.♕xe6† ♔h8 22.♘c2 ♖d3 23.♘e1 ♖d4 24.♘c2 ♖d2 25.gxh4 ♕xh4 26.♕e3 ♘f6 27.♕g3 ♕xg3† 28.hxg3 ♘e4 29.♘b1 ♖e2 30.♖fe1

30...♘xg3 31.♘c3 ♖xe1† 32.♖xe1 ♘f5 33.♘e3 ♘d4 34.♔f1 ♖e8 35.♘b5 ♘xb5 36.cxb5 ♗f3 37.♘c4 ♗g2† 38.♔xg2 ♖xe1 39.♘xd6 ♖a1 40.a4 ♖a3 41.♘c8 ♖xb3 42.♘xa7 c4 43.♔f1 c3 44.♔e2 h5 0–1

Vladimir Kramnik:

"This was my first appearance in a tournament at national level and thus the first major youth tournament in my life. The Soviet U18 Championship was the strongest youth tournament in the Soviet Union, and at that time also the world. All the up-and-coming stars were in the starting blocks: Gata Kamsky, Alexei Shirov and Peter Svidler, to name but a few. A total of 60 players took part and on average they were four to five years older than me. I was just twelve years old, but nevertheless took an outstanding fifth place. It was my first big success. After it, everybody in Russia knew that there was a talented player from the depths of the Russian provinces.

My 16-year-old opponent, Handszar Odeev, was one of the best juniors of the day. The game is another good example of my style: active, positional and for the age, quite accurate play. I had the bishop pair and was able to outplay him. In the endgame I displayed quite decent technique."

Vladimir Kramnik – Sergei Germanavicius

USSR U18 Championship, Pinsk 1989

1.e4 c5 2.♘f3 d6 3.d4 cxd4 4.♘xd4 ♘f6 5.♘c3 a6 6.f4 e5 7.♘f3 ♘bd7 8.a4 ♗e7 9.♗d3 0–0 10.0–0 exf4 11.♔h1 ♘c5 12.♗xf4 ♗d7 13.♕e2 ♖e8 14.a5 ♖c8 15.♗e3 ♗f8 16.♗d4 ♗g4 17.♕e3 ♗h5

18.♗xf6 ♕xf6 19.♘d5 ♕d8 20.b4 ♘d7 21.c4 ♗g6 22.♖ae1 ♗e7 23.♕a7 ♖b8 24.♗c2 ♘f6 25.♗a4 ♖f8 26.♕d4 ♘xd5 27.♕xd5 ♗f6 28.e5 dxe5 29.♘xe5 ♗xe5 30.♖xe5 h6 31.♗d7 ♕c7 32.c5 ♔h8 33.♖e7 ♖bd8

34.♕d6 ♕xd6 35.cxd6 f5 36.♖d1 f4 37.♗g4 ♗f5 38.♗f3 ♖f6 39.d7 ♔h7 40.♗xb7 h5 41.b5 axb5 42.a6 ♖b6 43.♖e8 ♖xd7 44.♖xd7 ♗xd7 45.♗e4† g6 46.♖e7† ♔h6 47.a7 ♗c6 48.♖e6 1–0

Vladimir Kramnik:

"I also played this game during the Soviet U18 Championship, just one year later. Even today I would not play much differently and would be happy with it: in the same positionally active style. You can see that within a year I had improved considerably, and this game ended in a nicely played victory."

Loek van Wely – Vladimir Kramnik

European Junior Championship (U20), Arnhem 1990

1.d4 e6 2.c4 f5 3.g3 ♘f6 4.♗g2 c6 5.♘f3 d5 6.0–0 ♗d6 7.b3 ♕e7 8.♗b2 b6 9.♘e5 ♗b7 10.♘d2 0–0 11.♘df3 ♘bd7 12.♕c2 ♖ac8 13.cxd5 cxd5 14.♕d3 ♘e4

15.♘xd7 ♕xd7 16.♘e5 ♕e7 17.f3 ♘f6 18.♖ac1 ♘d7 19.♖xc8 ♖xc8 20.♘xd7 ♕xd7 21.e4 dxe4 22.fxe4 ♗xe4 23.♗xe4 fxe4 24.♕xe4 ♗e7 25.♖e1 ♗f6 26.♖e2

26...♕d5 27.♕xd5 exd5 28.♔f2 ♔f7 29.♔e3 h5 30.h3 b5 31.♔d3 b4 32.♖e1 ♖c6 33.a3 bxa3 34.♗xa3 ♖a6 35.♗b2 ♔g6 36.♗c3 ♖a3 37.♖a1 ♖xa1 38.♗xa1 ♔f5 39.♔e3 g5 40.♔f3 g4† 41.hxg4† hxg4† 42.♔e3 ♗e7 43.♗c3 ♗d6 44.♗e1

44...♔e6 45.♔d3 ♔d7 46.♔e2 ♔c6 47.♔d3 ♔b5 48.♔c2 a5 49.♔d3 a4 50.bxa4† ♔xa4 51.♗f2 ♔b3 52.♗e1 ♔b2 53.♗f2 ♔c1 54.♗e3† ♔d1 55.♗f2 ♗a3 56.♔e3 ♗c1†

57.♔d3 ♗d2 58.♗e3 ♗e1 59.♗f4 ♗f2 60.♗e5 ♔e1 61.♔c3 ♔e2 62.♔b4 ♔f3 63.♔c5 ♔e4 0–1

Vladimir Kramnik:

"This was a very significant game for me in the U20 European championship. I was just 15 years old and at the end finished shared third. For my encounter with Loek, I received the prize for the most beautiful game in the tournament. This was my first international cup, of which I am very proud and which still has a place in my trophy cabinet. What was more important was that after it I received the support of Anatoly Bykhovsky, the head trainer of the Soviet youth team. The game against Van Wely was the deciding factor for him. Bykhovsky explained to me years later that because of this game he understood that I could become a really great player.

After it, he arranged some invitations to Russian tournaments which I would probably not have gotten otherwise. These helped my further development greatly. What is impressive about this game against Van Wely was that I was able to outplay the Dutch player, three years older than me, in a level position. After move 25 Loek offered a draw. I declined, because Black had a better bishop, was playing on both wings and was able to gradually increase his small advantages. At the age of 15 my endgame technique had already become refined. Later I went on to win many important games in my career in this style."

A Chaotic Genius

 8

A lot happened in the chess world in 1992. Garry Kasparov took his first step towards breaking away from the world chess federation, FIDE. On 28th June 1992, Mikhail Tal, the eighth World Champion died at only 55 years old.

1992 was also the year in which Bobby Fischer reappeared, twenty years after his legendary victory in Reykjavik. He played his final games in public for a prize fund of five million US dollars, two-thirds going to the winner, against Boris Spassky in Sveti Stefan and Belgrade. It was a rather meaningless show match which Fischer won easily 17½–12½ (10 wins against 5). Fischer seemed to have a real need of the money, which came from the Yugoslav banker Jezdimir Vasiljević. The match brought Fischer a lot of trouble since playing contravened a UN embargo against the remains of Yugoslavia, Serbia and Montenegro, where the venues were situated.

Fischer was threatened with arrest and a large fine, should he return to the US, with the result that he frequently changed his place of residence. Whenever it became known to the USA where Fischer was staying, the US authorities tried to get hold of him. After residing in the Philippines, Germany, Hungary and Japan, Bobby found his final domicile in Iceland. In Reykjavik, where he fought his greatest battle, he died on the 17th of January 2008, without ever having seen his homeland again.

The chess world was beginning to cast its spell on me. I already had experience in professional sports with footballers, boxers, handball and table tennis players. But chess was quite different. The top grandmasters have extraordinary abilities and strong personalities. They enjoyed enormous respect, even with the media. Everything was more intense and longer lasting. Moreover, they were real globetrotters. The game takes them all over the world, not like a footballer who visits another country two or three times a year for European Cup matches, should he be so lucky. No, chess was much more than that and not only on account of its grandmasters.

Looking back, I think the 1980s and the 1990s represented the golden age for chess. Computer-supported opening preparation was not yet important, in principle man was still superior to the machine. The players travelled to tournaments with books and their own notes. The grandmasters were meeting in the morning for breakfast in the tournament hotels. They came from all over the world and would talk shop about chess, sports or politics. After the games they often shared a glass of wine or beer. It was a "romantic," or perhaps better said, easy-going, time. Friendships developed and the company of Artur Yusupov, Jan Timman, Klaus Bischoff, Eric Lobron, Ivan Sokolov and others left unforgettable memories.

The playing conditions and the prize funds had improved considerably in this period, thanks partially to Bobby Fischer, who had set standards with his demands, forcing the organizers to show greater respect to the interests of the players. Fischer was often described as mad. Professionally speaking, that was in no way so, and Vladimir Kramnik does not think so either. Top grandmasters have profited to the present day from his initiatives. Fischer's successors, Anatoly Karpov and Garry Kasparov, picked up and ran with it. Their world championship matches added to the popularization of chess. At the end of the 1980s, beginning of the 1990s, it would have been possible – just as happened in tennis (ATP) or golf (PGA) – to lay the foundations for a prosperous future for professional chess. The fact that this wonderful chance was missed lies solely with FIDE, the world federation.

Of course, the world champion at the time, Garry Kasparov was a difficult partner. Back in 1987 he co-founded the Grandmasters Association (GMA) and displayed the first hint that he would break away from FIDE, something he finally did in in 1993. Kasparov had fair reasons, since FIDE understood little to nothing about marketing the world championship cycle and other top events. This has not changed. The frequent amateurish presentation and organization of top events continue to this day.

The entry of powerful computer programs into the chess world changed the atmosphere in a negative sense one move at a time. The use of large databases of previously-played games on the most up-to-date hardware advanced rapidly from the late 1980s onwards. Garry Kasparov in collaboration with the Hamburg-based company ChessBase were the key engines in this. Kasparov was the first to recognize the potential of the computers. For a few years they gave him opening preparation which brought him an advantage over his rivals. The approach he took then is nowadays as self-evident as the laws of chess.

Modern grandmasters use most of their time preparing their openings with computers. Conversations and post mortem game analysis hardly exist anymore. Chess software running on an average laptop is superior to the world champion. As a consequence, the tournament halls usually have less visitors these days. The spectators overwhelmingly prefer to follow the games at home in front of a computer. Even seasoned chess journalists don't necessarily go to the venue anymore.

None of which is attractive for commercial sponsors. It is high time for drastic rethinking by the world federation and other tournament organizers. Time-delayed internet broadcasts and high-quality standards, organization and presentation of top events must urgently be introduced. Most events do not meet the demands of modern marketing.

There is however a new hope. On October 3rd 2018, in Batumi, Georgia, former Russian Deputy Prime Minister Arkady Dvorkovich was elected as the new President of FIDE. This is the biggest hope for professional chess in more than 30 years. With experience from boosting chess in Russia, organizing two World Championship matches (2012 and 2014) and not least organizing the 2018 Football World Cup, this talented young man had unanimous support from the Association of Chess Professionals and most grandmasters from all over the world, including Vladimir Kramnik.

♔9

Back to Vladimir Kramnik. In 1992, when he began his unstoppable rise to the top with tournament victories in Gausdal (Norway), the Dortmund Open and in Chalkidiki (Greece), the chess world was still in good order. He was recommended for the Russian team in the Manila Chess Olympiad by Garry Kasparov. Mikhail Botvinnik and Yuri Razuvaev also advocated Kramnik. Nevertheless, his selection was hotly discussed within the Russian Chess Federation and the cause of fierce criticism.

In Russia there were 40 grandmasters and Kramnik had not yet been awarded the title. He would be a junior for several years, and was now upsetting the hierarchy. What made things more difficult was that due to the collapse of the Soviet Union, the Russians faced new and strong opponents such as Ukraine, Armenia, Latvia and so on in Olympiads and world team championships. The Soviet Union had won most of these tournaments in the past, with notable exceptions of 1976 (held in Haifa, Israel, leading to a boycott) and 1978, where Hungary narrowly surpassed the Soviets. But with so many hungry new rivals, there was no guarantee of gold medals.

Eventually Kramnik was selected and proved the confidence in him in a way that made even his harshest critics acknowledge his contribution. With eight wins and one draw as first reserve, playing on Board 4, he made a considerable contribution to the Russians' team gold. On 25th June 1992, his 17th birthday, he was awarded the Olympiad's individual gold medal for the best performance as the first reserve. His rise into the ranks of the world elite was so meteoric that FIDE did not have enough time to award him the titles of International Master and Grandmaster in succession. So, in Manila he got both titles simultaneously, something that has only happened a handful of times.

In these months of 1992, the chess world outside Russia became aware of Kramnik's talent. He was refreshing, enormously creative and equipped with an outstanding technique. He already belonged to the ten best chess players in the world, entering the top 10 officially for the first time on 1st of January 1993, occupying sixth position. For the next 22 years he would remain in the exalted circle of the ten best players, until a small dip in November 2014 took him briefly down to eleventh place.

What Vladimir lacked was direct confrontation with the top players, playing top tournaments and participating in the world chess championships cycle, in order to make further progress towards realizing his potential. This was Kramnik's mission, though the full development of his abilities would take a few more years.

At the end of 1992 Kramnik's contacts with Germany intensified. As well as the future regular participation in the Dortmund Chess Days, he was engaged by the Chess Bundesliga team Empor Berlin. He soon played on the top board and remained undefeated in eight games in his first season of the Bundesliga.

♔10

1993 was the year Kramnik had his first experience with matches. In Cannes he won a duel with the top French player Joel Lautier by 4½–1½. With the same score he defeated the Spaniard Miguel Illescas.

He played for Lyon and won the French team championships. In the super-tournaments in Dortmund and Belgrade he was undefeated, taking second place both times. Vladimir shared first in Madrid with Veselin Topalov and Viswanathan Anand. He seemed unstoppable.

That year I visited the tournaments in Linares, Madrid, Tilburg and Groningen. I got to know the scene better and to know Vladimir Kramnik personally.

Meanwhile, World Champion Garry Kasparov had had enough of FIDE and brought about the split. In London he defeated the English player Nigel Short by 12½–7½. The world federation FIDE have stripped him of the world championship title (and both he and Short of their rating for a short period), but everyone continued to view the Russian as the world champion. Under the "Professional Chess Association" (PCA), founded for the world championship match, Kasparov, with sponsorship from the computer giant Intel, set up a successful world championship cycle.

In Linares 1994 Kramnik won his first tournament game against Kasparov. This was a first milestone on the road to London 2000, the world championship match between the two Russians. In chess circles the discussion had begun: could Kramnik's potential take him as far as the world championship title?

Winning against the world champion in an important tournament brought Kramnik enormous self-confidence. From then on, unlike the other top players, he was no longer overly impressed by Kasparov. In the future he would become Kasparov's nemesis. He dethroned him and accumulated a positive score against him in classical chess.

In the PCA's "Intel Grand Prix" in 1994, tournaments played in Moscow, Paris, New York and London, Kramnik left everyone without a leg to stand on. He won in New York and topped the overall ranking in this well-funded competition in rapid chess. This was the last Grand Prix PCA would organize. It collapsed the following year.

My visit to the 1994 Olympiad in Moscow, played at Hotel Cosmos, remains unforgettable, though not only from a positive point of view. Let's mention that Russia again won the Olympiad, helped by Kramnik's fantastic eight points from eleven games.

What people remember is that under the presidency of Boris Yeltsin, anarchy reigned in Moscow. Muggings on the way from the hotel to the metro were commonplace. From the hotel you could hear shots fired at night. The Kremlin was unable to provide law and order, leaving this as a personal matter.

At this time Anatoly Karpov and Garry Kasparov were deeply involved in chess politics. I remember the legendary invitation from Anatoly Karpov. We were happy to leave the hermetically sealed Hotel Cosmos. In minus 30 degrees we waited for a bus, which took 50 of us to a small discotheque on the edge of the city, which was guarded by about 30 guards with semi-automatic weapons. On the roof of the building there was an additional unit with a machine gun. We were all a little uncomfortable but were well compensated. Karpov was trying (unsuccessfully) to force through the Frenchman Bachar Kouatly as FIDE President and provided caviar by the kilo, the finest champagne and acrobatic performances by the Moscow State Circus.

The way things worked in Moscow is well explained by the following example. The ticket price at the Bolshoi Theatre was roughly 100 roubles, the equivalent of 3-4 US dollars. However, the performances were always sold out. I paid over the 120 dollars on the black market to see *Swan Lake* being performed to the music of Tchaikovsky. In the auditorium there were almost 2000 seats, all sold out, but there were at most 300 spectators present. Certain organizations bought all the tickets for the entire season and sold them on the black market. The ordinary Russians had no chance of going to the Bolshoi.

♔11

Both the PCA and FIDE began new world championship cycles in 1994. Kramnik had reached third place in the world rankings and qualified for both cycles. In the Candidates matches organized by FIDE, in Wijk aan Zee, Netherlands, he won 4½–1½ against Leonid Yudasin from Israel.

Up to this point everything had run like clockwork, but two defeats struck the 19-year-old like hammer blows.

Firstly, in the quarter-finals of the PCA world championship he lost by 1½–4½ to his ex-compatriot Gata Kamsky, now representing the US. And shortly afterwards, in the FIDE cycle he lost by 3½–4½ to Boris Gelfand, at that time still representing Belarus. Vladimir was the clear favourite in both matches, but being young, Kramnik naturally lacked experience in match play. But there were additional reasons for these failures. One was that his lifestyle at that time was anything but professional.

In the mid-1990s Vladimir got to know Josef Resch, a German dealer in metals. Resch had grown up in the Soviet Union. After studying business management in Germany, he was living in Moscow, speaking Russian fluently. He knew the mentality of the people and gained Kramnik's trust. At twenty, Vladimir possessed the intellectual culture and maturity of a grown man, but lacked experience in dealing with the capitalist system of the West. There were also other weaknesses that prevented him from reaching his full potential in chess.

Resch describes the problems like this: "Volodja was always hungry, but ate unhealthily, quite often directly from the tin. He had a three and a half room flat in Moscow. There were continually lots of people living and spending nights there." He was going to bed in the early hours of the morning, not getting out of bed before 2pm. "But worst was that he paid no attention to his physical condition, leading a chaotic life," remembers Resch.

Kramnik has a lot to thank Josef Resch for. Unlike many other people whom Vladimir met, Resch had no financial interest and he was open and honest with him. Resch criticized his lifestyle and also told him to look after his assets, because otherwise he would never have any. He told him quite directly: "With this way of life you will never become world champion." Kramnik of course understood this, but at first remained stubborn. It was to take years before he would change his lifestyle.

For that to happen he needed a great challenge, which came with the 2000 match against Kasparov. Another problem was becoming increasingly important: he was a star in Russia and frequently surrounded by a lot of people, including some looking for personal benefits. Kramnik at that time did not find it easy to say 'no' and struggled to escape such people. Focusing on his career became almost impossible and – in such cases – that often represents the beginning of the end.

But at the time Kramnik did not see any problems. In 1993 he said about himself: "I am not very ambitious, that is in my nature." Despite these circumstances he worked hard, but not in an organized way. He was a strong analyst and even then advanced chess theory with scientific precision. Vladimir believed in correct chess, in the beauty of the game. He lived like a bohemian, his young body could keep up with it all and he felt at ease.

Yet slowly but surely a transformation took place, encouraged by his mentor Resch. As almost a reaction to his match defeats in 1994, 1995 was the year Kramnik erupted. Vladimir triumphed first in Dortmund, then in Horgen (Switzerland) and Belgrade. His performance for Empor Berlin in the Bundesliga was unbelievable. On first board he scored seven wins and three draws. German chess fans were astonished by the young Russian.

♔12

But all that glittered was not gold. Around the middle of the 1990s, Vladimir Kramnik put his trust in the wrong people. He was swindled out of the greater part of the fortune he had accumulated up to then, almost 400,000 marks (over $200,000). In the presence of a well-known chess journalist from Berlin, he had opened a bank account. According to Kramnik, power of attorney was given to someone associated with his Bundesliga team. While abroad, Kramnik had several times handed over cheques and cash to chess friends from Germany and asked them to pass them on to this person to pay them into his account. For a long time, Vladimir believed that his assets were secure in the account; however, he was never to see a penny of it.

Vladimir Kramnik thinks he was swindled by the Berliner: "He had power of attorney for my bank account and withdrew large sums without my approval. No matter what he claims to have done with the assets, I never gave him permission to do that!" Kramnik neither revealed who this person was nor started a criminal complaint. Kramnik's equanimity in those days, his uncertainty in dealing with the German legal system, and some embarrassment about the whole business, all played their part.

Even today, some people from the Berlin scene claim that Kramnik's money was transferred to the firm Spree-Capital GmbH in order to invest it. German grandmaster Joerg Hickl wrote a blog about it. Some chess players entrusted their hard-earned cash to Spree-Capital. After the fall of the Berlin Wall, the managing director is said to have set up on his own with that firm, and soon afterwards to have come under suspicion of embezzling money from his depositors. When Spree-Capital collapsed, its managing director was sentenced to five years in prison.

It was not only in 1990s Berlin that fraud seemed to flourish as common practice in the German chess scene. In its issue of 3rd November 1995, *Der Spiegel* revealed that the Germanist and art dealer Heinrich Jellissen had promised his investors a yearly return of at least twelve percent. Jellissen exuded the aura of a man of the world. More than a dozen German players and officials entrusted their savings to him, including Robert Hübner, Dr Helmut Pfleger, Stefan Kindermann, Raj Tischbierek, Artur Yusupov, Horst Metzing and Ralf Lau. In some cases all their savings. Jellissen suddenly died from a heart attack at the end of 1994. Of the three million deutschmarks he had acquired from chess players alone, none was found. *Der Spiegel* expressed it as follows: "Up to 680,000 marks per person was what their bargain-seeking mentality cost the sharp analysts."

Nevertheless, chess was booming in the 1990s. I attended tournaments in Novgorod, Riga and the Netherlands. The Dutch were suffering from chess fever more than anyone. With Wijk aan Zee, Amsterdam, Tilburg and Groningen they organized more top events than anywhere else in the world. However, the public showed the most enthusiasm at the Belgrade Sava Centar: 8,000 to 10,000 spectators were common.

♔13

Kramnik's fantastic 1995 tournament results brought him to first place in the world ranking list on 1st January 1996. Only 20 years old, this was a new record, which stood for 14 years, until broken in January 2010 by current world champion Magnus Carlsen. One major goal had been reached; the other would have to wait for a further five years. Kramnik and Kasparov both had a rating of 2775, but Kramnik was first, as he had played more games in the preceding six months.

After his tournament victory in Dortmund 1995, Kramnik took an unexpected decision: he agreed to sign on for the reigning world champion Garry Kasparov's team for his title defence against Viswanathan Anand. And he did so although at that time he was heading for the number one spot and was considered a serious contender.

This decision seemed suspicious to me. Vladimir would not have financial motives. With friends I discussed his possible motivation: is he again incapable of saying 'no'? Does he feel thankful to Kasparov? Why help the world champion, when he should be having ambitions for the chess throne? Why does the man not have higher aims?

On the top floor of the World Trade Center, Kasparov defeated the luckless Indian. Anand had taken the lead in Game 9, but Kasparov struck back hard with wins in Games 10, 11, 13 and 14, winning 10½–7½.

Later I understood Kramnik's decision, as I was at his side day by day for many years and came to understand his character. He had hardly giving any thoughts to his own chances to play for the title of world champion. He simply wanted to experience the match, and Kasparov, from the inside.

Five years later the experience he had gained in New York would give him important pointers, although this was not his intention. He understood how extraordinarily hard and professionally Kasparov and his team worked, with computer support. He experienced the rigour with which Kasparov dealt with his opponent; Garry's emotional outbreaks during the games; Kasparov, the actor, ready to give his all for victory. This was contrary to what Kramnik wanted to be. But witnessing Kasparov's actions made him immune to the theatrics of the 13th World Champion, on and off the chess board. Kramnik could not know whether and when he would play against Kasparov for the world championship. But the experience from New York was worth its weight in gold five years later.

Vladimir loved life, and art, and had many interests. After successes he liked to slacken the reins, celebrate and enjoy life. So after he took the top spot in the world ranking list, the steep rise of 1995 stopped. He was victorious in Dos Hermanas, where he won a madcap game with Black against Kasparov, and in Dortmund. But the rest of the year was below standard. The 21-year-old genius was not yet mature enough to undertake a serious attack on the world championship.

His trainer Sergey Dolmatov, 1978 World Junior Champion, was critical of his behaviour: "Kramnik has enormous undeveloped potential. He does a lot which wastes a lot of energy and at the same time does not allow him to concentrate fully on his game. He lacks ambition. It is time for Kramnik to crave winning and to show it."

The 1996 Olympiad was held in Yerevan, Armenia. Kramnik played Board 2 for Russia. Led by a fierce Kasparov, Russia took gold. Vladimir was in poor form and made nine draws, his worst Olympiad result.

At that Olympiad I met Miguel Najdorf for the only time. Together with grandmaster Adrian Mikhalchishin, we had a lively conversation. Najdorf was 85 years old. All chess players know of the Najdorf Variation in the Sicilian Defence, including young people who may believe that Najdorf is an exotic town, and not a Polish-born Argentinian businessman, who was one of the best players in the world after World War 2.

Sitting outside a café, we were joined by the Ukrainian ace Vassily Ivanchuk. "Chucky" is always thinking about chess and is sometimes not quite present. He ate a salad and presented Najdorf with a few ideas in the latter's variation. He failed to notice how salad leaf after salad leaf was landing on the trousers of the little Argentinian. Najdorf overlooked this faux pas, but after the conversation his trousers were fit to be changed.

Rarely in my journeys have I come across such poor conditions as in the Armenian capital. On the way to a meeting with some painters, I witnessed the consequences of the 1988 earthquake in the already hard-pressed region. In the windows, broken panes were covered by towels. In the hallways every second wooden step could be missing, having been used as firewood during the bitterly cold winters. Electricity and water were available only infrequently. My Armenian friends tell me the conditions have improved greatly, also outside Yerevan.

♚14

Despite a modest performance at the Olympiad, Kramnik received great praise from Kasparov in 1997, saying that he was his strongest opponent by talent. The demands on the young Russian were growing. During the Linares tournament he was asked why he was unable to take the final step. Kramnik replied: "Sometimes I play safely, sometimes active and open chess. If I were to understand which step I have to take, I could work on it. Then I could win a tournament like Linares. I believe that I could have won based on my play, but now I am simply disappointed."

Such statements show that Kramnik still judged things purely based on chess. He sounded ambitious but was not ready adjust order his habits, to prioritize success. His physical condition was desperate for a 22-year-old and his attitude to tournament chess not professional. "Between 1995 and 1997 I kept on telling him he would never become World Champion," remembers Josef Resch. Kramnik's answer remained the same: "That is not my aim!"

As I remember Vladimir, he really was not very interested in the title. Apart from a lack of ambition, Kramnik was aware that the title of World Champion meant not only fame, honour and money, but also responsibility and hard work. Resch said his attitude changed little by little: "He slowly started to expel spongers from his flat. Also he asked me for advice on how to sort out his financial affairs."

But even with one foot stuck on the brakes, Kramnik was a giant. From 1997 to 1999 he occupied second or third place in the world rankings. In 1997 he won Dos Hermanas, Tilburg and the strong 25th Jubilee tournament in Dortmund. It was his third win in a row in Dortmund. Why was he so successful in Dortmund? Kramnik replied: "In Dortmund we are all playing in a peaceful atmosphere, everything is quite relaxed. I have a good feeling and that helps me."

In 1998 he was victorious for the only time in Wijk aan Zee. The top Dutch tournament never suited Vladimir. We often spoke about why, but never came to any conclusions. Somehow things never clicked there, except for in 1998. While in Dortmund Vladimir notched up four tournament wins in succession. The only comparable thing with this is Kasparov's victories in Linares from 1999 to 2002.

Kramnik also won the lucrative blindfold and rapid chess tournament in Monaco, something he managed to do another four times, in 1999 and 2007 alone and in 2001 and 2004 tied with Topalov and Morozevich respectively.

In January 1998 Kramnik was once ranked number two in the world.

♔15

Once again a bad setback occurred. Vladimir played a match against Alexei Shirov, the Latvian now playing under Spanish colours. The winner was to challenge Garry Kasparov for the title of what was now called the Brain Games World Championship. In Cazorla, Spain, Kramnik lost the most important match in his career so far by an undistinguished 3½–5½.

Whenever you are not successful at the highest level, where small nuances decide, there are two possible explanations. Either your opponent is simply better, or you are not ready to do what it takes to succeed. I am convinced that in his innermost self, in 1998, Kramnik was not mentally nor physically focused on becoming World Champion.

In 1999 Vladimir took second place in Wijk aan Zee. Also, in Dos Hermanas and Dortmund he had to concede to 19-year-old Peter Leko, and take second place. Kramnik seemed not to be over the defeat to Shirov. At the roulette tournament in Las Vegas, the so-called FIDE World Championship, he was eliminated in the quarter-finals by the English player Michael Adams.

The only clear success in 1999 was the title defence in rapid and blindfold chess in Monaco. And in a blitz match against Kasparov in Moscow, Kramnik brought the millennium to a pleasing end for him with a good performance and a 12–12 draw. At 24 years old, on 1st January 2000, Kramnik was third in the world rankings.

The chess world was stagnating. The split between FIDE and Kasparov appeared unbridgeable, although the World Champion had not defended his title for four years. The crown princes, Anand and Kramnik, appeared to pose no great danger to Kasparov. Anand was *unable* to do anything against him and Kramnik somehow *unwilling* to. Everything was in tune with the motto, "Live and let live."

Just like Josef Resch, I kept discussing the changes required with Kramnik. Josef and I agreed: "If you continue like this, you will regret it one day. When you have children, you will ask yourself why you did not make the most of your unique potential." Kramnik understood we had his best interests at heart, but was not particularly interested.

However, towards the end of the 1990s he realized his lifestyle would harm his health in the long run. He was not ready for major changes, but at least was beginning to consider it. It was in the air. An old German proverb goes: "Opportunity makes the thief."

The opportunity arrived unexpectedly. Only a year later the chess world would have changed completely, and Vladimir too.

In Russia, the millennium ended on 31st December 1999 with the appointment of Vladimir Putin as president. Plagued with dementia and alcoholism, Boris Yeltsin had resigned. Conditions in Russia had become stable and the East-West détente was in progress.

Garry Kasparov – Vladimir Kramnik

Dos Hermanas 1996

1.d4 d5 2.c4 c6 3.♘c3 ♘f6 4.♘f3 e6 5.e3 ♘bd7 6.♗d3 dxc4 7.♗xc4 b5 8.♗d3 ♗b7 9.0–0 a6 10.e4 c5 11.d5 c4 12.♗c2 ♕c7 13.♘d4 ♘c5 14.b4 cxb3 15.axb3 b4 16.♘a4 ♘cxe4

17.♗xe4N ♘xe4 18.dxe6 ♗d6 19.exf7† ♕xf7 20.f3 ♕h5 21.g3

40

21...0–0! 22.fxe4 ♕h3 23.♘f3? ♗xg3 24.♘c5? ♖xf3! 25.♖xf3 ♕xh2† 26.♔f1 ♗c6! 27.♗g5 ♗b5† 28.♘d3 ♖e8!–+ 29.♖a2 ♕h1† 30.♔e2 ♖xe4† 31.♔d2 ♕g2† 32.♔c1 ♕xa2 33.♖xg3 ♕a1† 34.♔c2 ♕c3† 35.♔b1 ♖d4 0–1

Vladimir Kramnik:

"This game and the tournament too are in several respects memorable. Garry and I played against each other many times. This game was the only one in classical chess either of us managed to win with Black. The tournament had high level participants and was one of the strongest of its day. Almost all the top players participated. Being shared first in the world ranking list I was considered a favourite, but was at first unable to find my stride.

There were nine rounds. I started with five draws after experiencing some problems. Then one by one I won three games: with White against Anand and with Black against Kasparov and Ivanchuk. A hat-trick against the best players in the world, including two wins with Black, is a rarity in the history of chess. For this reason I managed to take first place in the tournament.

Against Kasparov I chose a sharp variation of the Meran System. At that time played this opening often, with good results. As usual Garry had an interesting novelty up his sleeve and played 17.♗xe4. After the recapture 17...♘xe4 he played 18.dxe6 and I had to think for a long time. The position is complicated with numerous possibilities. Everything looked dangerous for me so I decided on a counterattack. This was unpleasant for Kasparov. He is used to having the initiative. I had long since noticed that he did not always react with a level head when under attack. Because his opening preparation was so fantastic, this rarely happened to him.

After the sacrifice White was objectively better but, as said, Kasparov was forced to defend in a complicated position, which did not suit him.

He went wrong with 23.♘f3. He had a plethora of options; 23.♕e2 would certainly have been better, intending to meet 23...♗xg3 with 24.♘f5. White would have been better, but in a practical game with time pressure it was difficult to find. His idea was to play 24.♘c5, as he did. Everything would have worked beautifully for him, if I had not had the wonderful move 26...♗c6!!. He had either not seen it at all or else underestimated it.

That is understandable, because in positions of this type White is normally on the lookout for checks.

With 26...♗c6 Black may be a rook down, but already the attack is unstoppable. 28...♖e8 was a quiet but powerful and very beautiful move. I bring my last piece into the attack and still a rook up, White has no defence.

I would have been pleased if Garry had played 31.♗e3 instead of 31.♔d2. This would have led to a mating pattern which I had not yet seen in a practical game: 31.♗e3 ♕g2† 32.♖f2 ♕xf2 mate.

This game was designated as the most beautiful of the year 1996 by Chess Informant and I am still proud of it. I managed to sweep the World Champion off the board with the black pieces. He did not want to analyse the game in the press centre in front of the journalists, but invited me to his room. We studied the game for an hour and Garry was not so disappointed. I understood him well, because I too am far more annoyed when I play badly, than if my opponent has played brilliantly and the result is a wonderful game."

Metamorphosis and Millennial Victory

♚16

Remember the dramatic fears at the end of the last century? The world would come to an end – at least the Millennium Bug would cause a breakdown of all computers and plunge the world into chaos. If anyone will read this book in a hundred years, I can assure you that nothing like that happened.

But there were other powerful changes. Globalization was accelerating, leading to many indirect effects. Conditioned by the meteoric development of communications technology, and strengthened by religious and nationalistic radicalization, humanity finds itself in the middle of a period of major change. Nobody knows where it will lead, yet the change is happening with barely credible intensity, perhaps most easily comparable with the high point of the industrial revolution at the end of the 19th century. Still, at that time the great scientific breakthroughs were not joined by economic volatility and ideological upheaval.

Changes are at the core of any progress, and so it is also in the chess world. Everything was still calm, Kasparov still considered an unbeatable world champion and FIDE trying not to let itself be impressed by that. It continued to ignore what could not be ignored and produced its own world champions as if on a conveyor belt. That hardly anybody respected their knockout champions as the real champion was ignored by the officials.

Yet Kasparov had begun to display weakness. In 1997 he lost to the IBM computer Deep Blue by 2½–3½. Despite this defeat, which even today represents a turning point for chess, chess journalists represented the result as an accident. Garry put in an extra effort during the match and immediately after his loss in the second game accused the IBM team of cheating. IBM switched to stubborn mode, rejected all investigations and broke Deep Blue up into its constituent parts after the match. Some of these are in the computer museum in Silicon Valley today. So ended all cooperation between IBM and Kasparov. Also importantly: many insiders are convinced that by doing business with IBM, Kasparov annoyed his main sponsor Intel, causing them to withdraw from chess. Kasparov denied this vehemently.

Whether true or not, from 1997 onwards Kasparov was unable to produce sponsors for his own world championship cycle, nor did he have a suitable organizational structure.

Throughout 1998-1999 he was unable to find sponsors for the world championship match against Shirov. The 13th World Chess Champion was in a difficult situation.

After short celebrations with my family, I flew to Budapest in the early morning of New Year's Day 2000. Peter Leko, with the support of his sponsor RWE, was playing the newly crowned FIDE world champion Alexander Khalifman, the winner of the FIDE roulette in Las Vegas. The six-game match was rated and counted for the world ranking list.

I had been looking after the interests of Leko since 1998. At the tender age of 20 the Hungarian entered the top 10 in 2000 and became a fixture there almost without interruption for the following ten years. I really pumped up his motivation. In the capital of his native land, where the Polgar clan, Zoltan Ribli, Lajos Portisch, Andras Adorjan and above all the officials of the chess federation set the tone, Peter may have been the absolute number one in sporting terms, but despite his potential he was looked down upon. As a boy brought up and living in Szeged, he represented more of a threat for the ambitious people in Budapest than a great hope.

After the well-organized match in the ballroom of the Hotel Kempinski, where all seats were occupied, things changed: Leko took apart the grandmaster from St Petersburg, by 4½–1½. The national press was exultant and the elder grandmaster Andor Lilienthal described Peter as Hungary's greatest hope ever, a future world champion. Just weeks after Khalifman's victory in Las Vegas, the reputation of the FIDE crown plonked to rock bottom. Unintentionally, we had strengthened Garry Kasparov's hand.

♔17

Kramnik meanwhile returned to second place in the world rankings. He and Kasparov triumphed together in March 2000 in Linares. At the time, this tournament in Andalusia was the strongest in the world. Garry Kasparov allowed Kramnik to take the coveted trophy, a gesture which he eight months later would describe as the first in a series of mistakes.

It was Vladimir's first of three wins in Linares. He had begun a lifestyle change. He got up early and attended breakfast at Hotel Anibal in Linares. That was new. In the 1990s nobody dragged him out of bed before 13.00. He had also given up smoking.

There was a good reason for the changes in Kramnik's lifestyle. With no financing Kasparov had abandoned his world championship match against Shirov. Anand had been given an offer, but had hesitated, so finally negotiations about a possible match were taking place with Kramnik. The prospect of a duel with Kasparov inspired him. When Vladimir signed a contract for a title match against Kasparov on 5th April 2000, he experienced a mental transformation. He now wanted to do everything he could to succeed.

In July 2000 Vladimir travelled to Dortmund. Three months before the world championship match he was already in excellent physical condition. He had not lost any of his previous 79 tournament games. He pushed this unbeaten streak up to 82, before losing to Michael Adams. It was Kramnik's first defeat in Dortmund. He did not grieve about it particularly and still won the Dortmund tournament for the fifth time.

After the match in London, he described his loss to Adams as something which pointed the way to his strategy against Garry. Also, the unbeaten streak had created pressure on him, which now dissipated.

Previously, at the Chess Classic 2000 in Mainz, in Dortmund and afterwards in Cologne, on the occasion of a live game on WDR television, I spoke intensively with Vladimir about the match. He had made great changes, and not only externally. For the first time, I found him totally focused. His personality developed along similar lines: his appearance in public became more and more masterful. He began to impress people outwith his narrow circle of friends.

Kramnik asked me to organize a training camp for him and his team before the match. I gladly did so. I chose a peaceful locality on the North Sea coast of Germany, where there are no distractions.

Before talking about the London 2000 world championship match, it is appropriate to investigate its prehistory. This will clarify the chaos in the chess world under Garry Kasparov. This is necessary to understand decisions made by Kramnik once he became World Champion.

♔18

After Kasparov broke from FIDE and defeated Short in London, he scored a great success with a sponsorship agreement with Intel. This showed that a global firm with years of strategic experience could be won over to chess. As well as major showcase events in rapid chess, Intel sponsored Kasparov's new world championship cycle.

PCA 1995
Viswanathan Anand won Kasparov's Candidates tournament. The resulting world championship match with Kasparov was organized in 1995 on the top floor of the New York World Trade Center.

Anand took the lead in Game 9, but then things changed. In the tenth game the Indian ran into a variation prepared in depth by Kasparov, which won by force and equalized the match score. Kasparov had rattled out the first 20 moves in five minutes, jumping up after almost every move, leaving the room and banging the door. Nobody thought anything about this behaviour. There was secret muttering behind closed doors in the press centre, however the world champion was scarcely criticized in the reports. Most of the assembled journalists were on Garry's side and no longer capable of objective reporting. Kasparov likes to preach democracy and fairness, but the chess tsar took a lot of liberties. Finally, in Game 11, Anand was broken. He declined Kasparov's draw offer and blundered soon after, on move 30. Vladimir Kramnik, working for Kasparov in New York, did not excuse Garry's behaviour. But as a team member, he said nothing in public.

FIDE 1995

After his 10½–7½ victory over Anand, Kasparov had the recognition of the chess world. The whole chess world? No! Some chess officials tried to continue to ignore Kasparov. The president of the tiny Southern Russian republic of Kalmykia, Kirsan Ilyumzhinov, had in 1995 replaced Florencio Campomanes as FIDE President. Having defeated first Timman and now Kamsky, Anatoly Karpov vehemently stuck up for his own interests. Although foiled by Kasparov in four consecutive world championship matches, Karpov never tired of describing himself as the true world champion under FIDE's leaky roof.

Kasparov was unimpressed. He searched for an organizational structure of his own and a challenger. But it would take five years before he defended his title again. From 1998 the US sports agent Owen Williams represented him, having made a name for himself in professional tennis and by representing the well-known golfer Nick Price.

FIDE 1997

Kramnik did not take part in the first FIDE knockout world championship in Groningen 1997. He considered Karpov's privilege of being seeded straight into the final as unfair. The other 128 participants had to suffer through endless rounds. At the end, the challenger to the rested Russian, Anand, was completely drained. The Indian lost the final in Lausanne, a match played only three days after the semi-final play-off ended, in a different country.

By boycotting the event Kramnik became active in chess politics for the first time, with no personal advantage by sacrificing a decent amount of prize money.

WCC 1998

Kasparov's friend Luis Rentero, the Spanish organizer behind the Linares tournaments, supported him in a new cycle. Having excellent relationships with the government of Andalusia, he founded the World Chess Council (WCC) in 1998. The organization was a one-man show, which promised 1.9 million dollars for a world championship match with Kasparov and a further 200,000 dollars for a Candidates match. The latter went to the loser of the Candidates match. Supposedly, the winner was guaranteed a large part of the prize fund from a world championship match. Alexei Shirov and Vladimir Kramnik played in this match without any guarantees, trusting the magnificent promises of the Spaniard.

Kramnik – Shirov 1998

Losing badly to Shirov was more than a disappointment for Kramnik. Vladimir's career up to this point had gone almost exclusively upwards. Losing a shot at the world championship was a severe setback. Kramnik's trainer Dolmatov cited psychological reasons for the defeat and described Shirov as his bête noire. This sounded just as unconvincing as the speculations in the chess press about Kramnik being insufficient prepared.

The reason for the defeat was that Kramnik played rotten chess. In 1998 he had not yet found a good approach to such an important match. He was not playing freely and suffering from a mental block. He wanted to take this step towards the world championship title risk-free. But to do so he would have had to radically change his lifestyle. Vladimir was probably unconsciously wavering between a lack of insight and preparation. His supposed lack of ambition, with which he flirted a little in his circle of close friends, provided him with a welcome excuse.

Shirov's play too was generally average and on some occasions deficient. But Kramnik was inexplicably unable to exploit his chances. He was in desperately bad form and his performance the most disappointing in his career. From then on, Shirov was considered Kramnik's nemesis, which bears no relation to reality. Their head to head score in classical chess clearly favours Kramnik.

Shirov did not play the promised match against Kasparov, nor gain a single cent, not from the WCC nor from the coffers of the rich Andalusian.

Kasparov – Shirov 1998-1999
After Shirov's victory over Kramnik, the government of Andalusia lost interest in financing the world championship. Garry Kasparov brought the affair to a final conclusion, after several unsuccessful attempts at finding sponsors, by describing Shirov as too weak to play him. The chess world was amazed, but as usual Kasparov escaped with muted criticism and loss of face.

The unfortunate Shirov has to bear a share of the guilt. According to what he himself has said, he declined an offer from Los Angeles with a prize fund of 600,000 dollars. History shows that he should have seized the chance; this amount was certainly not peanuts.

Braingames 2000
The efforts to organize a world championship match between Kasparov and Shirov had failed. Kasparov now wanted a title defence against Anand, who in 1999 again occupied second place in the world ranking list.

The Canadian promoter Serge Grimaux, together with Kasparov supporters such as Bessel Kok and the Swiss William Wirth, issued a press release in March 1999, announcing a world championship match with a prize fund of three million dollars between Kasparov and Anand in October 1999. In June 1999, Grimaux announced that Anand had accepted.

One can only speculate what moved those responsible to make this announcement, since the Indian player refused to sign the contract immediately afterwards. Anand had decided to take part in the 1999 knockout world championship in Las Vegas, accepting a clause in the contract which forbade taking part in any world championship match outwith FIDE, unless the event in Las Vegas would not have been concluded. Anand failed in the FIDE world championship, won by Khalifman.

Next up, English grandmaster Raymond Keene tried to organize a world championship encounter between Kasparov and his favoured opponent Viswanathan Anand. Raymond Keene, David Levy and Tony Buzan had founded the MSO (Mind Sports Organisation). There was an argument between Keene and his brother-in-law Levy. The latter accused Keene of having used deposits from the MSO to the tune of 50,000 pounds without his knowledge in order to found the competing firm Brain Games Network plc.

Keene paid no attention to the accusations and with Braingames found backers for a world championship match between Kasparov and Viswanathan Anand. The Indian, advised by his wife Aruna, hesitated again and demanded an advance of 300,000 dollars from a prize fund of 2.4 million US dollars. Braingames set Anand a final deadline of 21st March 2000. The deadline passed, after which there was no way to ignore Vladimir Kramnik.

Kramnik accepted all the conditions on 5th April 2000, partly because the prize fund was placed in an escrow account. Why Anand had declined a contract with such excellent security remains incomprehensible. In addition to this safety net, another clause meant that the winner of the match would play for a million dollars in Bahrain against the strongest computer in the world. On top of this Braingames was committed to organizing further world championships with the concomitant qualification tournaments. The loser of the duel agreed to take part in a Candidates tournament organized by Braingames for the next cycle.

Immediately after this agreement, Kramnik was sharply criticized, in particular by Alexei Shirov. Kramnik replied: "Braingames wanted the match to be between Kasparov and me. That was what they were interested in, not in what happened two years ago. The situation has changed completely. My results over these two years were stable, better than all others with the exception of Kasparov. It is true that I lost the match against Shirov. That happened two years ago! In 1994 I also lost a match against Gelfand, and he is not claiming that he should play against Kasparov instead of me. There is financing for a world championship match between Garry and me. Two years ago, Shirov declined to play for less money. He wanted more, additional sponsors. He did not manage to do so and hardly anybody remembers."

And he added a sentence which was revelatory: "For me, playing Kasparov is not about money. I would play for nothing!" With his tournament wins in Linares and Dortmund, Kramnik was back to second place in the July 1st rating list. He was happy and so was Kasparov. For five long years Kasparov had not defended his title. It was high time to do, if he did not wish to completely lose his credibility. The time had come.

The world championship match in London took place from the 8th October to the 2nd November 2000, with a magnificent victory for Vladimir Kramnik. In it he climbed the Mount Olympus of the chess gods to become the 14th World Champion. For those of us who had observed and supported him closely in 2000, the triumph was anything but a sensation.

Kasparov was presented in the media as the absolute favourite, although his score against Kramnik wasn't outstanding. (At the end of Kasparov's career, Kramnik would hold the upper hand over the 13th World Champion in classical chess with five wins to four). Moreover, in the preceding tournaments Vladimir had had first-class results. To my mind, Kasparov was already operating at his peak, but Kramnik still had some leeway. And as a member of Kasparov's team in 1995, Kramnik was to a certain extent immune to the world champion's histrionic talent, his grimaces and psychological tricks. Kasparov would not be able to put Kramnik off with fits of anger or by banging doors.

Kramnik prepared quietly. Only a few trusted people had the chance to observe the enormous changes he was making. Publicly his image was that of a sloppy genius. The chess world saw him in this light. *Der Spiegel* had done a lot to promote this image. Informed by Kasparov's friends, it disrespectfully described Kramnik, who used to have long hair, as a Newfoundland dog after a heavy shower. It photographed him at the chess board with sunglasses and accused him of drinking kirsch schnaps.

At times, criticism of Kramnik's lack of professionalism was justified. Of course, this was less than insulting and unfair. But in a certain way it played into Kramnik's hands. Those around Kasparov did not take the challenger seriously and Kasparov himself did not consider the possibility of a defeat in his calculations. This could be seen during the contract negotiations. There he could easily have negotiated for a rematch in the event of defeat after his 15 years on the throne. And it was most definitely Kasparov who demanded that the loser take part in a Candidates tournament in the subsequent world championship cycle.

Though there were signs that Kasparov was over-confident, Kramnik nowadays is convinced that Kasparov not only respected him, but was almost afraid of playing against him. That possibly occurred during the match, but there was little to indicate so before the duel.

Not considering defeat against such a powerful player as Kramnik shows at the same time the great strength and also the great weakness of the chess tsar. Things were not so clear among the professionals. Viswanathan Anand rated Kramnik's chances. In the 1990s, Kramnik regularly won against Kasparov. He was the only top player who managed this. After beating Kasparov in Novgorod 1997, he talked to the Dutch chess journalist and editor of the leading magazine *New in Chess* Dirk Jan ten Geuzendam in an interview: "The assumption that Kasparov is so extraordinary was created by journalists. He is not. He would lose more often if everybody understood that."

In another interview with Ten Geuzendam, six months before the match, Kramnik said: "The most difficult moment was my match against Shirov. That was a big blow to me. Everybody started to doubt if I ever could play some kind of world championship match. Or if I ever could be World Champion. For two years after this match I had no opportunity to prove that this is no longer the case."

The transformation of Vladimir Kramnik from an unambitious genius into a professional prepared to give his all, to suffer, began when he signed the contract. Unexpectedly he had the path to the greatest goal a chess player can have directly in his mind's eye. This shock was precisely what Vladimir needed to change his lifestyle.

After signing the contract, hardly any thought was given to the handsome prize fund. Kramnik saw his responsibility as follows: "I feel that I must work really hard for this match. And that is precisely what I always wanted to do. But so far I have been unable to force myself to do so. And apart from improving my chess, I will give up smoking, train hard physically and be more organized." Kasparov should have pricked up his ears.

The preparations in Germany were productive. With a smile, Kramnik attributed this to the heavy rain and loneliness of the North Sea coast. "The weather was so bad that we were forced to concentrate on the training," is how Vladimir remembers it.

Physically, mentally and in chess, Kramnik gradually achieved top form. Earlier training programmes had been frequently interrupted and not adhered to seriously, but this time he was focused. Swimming, running and regular visits to the gym. When the match began, he looked like an athlete. From his physical form, his condition and his body language, you could tell that this time he would not make random mistakes or lose concentration.

In London, Vladimir's team occupied a house in Chiswick. Grandmasters Evgeny Bareev (Russia), Miguel Illescas (Spain) and Joel Lautier (France) were responsible for the chess. Lord Rennell of Rodd was the delegation leader and Antonio, the Spanish cook, was valued by the team for his sense of humour, though unfortunately he could not cook.

Besides his London team, Kramnik worked with other grandmasters, including Peter Svidler, Alexander Morozevich and Sergey Dolmatov. With Dolmatov he prepared the Berlin Defence, which turned out to be a deciding factor in the match. At the start of the world championship, the members of his London team knew absolutely nothing about this ace. Dolmatov had seconded Kasparov in his world championship matches against Karpov and could provide valuable inside information. Bareev worked on preparation for White, Lautier on the Scotch Game, and Illescas did outstanding work on the Grünfeld.

Kramnik's preparation was not really universal. In all his world championship matches, he established certain priorities. He calculated that Kasparov would exclusively play 1.e4, opening with the king's pawn on the first move. He hardly spent any time looking at 1.c4 and 1.d4. This method almost cost him the 15th game, but in this assumption Kramnik was more than 90% correct.

This way of proceeding has a flipside. In his world championship matches against Leko in 2004, Topalov in 2006, and above all against Anand 2008, Kramnik fell victim to his opponents' opening strategies and got into serious difficulties frequently. At the highest level, attempts are made to "read" one's opponent, which involves more than a little speculation. Priorities are necessary since all-embracing opening preparation would naturally be too widespread and thus superficial and counterproductive on account of the vast amount of possibilities.

In London, Kramnik's match strategy worked perfectly. Also, from a chess viewpoint the team was ideal. All three grandmasters were hard workers, and on a human level they complemented each other and helped motivate Vladimir by their example. They did not have the same potential as he, but with hard work they had gotten far. Lautier had always done well against Kasparov, simply because he was not afraid of the World Champion and ready for a fight. This attitude became the leitmotif for the match plan: hang in there, don't be afraid and fight until the last cartridge!

Kasparov's on-site seconds were grandmasters Andrei Kharlov, Mikhail Kobalia, and Yury Dokhoian. The latter remained by Kasparov's side as permanent second until the end of his career in 2005.

♔20

On 8th October 2000, at the Riverside Studios in the London borough of Hammersmith, the world champion and his chosen challenger were standing opposite each other.

The aggressive Kasparov wanted to overrun his opponent: "He may be a nice lad. But the title belongs to me. We are professionals. He wants to kill me, and I want to survive. And the only way to survive is to kill him."

Facing him was the calm Kramnik, whose subtle understanding was tuned to turning the smallest positional advantages to his favour.

Game 1
Kasparov played White and as expected moved his king's pawn to e4. Kramnik surprised Kasparov and his own team, when in the Ruy Lopez he played into the Berlin Defence, later called the Berlin Wall in many books.

It was played rarely and considered dubious for Black. The white structure looks impressive, whilst Black is only one or two steps away from the abyss. Only the Hungarian grandmaster Almasi would regularly play the Berlin with Black at that point.

Kramnik had chosen a brilliant strategy. He was well prepared and managed to lure the World Champion onto unaccustomed terrain. Kasparov used computers in his preparation better than anyone else. But in the Berlin Defence the computers were close to useless. They kept on stating that White had a positional advantage, but they did not understand the positional subtleties. The computers will give an evaluation based on the parameters set by the programmers. Later on, they would adjust their programming, learning from the match.

The game was drawn after only 25 moves.

Kramnik had killed three birds with his one stone: Kasparov did not feel at home in positions of this type; his team had not spent a single second analysing the "Berlin Wall"; and Kasparov's monster computer conclusions would be missing all of the core subject on this defence.

Score: ½–½

Game 2
Vladimir had nothing extraordinary up his sleeve for White but wanted to play precisely and take advantage of any chances on offer. Kasparov chose the Grünfeld Defence, a main opening system which both players knew really well.

After the opening phase White had some pressure, but in principle it looked like a draw until on move 34 Kasparov played what Kramnik suspected was the decisive mistake (34...♖d7 instead of 34...♗d6).

Having landed in time trouble, Kasparov then practically gave the game away with a major blunder just before the time control (39...♔e7?).

Kramnik took the lead to the amazement of the chess world.
Score: ½–1½

Game 3
Kasparov had fallen behind, not for the first time in a match. His fans did not yet feel anxious.

Once again, the Berlin Defence appeared on the board.

Kasparov made a serious attempt; for 53 moves he exerted pressure on the black king before finally offering a draw.

Once again, the position had looked hair-raising for Black. Nobody could or wanted to believe that there would not be a way for Kasparov to break through. But the slow technical play did not suit the champion, and his team found it hard to come up with any powerful innovations during the match.
Score: 1–2

Game 4

In the fourth game, Kasparov landed in a critical position. Vladimir outplayed him in a slow variation of the Queen's Gambit Accepted. After 74 moves and a great struggle, Kasparov saved the draw as though only by a miracle. Kramnik played brilliantly up to the first time control, where he missed the first chance to win the game.

Later, his 49th move (49.♘e4?) was a big mistake, throwing away the win. The position was still difficult for the champion, but he managed to hold a draw with the narrowest of margins.

Both players should be praised for their fighting spirit. Kasparov had defended with tooth and claw, seen by the self-styled psychological experts as a plus for the title defender and continued to bet on him. Years later, Vladimir told he had been quite disappointed not to win this game, but still described this as his best of the match.

Score: 1½–2½

Game 5

On the morning of the fifth game, Kramnik received a note from the organizing team. Some sort of provocation concerning his toilet visits was said to be planned by Kasparov. Vladimir was late out the door and the driver did not know the way and got lost. Kasparov had already made the first move when the organizers stopped Kramnik on his way to the playing table, telling him: "Because of a demand from Kasparov's team, from now on you will be accompanied to the toilet by a security man." Obviously, this was a typical psychological manoeuvre from Kasparov. Kramnik reacted calmly: "You could have told me that a long time before the start of the game and not while my clock is running. Let us talk after the game."

However, they demanded that it had to be decided then. Kramnik agreed, but demanded the same conditions for Kasparov. Soon all involved understood that the whole business was a simple nuisance. No more was heard of it and it finished as a storm in a teacup. Kasparov opened with 1.c4.

But after 24 moves he agreed to the draw offer from Kramnik. The World Champion and his team obviously still had no idea how the Berlin Wall could be torn down.

Score: 2–3

Six years later, the "toilet question" would return with increased intensity. "Toiletgate", the greatest scandal in the history of chess, had in Vladimir's view its origin in this minor incident in London. Kramnik's longstanding habit of leaving the playing table after almost every move and staying in his restroom, walking up and down to work off his emotions and tensions, constituted a fertile breeding ground for conspiracy theories.

Game 6
Kramnik had White and on move 13 came up with a new idea in the Queen's Gambit in the form of 13.h4.

Kasparov reacted correctly, and the game moved along peaceful channels. After 40 moves and the first time control, the game was level. Then the World Champion made some small mistakes and was once again on the defensive. Later Kramnik had many promising options and chose the wrong one.

50.♕f8! (instead of 50.♖xh7+?) followed by a series of accurate moves would have won the game, for example. There were chances later, but this was the biggest one.

Although Kasparov had been harmless with White up till then, he had defended strongly with Black. Again Kramnik exerted tremendous pressure in the endgame, trying all he could tactically and positionally, but Kasparov found so many "only" moves during this game that he was justifiably congratulated for this 66-move draw by the commentators afterwards, with grandmaster Julian Hodgson stating it was the greatest game he had ever seen.

Kramnik lamented: "He is so lucky. How can he get away with such blunders?"
Score: 2½–3½

Game 7
Kasparov with White again sidestepped with 1.c4. Only eleven moves were played before Kasparov offered a draw.

It was a rare moment when Kasparov was faced with massive criticism in the chess world. This time his propaganda machine *kasparovchess.com* with the American Mig Greengard as opinion-former was of less use. Disgrace was the topic. The World Champion was even accused of dishonourable conduct. The game only lasted 48 minutes. And this was the day match director Raymond Keene had invited potential sponsors. They experienced the shortest world championship game since Botvinnik – Petrosian 1963, which must have suited Kramnik. One can have some understanding for Kasparov's motives. Especially with the immense pressure of a world championship match considered.

I experienced three world championship matches from the inside and can comprehend Kasparov's behaviour. He was visibly despairing; day and night he and his team and the computers were working on how to tear down the Berlin Wall. This alone was costing a lot of time and an incredible amount of energy. In the seventh game Kasparov wanted breathing space, a time-out, especially since he was beginning to tire from the middle of the match. However, 1.c4 was hardly the appropriate way to play for a win against Kramnik. Perhaps he should have switched immediately to 1.d4. But certainly pride played a part too.

Score: 3–4

Game 8

Kasparov chose the Nimzo-Indian Defence as Black and emerged from the opening with some positional advantages. 16...♞c7 was a strong innovation and the body language of the World Champion displayed confidence and strength.

For the first time his preparation was working, at least with Black. Kasparov spent only five minutes in the opening, Kramnik more than an hour. A win for Black would have caused a turn-around in the match. Kramnik defended prudently, sometimes brilliantly, and in doing so sacrificed a pawn for space and counterplay. When the knights were exchanged the game went to a rook ending with bishops of opposite colours and an extra pawn for Black. All the experts and even both players thought after the game that Kasparov had missed a win. But in the subsequent analyses no win or anything close to it was found. It was the first time that Kasparov had looked on the way to winning a game, yet Kramnik had withstood a powerful storm.

Score: 3½–4½

Game 9

Kasparov returned to 1.e4 and thus we had another Ruy Lopez. Although most were certain he must have found something against the Berlin Defence by now, Kramnik was unimpressed and played "his system". The World Champion wanted to show Kramnik that the Berlin Defence could not prevail against him. This stubbornness was one of the reasons he lost the title. But history repeats itself: Kramnik lost only one world championship match, roughly eight years later. The main reason was a similar stubbornness!

Kramnik had spent weeks looking into the Berlin Defence; he was aware of Kasparov's impatience and he knew precisely how infinitely difficult it would be for the title defender to find an antidote during the match. Moreover, the early exchange of queens in these variations suited Kramnik. His feeling for positional play came into its own, whilst the aggressive Kasparov was robbed of his tactical and active powers by the exchange of the strongest piece.

The game ended in a draw after 33 moves (the diagram shows the position after 22...☐d3). Later Kramnik expressed the idea that the position had been dangerous for him, but that Kasparov's attack had been too weak.

Score: 4–5

Game 10

The chess press still considered Kasparov as the favourite. Even the psychological breakdown of Kramnik was being predicted. In any case, the majority were convinced that Garry's experience would bring him the upper hand. A chess world without Kasparov as champion was totally unthinkable for most.

Kasparov again defended with the Nimzo-Indian. But this time Kramnik was prepared. The World Champion was surprised by 4.e3, the Rubinstein Variation, which had never been part of Vladimir's repertoire.

Kasparov deviated from theory with 14...♘xf6 (the usual move here being 14...♗xf6), and after 15.♗xe6

came the decisive mistake with 15...fxe6 (15...☐c7! would have been okay for Black).

Kasparov was in despair, shaking his head several times. One might have expected that Kasparov had prepared this, but both players probably found themselves in unexplored territory. Be that as it may, Kramnik played accurately. Kasparov made the final mistake on move 23 with 23...♖f8. With the resignation of the World Champion it was all over after 25 moves.

Score: 4–6

Game 11

The playing hall in the Riverside Studios was sold out.

Vladimir came up with a fresh surprise, employing the Neo-Archangelsk Variation in the Spanish Opening, a system which had been gaining in popularity in the 1990s. Kasparov was prepared and played aggressively, but Kramnik defended prudently and after 41 moves a draw was agreed. In the subsequent press conference, there was a lively discussion between the two protagonists.

Kasparov claimed to have missed a clear win.

Instead of 23.♔f2 he should have played 23.♖a1. "I am playing poorly and everyone can see that." Kramnik contradicted him in his calm fashion: "We had seen 23.♖a1 in our preparation and I analysed the position deeply. I am of a different opinion." Everybody could then see Kasparov's psychological suffering. Kramnik continued: "I will offer the same position in a future game. Then we will see!"

Score: 4½–6½

Game 12
Kramnik looked anything but prepared. Again facing the Nimzo-Indian Defence with the white pieces caused him problems. Obviously his preparation was not working here, or else he simply overestimated the position. It developed into an exciting game, once again in front of a full house. More and more grandmasters from all over the world were guests for the decisive phase of the match. Kramnik played for a win, wanting to clarify everything. This time the queens remained on the board. Kasparov fought back and both players got into considerable time trouble.

The World Champion took the initiative with 23...a6, which was followed by inaccuracies by Kramnik. Kasparov missed some great winning chances in what followed. In time trouble, Kramnik's play was once more of the highest level. Kasparov had increased the pressure and set a trap with 28...♘b6.

Kramnik found a strong defence in this dramatic situation, first 29.♖4c3, and after 29...♖b4 he played 30.♘d2! to protect the white bishop on e4 and at the same time blockade the passed pawn on the c-file. Frustrated, Kasparov, who once more saw his hopes dashed, made the inaccurate moves 30...f5 and 31...♘a4, which led to a draw after 33 moves.

Score: 5–7

After the game Vladimir went home on foot through a park. A group of aggressive men followed him. He started to become fearful and ran away, with the young men on his heels. In this situation too, his physical condition paid off. He was simply faster, and on one and the same day he escaped not only Kasparov, but also a group of thugs.

Game 13

Kasparov is very superstitious, as are most chess players. His lucky number is 13 – he was born on the 13th of the month, became the 13th World Chess Champion, and in earlier matches his mother Klara had always sat in seat 13 of the 13th row. So in the 13th game, it should all work out. But in this world championship match, even the 13th game did not come to his aid.

Once again, the Berlin Defence appeared on the board. Kramnik again changed his move order in the opening.

Objectively it was probably not so good, and neither Kramnik nor any other top player ever repeated this set-up. But Kasparov had nothing prepared for it and looked very uncertain. He was simply not prepared to play and after only 14 moves he conceded a draw. Once more, to the disappointment of his fans, Kasparov refused to fight with the white pieces.

Score: 5½–7½

Game 14

Nothing is more difficult than turning a supposedly won world championship match into a final triumph. Once they are on track for a win, all top sportsmen start to feel anxious. The more important the competition and the greater the lead, the greater the tension. Thinking about the possible disgrace of letting a sure-fire success slip out of one's hands takes over.

In my experience, this pressure is greater in chess than in physical sports. Movement creates a safety valve unknown to chess players. No grandmaster can escape these fears, and Vladimir was feeling the burden. Growing tension took a hold over him. He was finding it hard to sleep, and doubts gnawed away at his confidence.

This was the situation before the 14th game. Kramnik played 1.♘f3 and Kasparov transposed into the English Opening.

Vladimir lost material with White, but Kasparov was no longer himself and unable to turn the extra pawn into a win against the young contender's stubborn defence. For the first time, Kramnik showed signs of nerves. Vladimir's preparation with White was again not the best; he played without confidence and Kasparov got a decent advantage. Kramnik's mistake on move 51 with 51.罝g7 could easily have lead him into dangerous troubles, where any additional mistake would have cost him the game.

But Kasparov too was no longer seeing everything he might and after the mistake 55...♔f5 the chances had evaporated. Instead 55...♔f6 was winning according to Kasparov, but deeper analysis showed that White still had enough defensive resources left, although it would have been challenging to find them all at the board.

The following story epitomizes the mood of the World Champion. When a threefold repetition appeared on the board, Kramnik pointed it out. Kasparov's reply was strange: "Perhaps, perhaps..." Kramnik went to the arbiter and claimed a draw.

After the game there was the following dialogue.

Kramnik: "But you could have gone to d5 with your king."
Kasparov: "Where is my king, on e6?"
Kramnik: "Yes, e6."
Kasparov: "Yes, then perhaps... yes, I could have played that."

Kramnik had never seen the 13th World Champion so distracted. Kasparov was on the point of going down. Kramnik: "He was terribly tired and no longer capable of playing a long game. Four or at the most five hours was enough for him."

Score: 6–8

Game 15
Late in the afternoon of 2nd November 2000, Kramnik for the first time in his chess career pumped his right fist into the air – a gesture made by many great icons of sport. On another two occasions, Vladimir would show his feelings in this for him uncharacteristic extroverted way after his successful title defences against Peter Leko and Veselin Topalov. The 15th game was the last one in the match. The draw after 30 moves was not as peaceful as one might have suspected. Kasparov had surprised Kramnik with 1.d4. Apparently without any special preparation, Kramnik went into the Catalan Opening. Strategically speaking, Kasparov's position was so good from the opening that he ought to have won this game.

But the World Champion had no more energy; his moves were lifeless and inaccurate, and Kramnik defended with precision.

Final score: 6½–8½

♔21

History had been written. On only one previous occasion had there not been a single victory for the titleholder, when José Raúl Capablanca defeated Emanuel Lasker with four wins and ten draws in Havana 1921. Kramnik's strategy had worked perfectly: "Bore him to death with Black and strike mercilessly given a chance with White."

Kasparov, who was used to emerging from the opening with an advantage as a stepping stone to winning the game, faced an opponent prepared up to his eyeballs who made better use of his chances. In 2000, half the chess world was working for Kasparov. He was using the best chess software on the strongest performing computers. Nowadays, all top players work the way he did back then. In the 1980s and 1990s he had a head start over his competitors.

Despite all these advantages, Kramnik showed no sign of fearing Kasparov and his machines. He was readier for the struggle than at any previous time in his career. With the big prize in sight, he drastically changed his lifestyle and did everything possible to ensure success. His analysis of Kasparov's strengths was crystal clear, and he brilliantly neutralized them.

Immediately after the match, Kramnik expressed himself as follows: "Naturally Kasparov was the favourite. Not as far as his chess playing strength was concerned. In our games before the match I never had the feeling that he was the better player. But there were factors which had nothing to do with chess, or only indirectly so. He had a colossal amount of experience of match-play, something you cannot compensate for. In addition, there was a group of seconds who over the years had worked out an effective system of preparation and a strong opening repertoire. I was not certain whether I would be in any position to win. But I wanted to do all I could to put him to the test. In no way did I want to have to reproach myself for not having seized my chance because of any lack of effort. To that extent I could have lived with a defeat. I would have proof that I could not reach that level."

Long after the match there was still speculation in the chess world as to how this result came about. Kasparov himself said: "I was completely out-prepared, Vladimir chose bold openings and I was having to work on my preparation ten hours a day. I was not outplayed, but out-prepared. But the 14th game had the most dramatic effect on me when afterwards on the way home, I realized I had had a winning position." (Actually, he didn't).

There were many rumours as to why the ex-World Champion had played with such lack of energy. But at the end of the day there was only one single reason for his defeat – Vladimir Kramnik. Some years would pass before the chess world recognized that in London, Kramnik was simply the better player and his victory totally deserved. At that time, Kasparov's influence was too great. Most tournament organizers, journalists and even competing top players ate out of his hand. For years they all got a few crumbs from Kasparov's cake.

Grandmaster Evgeny Bareev was one of the few who hit the nail on the head and publicly praised Kramnik's performance: "If you purely go by the depth of his talent and evaluate his contribution to the development of chess in theory and practice, there is no doubt that Kramnik is a genius. It would otherwise have been impossible to defeat Kasparov in this way at the high point of his career."

Kasparov himself offered fair and honest congratulations after the loss of his title: "Kramnik is the real world champion and you can throw all the FIDE ranking lists into the dustbin."

In my opinion, Kramnik played an almost ideal match against Kasparov; an optimum performance, so close to perfection that even a World Champion will only reach that level a handful of times in his life. Or less. He saw things with crystal clarity. From then on, he knew better what he wanted or did not want. He even learned to say 'no', and his personality developed accordingly.

I like to compare the London match with the boxing world championship bout between George Foreman and Muhammad Ali in 1974 in Kinshasa, Zaire – *The Rumble in the Jungle*. Outsider Ali let himself be pummelled against the ropes by Foreman, as was Kramnik's tactic with Kasparov. Vladimir's ropes were the Berlin Wall and he knew, just like *the greatest that ever lived* once did, precisely what he was doing. All Kasparov's energy bounced off this wall until the 13th World Champion became exhausted and suffered a decisive blow in the tenth game. After that, Kasparov had no energy to turn things around and was as tired after the match as Foreman against Ali. Visualize George Foreman leaving the stadium in Kinshasa and you know what I am talking about.

For some years Kramnik acquired nicknames such as the "Rock" or the "Iceman". A maximum of coolness was attributed to the highly emotional Russian. Vladimir in any case began taking responsibility: "I am the World Champion and I will fulfil my contract," he said in one interview.

According to his commitments, Kramnik defended his title, but not under the Braingames banner. Four long years would pass before the title defence finally happened. A stony path lay ahead. But first, for the first time in his career Vladimir was awarded the Chess Oscar, for the year 2000. This award is decided worldwide every year by a few hundred chess journalists, and had been won almost exclusively by Kasparov and Karpov for decades.

Kasparov's great era as World Champion thus finally came to an end. But at the time nobody could know that. Garry had dominated the chess world for almost 20 years and held the world title for 15. His great world championship matches against Anatoly Karpov between 1984 and 1990 will never be forgotten.

I congratulated Kramnik on his victory and invited him to a rapid chess match in Budapest against Peter Leko at the beginning of year 2001, only a few weeks after his great triumph.

Vladimir Kramnik – Garry Kasparov

World Championship, London (10) 2000

1.d4 ♘f6 2.c4 e6 3.♘c3 ♗b4 4.e3 0–0 5.♗d3 d5 6.♘f3 c5 7.0–0 cxd4 8.exd4 dxc4 9.♗xc4 b6 10.♗g5 ♗b7 11.♖e1 ♘bd7 12.♖c1 ♖c8 13.♕b3

13...♗e7?! 14.♗xf6! ♘xf6 15.♗xe6! fxe6? 16.♕xe6† ♔h8 17.♕xe7 ♗xf3 18.gxf3 ♕xd4

19.♘b5! ♕xb2 20.♖xc8 ♖xc8 21.♘d6 ♖b8 22.♘f7† ♔g8 23.♕e6 ♖f8 24.♘d8† ♔h8 25.♕e7 1–0

Vladimir Kramnik:

"Before this game I was very tense and the match situation rather unclear. Previously I had missed outstanding chances to score wins, above all in Games 4 and 6. I was dictating the match, but had not obtained a decisive advantage. This was nagging me. If the match was drawn, Garry would retain his title, and he only needed a single win for that to happen. Game 10 changed this, in my favour.

It was a strange game in many respects. I chose the Nimzo-Indian Defence with 4.e3, because his statistics against it were poor. My own knowledge of it was only superficial, but I caught Garry completely on the wrong foot. After 13.♕b3, which had been played rarely only, there are several ways to equalize. Theory in this sub-variation was not well developed in 2000. Garry obviously did not know it and went wrong with 13...♗e7. Nowadays 13...♗xc3 14.♖xc3 h6 is quite popular and even then it was well-known. When playing 13...♗e7 he had underestimated 14.♗xf6.

66

It was the decisive situation for the match. The moment where everything began to go against him. He was trailing, feeling the weight on his shoulders. Somehow he was unable to cope and began to make unusual tactical errors. Garry as a rule only entered complications when he had prepared for them thoroughly at home. This time he had not done so and that was simply psychologically too much for him.

His play closely resembled that of a mental collapse. Time after time he missed the best defence. For example, I played 15.♗xe6 and Black had the resource 15...♖c7 16.♘g5 ♗d6. If he had played this, Kasparov would have been a pawn down, the f7-square would have been weak, and the position would have looked pretty scary. But according to present-day theory, Black's position would have been fine with good chances of a draw. Okay, this was very hard to find at the board, but not impossible. He played the solid looking 15...fxe6, which in the subsequent variation allows White 19.♘b5, a move which he perhaps underestimated.

After this he probably became panic-stricken. If he had kept a cool head and not been so emotional, he would probably have found 19...♕d2. That also appears dangerous, but it is a natural move. After it, White still has an advantage, but with accurate play a draw is still possible for Black. Black's next and decisive mistake was 21...♖b8. The correct move would have been 21...♖a8. After 21...♖b8 it was practically impossible for Black to hold the game. The next blunder 23...♖f8 resembled a collapse and ended the game after only 25 moves.

After I played my last move 25.♕e7, I went to my restroom. It was clear to me that the game was won, but nevertheless I felt quite strange. I simply could not believe that everything had gone down so quickly and easily. The applause broke out in the auditorium. I went to the table; Garry had resigned and was signing the scoresheet.

After this win I was leading the match by two points. There were only six games left and it was clear that I had every chance of winning against such a fantastic player and becoming the next World Champion. Correspondingly, Garry became less tense, his play was freer and he exerted pressure in the final games. The whole business became psychologically more difficult from then on, as nothing is mentally more demanding than taking the final step towards a great triumph. But all in all, I managed to get there.

In any case, on the route to the World Champion title, Game 10 was the greatest moment. From a psychological point of view, success could be equated to the annihilation of my predecessor. There were a lot of interesting games in the match, but this was the decisive blow which ensured success."

The Monster of Bahrain

♔22

One thing was crystal clear after the world championship match in London: Vladimir Kramnik would go down in the history of sport. He had dethroned the supposedly strongest chess player of all time. In the 1990s, Kramnik was considered to be a universal, though unambitious, chess genius. However, the opportunity to fight against Kasparov made him change his attitudes – Vladimir Kramnik learned about professionalism!

His playing style also altered correspondingly. In the past he had not avoided exchanging pieces, but during the world championship he preferred subtle positional play and logically stuck to that strategy. This approach brought the almost unbeatable Garry Kasparov to despair. In the 38th match for the world championship since 1886, Kramnik became the 14th World Chess Champion.

A lot had been achieved from a sporting point of view. But years later, another high point would appear to transcend the year 2000, at least emotionally.

But at this point Vladimir began to feel a certain emptiness, as can happen with successful people after they have achieved a great goal. Questions appear, such as: What can I still achieve? Why should I again put myself through such never-ending tribulations?

When Kramnik fell into this psychological dip, he gradually realized that he did not particularly relish the role of World Champion. One of his predecessors, Boris Spassky, had once told him that his years as World Champion had been the unhappiest ones in his life; too much responsibility had rested on his shoulders. Vladimir now saw personally what he had meant. The increased media interest along with loss of privacy, topped with agonizingly drawn-out chess politics, made life difficult for him.

Before the match with Kasparov, Kramnik had signed a contract stating that the next challenger was to be decided in a tournament between the best players. Kasparov had demanded this, before the world championship match, and committed himself – just like Kramnik – to take part in such a tournament in the event of a loss. But after his defeat, the ex-World Champion was no longer interested and vehemently demanded a direct return match. Many of his supporters and "his" journalists joined in the chorus. After a 15-year reign on the chess throne, Kasparov handed over not only the responsibility, but a certain vacuum. Garry had been a dominant titleholder and his successor would need a certain amount of time to assume this position.

After his match against Anand in New York 1995, Kasparov had taken five years before defending his title. That led to unease in the chess world, but he still had the advantage of being seen as the real World Champion, a part of the traditional sequence. No matter what FIDE organized, Kasparov was the man to beat. Kramnik may have defeated him convincingly in London, but he still lacked the scope of his predecessor's reputation.

Kasparov's friends saw the defeat of their idol as some sort of accident. They missed no opportunity in praising Kasparov as the "real" number one and disparaging Kramnik as a weak world champion.

In doing so, Kasparov played into the hands of his arch-enemy, FIDE, with president Kirsan Ilyumzhinov at the helm. That did not seem to matter to him, since Garry's interests lay elsewhere. His campaign against Kramnik did not make him only friends; some insiders on the chess circuit were well aware of what drove him down such an inconsistent approach. But they kept quiet, like the overwhelming majority of chess journalists. In any case, the officials in FIDE made use of the situation; immediately after Kramnik's world championship success, they joined the plan and began to act against Vladimir.

Vladimir Kramnik would have liked, in conjunction with his contractual partner Braingames, to have brought about the unification of the chess world through a match between him and the FIDE titleholder. However, FIDE wanted to continue their unravelling of long chess games with classical time controls and the tradition of deciding the world championship with a big final match. These were and are precisely the traditions which have worked successfully in promoting professional chess; a format that has led to chess becoming an important cultural fixture.

FIDE argued that these changes would serve to establish chess as a sport for TV and as an Olympic sport. Both aims sound wonderful, but they were and are unrealistic. Anyone who has looked into this subject professionally is well aware that chess will never be a TV sport; not as long as the spirit of our times preaches instantaneity and superficiality.

Ilyumzhinov and his followers considered that this only advanced their arguments. It is quite simple to interpret FIDE's method: a strong World Chess Champion was a thorn in their flesh. He would enjoy public recognition on all continents, all the way up to the highest government circles. His position had to be weakened. The best way to achieve this was to deprive him of his major showcase – the world championship matches. So FIDE organized a conveyor belt of "roulette tournaments" and produced their own titleholders, who were taken seriously by hardly anybody. Now that Kasparov had been replaced, they saw a one-off chance to break the traditional line of World Chess Champions.

I discussed these matters with Kramnik several times and in great detail. He found himself in the middle of a highly complex intrigue in chess politics and took an important decision. From then on, he would consistently work for the reunification of the chess world and for the maintenance of the classical line of chess world champions. This was honourable, but caught between Kasparov and FIDE, and tied to a weak rights-holder in Braingames, the situation was problematic.

Kramnik loves life in all its facets, but has always found it hard to accommodate himself to lazy compromises. Thus he wasted a lot of energy on nothing: amongst others on senseless meetings with officials who promised him heaven and earth, lied to him, and documented their own importance by appearing at his side.

♔23

Vladimir realized what Boris Spassky had meant – the job as world champion would be anything but a cakewalk. Especially for him, since he was following in Kasparov's footsteps outside of FIDE and reliant only on his own resources. As history shows, the only way forward was to be principled and steadfast.

The reunification of the chess world came six years later, and according to Kramnik's conditions. His central demands were implemented: even today the final match for the world championship is played under classical time controls.

That FIDE would never again be well disposed towards him could be predicted back then. This was later seen during the world championship match against Topalov, where the greatest scandal in the history of chess broke out with the help of influential officials.

During the Dortmund tournament of 2001, Vladimir, Josef Resch and I had a first discussion about how Kramnik might get better organized. Some meetings followed and I became more and more involved in specific subjects. At the end of 2001, during the Botvinnik Memorial event in Moscow, Vladimir and I finally agreed to work together.

However, the chess year 2001 had begun much earlier. On January 5th I had the pleasure of meeting Bobby Fischer in Budapest for the first and only time; something unfortunately denied to Vladimir Kramnik. Vladimir repeatedly planned to visit Fischer during his final years in Reykjavik. But commitments got in the way of this journey and with the death of Fischer on 17th January 2008, the opportunity was suddenly gone.

I was luckier. At the beginning of the millennium, Janos Rigo – an international master from Budapest – was looking after the chess legend, who had lived for several years incognito there. Janos called and asked if I would like to meet Bobby. He had asked Fischer, who had agreed. Fischer was a bit of a phantom: he frequently changed his domicile and hardly ever agreed to meet anyone. While organizing the Kramnik – Leko match I immediately went to see them.

Bobby was sitting with Janos and the latter's wife Kata in Anna Cafe on the Váci utca, the big Budapest pedestrian zone in the part of the city called Pest. Had I not known that I was to meet Bobby Fischer, I would not have recognized him. He had put on a lot of weight and his face was puffy. The hair on his head was thinner and he appeared rather unkempt.

It was no surprise that even in the Hungarian capital, so enthusiastic about chess, Fischer was not attracting much attention; you could hardly recognize him. I said: "I am very pleased to meet you, Mr Fischer. I know that you have already met Peter Leko. I am his manager and am organizing the rapid chess match between him and world champion Kramnik." He replied: "Ah yes, okay."

I took his hand, which after a short moment without any counter-pressure he withdrew. He took no more part in the short conversation between Janos and me. It was visibly unpleasant for him to have a stranger in front of him. After this meeting, Janos said to me: "It is mad, but when you had left he claimed that your involvement with Leko is only a pretext. In reality you are an agent of the American secret service. Bobby spotted that from your body language and other details." Once decided, Fischer would not tolerate a different view on that issue.

The rapid chess match had begun a few days beforehand, on 2nd January 2001. Once more outstandingly staged in the ballroom of the Budapest Kempinski Hotel by the German energy firm RWE. The importance of internet broadcasts was growing meteorically. More and more chess fans from all over the world were logging in. Although the medium was still in its infancy, already more than 100,000 people were following the rapid chess games between Leko and Kramnik live on the internet every day.

For a match of rapid chess – around 30 minutes thinking time per player per game – the match was contested at a very high level. The 21-year-old Leko was already Number 6 in the world and definitely not without chances. However, Kramnik warded off the attacks of the young Hungarian, professionally and calmly. He lived up to his role as favourite and won by 7–5. Both players would measure up to each other afresh in a much more important match only four years later: the dramatic match for the world championship in Brissago, Switzerland.

When I met Kramnik in Budapest, he again seemed changed, even slightly melancholy. Physically he was still in decent condition. He never wanted to fall back into his old habits. Here and there a small glass of red wine, okay, but no more carousing till the early hours of the morning. We spoke superficially about the match against Kasparov, the present situation in the chess world and his participation in the 2001 Dortmund Chess Days. I felt that chess politics and his status as World Champion were beginning to weigh on him. He was isolating himself in order to escape endless questions from journalists.

After the RWE match and a flying visit to my family, I travelled to Wijk aan Zee in the Netherlands on 13th January. Peter Leko had caught the flu. With a temperature of over 40 degrees Celsius he was in no condition to play. The next day he just happened to have to play against Kramnik. I had a word with Vladimir. He did not want to get a point by walkover against one of his closest rivals and agreed to a short draw.

This gesture may have cost him the victory in the tournament, because in 2001 he took third place, half a point behind Kasparov and Anand. This was the first and only occasion in my time as a chess manager that I arranged the result of a game. The incident shows one thing above all: the profoundly human side of the world champion Kramnik, unwilling to take advantage of his opponent's illness.

Vladimir made up for this with a magnificent victory in Monaco shortly after.

In the spring of 2001, in the final round of the extremely strong tournament in Astana, Kramnik lost to Garry Kasparov in the Berlin Defence, the symbol of Vladimir's world championship victory in London. This released any restraint Kasparov may have put on himself. He claimed to be the best player in the world and that Kramnik was morally obliged to give him a rematch. For weeks Kasparov's demands and hostile comments dominated the chess press. Kramnik pointed to the contractual obligations both players had signed, and tried to ignore Garry.

In the summer of 2001 in Mainz, Vladimir played a rapid chess match against Anand, which ended peacefully with a score of 5–5. In the meantime, I had got the green light from Dortmund: my hometown would organize the Candidates tournament in 2002, and the winner would receive the right to challenge Vladimir Kramnik. The Braingames adviser, Grandmaster Raymond Keene, was also staying in Mainz. He was really happy about this development, since he had been unable to make any progress on behalf of Braingames.

First, Kramnik won the Dortmund tournament of 2001 in great style; his sixth win since 1995, only interrupted by Peter Leko's victory in 1999. Anand had meanwhile become FIDE World Champion, but had collapsed completely in Dortmund. Neither before nor after did the Indian have such a bad tournament. With four losses – including against Kramnik – and no wins he was relegated to last place.

♔24

The terror attacks of 11th September 2001 changed the world. We can feel the effects to this day in almost all areas of our daily lives. At first independently of these events, the western capitalist system had begun to crumble. During the crash of the New Economy Markets many people lost a lot of money, some of them their entire fortunes. This was one of the biggest stock market crashes in history. An astonishing number of companies declared bankruptcy. The technology balloon has been over-inflated, mostly with hot air.

The resolution of the dotcom bubble was delayed by the somewhat sick capitalist system. For example, the Deutsche Börse (German stock market) tried to cover up the problem by delisting penny stocks. As a result innumerable private investors were taken to the cleaners with the active help of the banks. After this collapse, the god of money temporarily disappeared from the scene.

The effects of such a crash on the world of professional chess are even more serious than the effects on major TV sports. Receipts from ticketing and TV rights are negligible in chess, but the declining commitments by sponsors and patrons in such a crisis always leads to considerable problems.

But first Kramnik played the Botvinnik Memorial in Moscow, in November 2001. Against Garry Kasparov he scored 2–2 (four draws) at classical time controls, and 3–3 in rapid chess. In blitz chess (five minutes per player for the entire game) Vladimir lost by 3½–6½. This match took place in the famous Hall of Columns in the House of the Unions. In it the powerful men of the Communist Party of the Soviet Union (CPSU), including Joseph Stalin, had lain in state after their deaths. The Hall of Columns also hosted the first world championship match between Karpov and Kasparov.

Parallel to the Botvinnik Memorial, FIDE was organizing their knock-out world championship in the Kremlin Hall of the former CPSU.

During the match against Kasparov, I met Kramnik backstage. Kramnik and I met again in the Moscow sauna owned by Josef Resch. After a short conversation we reached an agreement and I consequently took over the management of the 14th World Champion.

Meanwhile the German Minister of the Interior and avid chess fan, Otto Schily, was visiting Moscow. I met him in the Kremlin and he was not at all happy about the split in the chess world. In return, the FIDE President was unhappy that Schily should express his displeasure so openly. Schily quickly developed a feel for the state of affairs in the world federation, and promised general support from the federal German government for the Candidates tournament in Dortmund. Kramnik and I visited him at his Berlin office in 2003. He cancelled all his appointments and we had a lively conversation lasting almost two hours.

I began working for Vladimir immediately after returning from Moscow at the start of 2002. I took a look at Vladimir's contracts. As I did so, ice-cold shivers ran down my back. His tax advisers had gotten him into an awkward situation. A demand from the tax authorities in London had not been followed up. It was only after some months of delay that Vladimir received news of a five-figure tax demand via his place of birth, Tuapse. I was able to clear things up with the tax authorities without complication, especially thanks to the understanding shown by the lady in charge of the dossier in London.

As far as the defence of his title, the situation was deadlocked. Vladimir was unable to act without Braingames. They possessed the rights to the world championship. Vladimir would only be able to terminate the contract if they failed to fulfil their contractual obligations. Braingames had no money and what was worse, they were not particularly active. Right up to the Candidates tournament in Dortmund, which we had brought about, not much happened.

So we were pleased when the Einstein Group plc of London, showed interest in taking over all rights and obligations from Braingames. They quickly come to an agreement with Braingames. Vladimir and I flew to London and on 28th February 2002 we signed a contract with Einstein. The following day there was a press released and Vladimir played a short exhibition match against eleven-year-old David Howell (who is today rated in the top 60 in the world). We were relieved, since the Einstein deal had at least temporarily improved our position with respect to FIDE.

After the London agreement, Vladimir moved to Bochum in Germany, quite close to where I live. He began to set up house and was able to provide lodging for his training partners. It was high time to leave Moscow. His lifestyle might have changed, but both his real and false friends left him no breathing space. On the streets of Moscow, everyone recognized him and all wanted something from him. He could not continue to live there.

♔25

In the meantime, Nahed Ojjeh had entered the chess life of Vladimir Kramnik. The multi-millionairess with Syrian roots lived in Paris and had fallen in love with the royal game. She founded the NAO Chess Club in Paris. Almost all the French grandmaster scene fluttered around Madame like moths to the flame. Kramnik made her acquaintance via Joel Lautier and was immediately engaged as top player for the NAO team, which went on to win a succession of French team championships as well as the European Club Cup in 2003 and 2004.

Madame was a diva, shimmering and sometimes unpredictable. But she meant well with Kramnik and guaranteed the prize fund of more than 400,000 euros for the forthcoming Dortmund Candidates. This was a great relief for the Einstein Group, headed by Steve Timmins.

However, much more significant was that Kramnik was showing strength. With the multi-millionairess, the Candidates tournament financed and the Einstein Group at his side, he was suddenly much more than a thorn in the side of the world federation.

From a chess point of view not much happened. In Leon in Spain, Kramnik defeated Anand 3½–2½ in so-called Advanced Chess, where the players get advice from a computer during the game. Personally, I find this variation of chess completely superfluous and the format did not last long.

After that, at the end of April we travelled to Prague. Bessel Kok, now Chairman of the Czech telecommunications company Eurotel, had invited the best players in the world to a rapid tournament. Not only did they all come, but they were accompanied by a complete "Who's Who" of the chess world, including the FIDE President.

Bessel Kok was a close friend of Kasparov and wanted to catapult Kasparov back into world championship contention, with the support of some of Kasparov's friends, above all the American grandmaster Yasser Seirawan. Einstein and Kramnik had declined Garry's demand for a return match, so now Plan B came into force.

In my entire career in chess, I never again experienced such a performance. To be brief: on 6th May 2002, among others Kirsan Ilyumzhinov (FIDE President) and Vladimir Kramnik signed the so-called Prague Agreement, a document which is famous, even legendary, in the chess world. During hours of negotiation, I sat next to Vladimir, advised him and was in a position to admire the theatrical performances from some of the actors from this front row seat.

Contrary to the hopes of Kasparov and Ilyumzhinov, this agreement was the best thing which could have happened to Kramnik. It contained a decisive plan for the reunification of the chess world (Annex A). We paid attention to the wording according to which Vladimir was clearly recognized by FIDE as the classical World Chess Champion. In cases of future conflict, this would hold up in any sporting tribunal in the world.

To this day, I am not sure whether our opponents underestimated the consequences of this recognition. FIDE and Kasparov had joined together. They felt strong. At the start of the negotiations they had excluded our partner Einstein, but had gone on to recognize Kramnik, his title and also the Dortmund Candidates tournament.

I rejoiced internally. The Prague Agreement represented the legitimization of Kramnik by FIDE. Kramnik was to defend his classical world title against the winner of the Dortmund Candidates tournament. The new classical World Chess Champion would then play the winner of a match between Kasparov and Ruslan Ponomariov (the Ukrainian teenager had recently won the FIDE title). FIDE took responsibility for organizing this match.

That was the agreed route to reunification, euphorically greeted by the chess world. There would soon be only one world champion, recognized by all chess players under the aegis of the world federation. A good thing! But Kramnik was far less optimistic. And sadly proven right. It would take another four years before reunification finally happened.

The 2002 Candidates tournament in Dortmund was opened by Otto Schily. In the Gold Room of the Westfalenhallen, the prize for the best game, donated by Chancellor Gerhard Schröder, went to Peter Leko. The Hungarian had the strongest performance of his career. Over 14 games he dominated. He qualified from the preliminary group, consisting of Evgeny Bareev (Russia), Michael Adams (England) and Alexander Morozevich (Russia). In the semi-final he crushed Alexei Shirov from Spain, who a few years before defeated Kramnik, by 2½–½, and in the final he beat the Bulgarian superstar Veselin Topalov by 2½–1½.

Madame Ojjeh visited Westfalenhallen, as did other celebrities from politics and sport, including Vitaly Klitschko, the heavyweight boxing world champion. I had organized this visit with Klitschko's manager, Bernd Bönte, whom I had known for several years from his previous activities at the former marketing firm Sportfive and the Pay-TV broadcaster Premiere (now Sky Deutschland). Vitaly and Vladimir played a few moves of chess from which photos ended up in all the major international media.

This PR meeting developed into a long-lasting friendship. The brothers, Vitaly and Vladimir Klitschko, are real chess enthusiasts. They supported us on PR occasions and visited chess events. Be it in Dortmund, Munich, Wiesbaden, Gelsenkirchen or Cologne: Kramnik and I often sat ringside at their great bouts, with fingers crossed.

On the final Saturday of the Candidates tournament, Vladimir was fetched by a limousine to go to the popular TV programme *Aktuelle Sportstudio*. The ZDF channel produced an interesting introduction to Kramnik and chess where the former German international goalkeeper and enthusiastic hobby player Jens Lehmann participated.

TV presenter Michael Steinbrecher was well prepared and more than eight million people saw a majestic world champion in the interview. Vladimir won applause when in a penalty shootout he defeated the trainer of the then Bundesliga team VfL Bochum, Peter Neururer, by 2–1.

Afterwards things were a little difficult for Neururer, who had his leg pulled a bit – a professional footballer should not lose to a chess player. Nobody knew that in his youth Kramnik had been a very talented footballer with pronounced defensive qualities.

Things were absolutely fine for us. Kramnik and Leko were to play for the world championship, the Einstein Group was committed to staging the match, it had Madame Ojjeh on board, and the Prague Agreement gave us its blessing. So what could go wrong?

Everything!

Einstein got into escalating financial problems. Participants in the Candidates tournament, such as Boris Gelfand (Israel) and Alexander Morozevich (Russia), received their prizemoney months late. And Madame Ojjeh withdrew her support for the Einstein Group. Such a piece of stupidity. We were simply shocked.

At the start of 2003, my situation became difficult. I had contracts with both Kramnik and Leko, who were to play each other for the world championship. We had to act, but our financially-weakened partner had the rights to the world championship and was responsible for the organization. They still had to agree to everything. Officially we could not do much, but at the same time we were under considerable pressure.

♚26

But first there was a different highlight in our programme. Before the world championship match of 2000, the winner signed on to a match against the strongest chess computer in the world, scheduled for October 2001. The events of 11th September 2001 pushed this match into 2002. Again it did not come to pass.

When I began to deal with Kramnik's affairs, I was not very optimistic that this man vs machine match would ever take place. That changed when I met Yousuf Al Shirawi at Düsseldorf airport. Formerly a minister in the government of Bahrain, he loved chess and admired Kramnik, and so obviously wanted to see this match come to Bahrain.

The contracts were drawn up; the match would be held from 4th to 15th October 2002. Representing the computer was the Hamburg-based software company ChessBase, running on a Compaq computer. The newly developed Deep Fritz – later released as Fritz 7 – was the strongest chess engine at the time. The monster was able to calculate up to four million positions per second.

The prizemoney consisted of a million dollars. Kramnik would get $600,000 in the event of a defeat. $800,000 for a draw, and a full million for a win.

Even in 2002, a match against the machine was anything but a walk in the park, even for the world champion. This had been shown by the 1997 duel between Kasparov and Deep Blue, when the former champion lost 2½–3½, which sent shockwaves way beyond the chess world. That may only have been five years earlier, but in the digital world this is an eternity. Computers were now considerably faster, but above all, the positional understanding of the chess software had mightily improved. In order to have a whiff of a chance this time around, Kramnik had to prepare extremely precisely for the encounter.

Kramnik's team consisted of grandmasters Christopher Lutz (Germany), Tigran Nalbandian (Armenia), the physiotherapist Valery Krylov (Russia), the bodyguard and former kickboxing champion Aziz Abu Luay, and me. We set up our tents in a training camp in Sporthotel Weiskirchen in Saarland. The recommendation came from football trainers, Ottmar Hitzfeld and Michael Henke, whom I knew from the good old days in Dortmund. The Bayern Munich football team and other top athletes prepare for important events there, secluded on the edge of the forested mountains of Schwarzwälder Hochwald. Kramnik felt at home in the relaxed atmosphere there; Sporthotel Weiskirchen served us again and again after 2002 before major matches.

With the motto "Brains in Bahrain," the duel between man and machine brought enormous worldwide attention. The news magazine *Der Spiegel* has a four-page interview with Kramnik. The match electrified the public with all hopes resting on the world champion. With Kasparov's loss to Deep Blue in mind, the honour of mankind was on the line – at least this was how the print media reported it. Oh well. In spite of the obvious advantages of the machine, Kramnik's chances were not nil. Based on his strategic abilities, the new world champion was reckoned to have better chances than even Kasparov, not to speak of all other players in the world.

On 26th September 2002, we got on a Gulf Air plane in Frankfurt. From the very beginning, the organizers, the ruling house of Bahrain with King Hamad bin Isa Al Khalifa at the head, did things in style. We flew first class. A good two dozen journalists were lodged and fed at the cost of Bahrain for the duration of the match. Everyone was put up in the Gulf Hotel, a five-star palace in the capital Manama. My own quarters consisted of a 60-square-metre suite. After checking in, I went looking for Vladimir at his suite. At first I could not find him. In the Amiri suite, where the king had stayed, there were three living rooms, three bathrooms as well as other facilities.

I think back to the match with mixed feelings. On one hand we saw unimaginable riches. On the other we experienced great poverty. Pakistanis, Indians and Bangladeshis were risking their health in the tough hot conditions on the building sites of the island.

Ours was the side of splendour. A Mercedes Pullman from the royal fleet was at our disposal day and night. But apart from going to the playing hall, once to go swimming and returning to the airport, we would make no use of the stretch limousine in the three weeks of our stay. Nevertheless, ready it was, 24 hours a day. When I tried to explain to the organizers that this was not necessary, I got my answer: "But it is not a problem. The king has more than 200 of these vehicles in his fleet."

Officially, there was no alcohol. But in the detached bar of the hotel, a cosy English pub, exceptions were made. Every Thursday evening the Saudis came to Bahrain for the weekend and stayed in the sinfully expensive Gulf Hotel. All just to be able to enjoy a few drinks. In Saudi Arabia this was impossible. Half a litre of beer was correspondingly expensive; it cost the equivalent of twelve dollars.

Meanwhile the construction of the Formula 1 circuit in the Bahraini desert outside Manama was just about finished. We participated in some PR events for it. The first Bahrain Grand Prix was held in 2004.

We found the climate difficult. Even though it was October, the thermometer climbed above 40 degrees, and did not descend much below 30 degrees at night. This heat, along with over 90% humidity, cost Kramnik a lot of energy. Walking a kilometre in the evening made us sweat so much we had to take a shower.

Vladimir only once dared to leave our air-conditioned hotel on a rest day. We drove in armoured limousines to a resort on the Persian Gulf. The whole beach was cordoned off for us; we were the only visitors. The water temperature was over 30 degrees, just like a bath tub. You did not have to move much when swimming, because of the high concentration of salt in the water. Still, we did not endure for long... And also the hope, after weeks of abstinence, that we would perhaps see a lightly clad woman, was unfulfilled.

When the match finally got underway, Kramnik showed himself, as against Kasparov, first of all to be an outstanding match strategist. He developed an "anti-computer strategy" based on exchanging the queens as rapidly as possible, aiming for a positional continuation of the game. This strategy suited Vladimir since he was able to develop a "human" plan, and to a large extent elude the machine's calculations. Deep Fritz's calculations became hot in the truest sense of the word: at the start of the match, a game had to be interrupted because the machine was overheating.

Even the chess pieces could not stand the high temperatures. In the test runs before the match, the broadcasting from the digital chess board (by now considered essential) to the large screens in the tournament halls and the internet regularly failed. Even in 2002, millions of people logged on in anticipation before big games! Many of the biggest news portals routed the signal from the live broadcast from Bahrain onto their websites. This way, more than 100 million people were able to follow the match move by move. It was simply fantastic. ChessBase had developed a wonderful app for the match. But first the problem of the broadcasting had to be solved. Some bright spark came up with the idea of cooling the chess pieces; the sensitive sensors simply could not withstand the heat. So from then on the pieces were kept in a fridge, when not in action in the air-conditioned playing hall.

Kramnik easily drew the first game. He won the second and third games to the joy and the amazement of chess fans all over the world. The early exchange of queens and Kramnik's positional skills were decisive. After a draw in Game 4, Kramnik was leading 3–1 at half-way. His strategy had worked perfectly and the whole world was surprised.

After this, the computer experts from ChessBase delved into the "mechanism" of the machine, because as things were, their calculating monster was unable to compete. This was within the rules agreed in the contract. One reason for this was to avoid always seeing the same variations and opening systems on the board. For that purpose, Deep Fritz had so-called hash tables, within which certain priorities in the opening databases of the software could be altered. From then on, the machine avoided rapid exchanges of major pieces and aimed for positions in which its ability to calculate would be more valuable.

However, this intervention was not the cause of the world champion's ineffective play in the second half of the match. In the fifth game Kramnik overlooked the loss of a piece. Emotional and angry at himself, in Game 6 he played diametrically opposed to the match strategy, uncompromisingly attacking, even sacrificing a piece. Deep Fritz was in its tactical element; it defended precisely and obtained an advantage. Kramnik resigned after move 34. There were discussions after the game as to whether this resignation was premature, but this was of a purely theoretical nature. No human could have held this position against a computer.

Kramnik did the only correct thing and saved energy. He needed to do so since with the score at 3–3, the match was trending in favour of his opponent. To be honest, after the sixth game I had written the match off. Kramnik was tired and the climate wearing him down. Mistakes of the type seen in Game 5 were a real possibility and would be mercilessly exploited by the machine.

Parallels to the Deep Blue match of 1997 began to appear. In that match, Kasparov was almost in a state of psychological collapse at the end. In addition, in this match Kramnik was showing a weakness which would cause him some problems later: emotions. In the sixth game he wanted to destroy the monster, to "play like a man". Which of course made no difference to Deep Fritz. Fortunately, Kramnik was able to pull himself together, make draws in the last two games for a final score of 4–4.

The honour of humanity had been restored. But it would be the last major duel against the machine in which the human still had a genuine chance. Vladimir realized that at the time and replied to a relevant question: "For me it is not a problem that soon we will no longer have a chance against the machine. After all cars are also faster than people. Nobody finds that interesting. And in the foreseeable future what will be important in chess too is which person can play the best."

For Kramnik personally, the match was an incredible success. The press response was almost greater than it had been for the victory over Kasparov. After Kasparov's disaster in 1997, Kramnik had established the principle of how to play against the machine. The result made him 800,000 dollars richer, though it took some time for the money to reach his account. 200,000 dollars of the prizemoney were to go to ChessBase. They are still waiting for it to this day.

The kingdom of Bahrain, with its 33 islands, still exudes a magical aura. There things are not as ostentatious and artificial as in Dubai, Abu Dhabi or Doha. The people of Bahrain are cordial and more open to the world than the Western press sometimes indicates. For travellers with an interest in history, the paradise of Dilmun is worth a journey. On its shores, once upon a time, the great Sumerian King, Gilgamesh, was stranded, according to one version of the Epic of Gilgamesh. In the National Museum of Bahrain there are impressive displays on the beginnings of modern civilization.

Shortly before we departed, the shisha bars in Manama began to fill up in the evenings with American GIs. Important vessels from the American navy were stationed in the Persian Gulf. I chatted with their officers. We saw the first signs of the Iraq war, which would break out a few months later.

It was time to leave this fairy-tale country. When we disembarked the plane in Frankfurt, the temperature was seven degrees. Accustomed to something entirely different, we were all freezing.

♔27

Kramnik required some time to recover from the Bahrain match, but in January 2003 he played in Wijk aan Zee. Things did not go as well as he would have liked, and he had to content himself with a disappointing fourth place. But in Linares, Vladimir more than made up for it. He won the strongest tournament of the year together with Peter Leko, ahead of Garry Kasparov. He let Leko have the trophy, who celebrated his first and only win in Linares.

In Spain, Kramnik and I were under strong pressure. Everybody wanted to know when the world champion would defend his title against Leko. Although we had no idea, we presented an optimistic and confident front to the press. For some time we had been aware that Einstein had nothing to offer. This was particularly delicate for me; since I represented the interests of both players, everyone expected me to have a solution. I conducted discussions with Belgrade, Shanghai, Budapest, Moscow and Abuja. The negotiations kept on failing. This was partly to do with mismanagement by the Einstein Group, and partly because some representatives were not serious but unscrupulous, sensing either easy profits or publicity.

Ilya Levitov, a Russian parvenu who had gained the trust of some Russian grandmasters and therefore from time to time had Kramnik's ear, assured us that Khanty-Mansiysk, the Siberian biathlon mecca, would definitely stage the Kramnik – Leko match. There would be at least a million-dollar purse. I flew to Moscow only to establish that it was all hot air.

FIDE was up to its usual shenanigans. They had undertaken to organize a Kasparov – Ponomariov match, but never got around to doing it. Einstein CEO, Steve Timmins, and I met the FIDE board in Bucharest. The officials had nothing to offer, but had their usual arrogant attitude. They announced publicly that the Kramnik – Leko match would be played in Buenos Aires. They had no rights in the matter, the Einstein Group knew nothing of this, we knew nothing, and the city of Buenos Aires was totally unaware. We would have laughed at this, had these things not negatively affected Kramnik's career and reputation.

Meanwhile, Vladimir took second place in Dortmund. The sensational winner Viorel Bologan from Moldova had qualified via his victory in the Aeroflot Open in Moscow.

But the high point of 2003 for Kramnik was an interview with the *Le Figaro* by Marie-Laure Germon. They fell in love and Vladimir moved soon after to Paris. The Frenchwoman is the great love in the life of Vladimir Kramnik. They married in 2007 in the Russian Orthodox church in Paris. Today they live with their two children, Daria and Vadim, in Geneva, Switzerland.

In the summer of 2003 we realized that the problems of the Einstein Group were greater than we had thought. They were on the brink of insolvency. Kramnik made use of this opportunity and we terminated the contract. From September 2003 we were finally free to act. Due to the failure of our former partner, all rights to the classical chess world championship had reverted to Vladimir Kramnik.

From this point onwards, everything ran smoothly. I met Christian Burger, a powerful man in Burger Söhne AG in Switzerland, an internationally established tobacco firm which, among other things, is known as the third biggest producer of cigars in the world. The luxury brand Dannemann is part of their range. On the shores of Lago Maggiore lay a jewel: Christian Burger had set up the Centro Dannemann, which was involved in numerous cultural activities. Including chess. In January 2003 a match was organized between future women's world champion Alexandra Kosteniuk, and the talented 13-year-old Sergey Karjakin (who challenged Magnus Carlsen for the world championship in 2016, but lost in a tie-break play-off).

I got to know Christian Burger and his son Beat better. Unfortunately, Christian died much too soon in 2007. But before that, in the wonderful ambiance of the Centro Dannemann on Lago Maggiore, the world chess championship match between Vladimir Kramnik and Peter Leko would be played in 2004.

Vladimir Kramnik – Deep Fritz

Manama (2) 2002

1.d4 d5 2.c4 dxc4 3.♘f3 ♘f6 4.e3 e6 5.♗xc4 c5 6.0–0 a6 7.dxc5 ♕xd1 8.♖xd1 ♗xc5 9.♔f1 b5 10.♗e2 ♗b7 11.♘bd2 ♘bd7 12.♘b3 ♗f8 13.a4 b4 14.♘fd2 ♗d5 15.f3 ♗d6 16.g3 e5 17.e4 ♗e6 18.♘c4 ♗c7 19.♗e3 a5 20.♘c5 ♘xc5 21.♗xc5 ♘d7 22.♘d6† ♔f8 23.♗f2 ♗xd6 24.♖xd6 ♔e7 25.♖ad1 ♖hc8 26.♗b5 ♘c5 27.♗c6 ♗c4† 28.♔e1 ♘d3† 29.♖1xd3 ♗xd3 30.♗c5 ♗c4 31.♖d4† ♔f6 32.♖xc4 ♖xc6 33.♗e7† ♔xe7 34.♖xc6 ♔d7 35.♖c5 f6 36.♔d2 ♔d6 37.♖d5† ♔c6 38.♔d3 g6 39.♔c4 g5 40.h3 h6 41.h4 gxh4 42.gxh4 ♖a7 43.h5 ♖a8 44.♖c5† ♔b6 45.♖b5† ♔c6 46.♖d5 ♔c7 47.♔b5 b3 48.♖d3 ♖a7 49.♖xb3 ♖b7† 50.♔c4 ♖a7 51.♖b5 ♖a8 52.♔d5 ♖a6 53.♖c5† ♔d7 54.b3 ♖d6† 55.♔c4 ♖d4† 56.♔c3 ♖d1 57.♖d5† 1–0

Vladimir Kramnik:

"The match against the machine in Bahrain was strange for me. It was my first big match against a computer and to that extent a new experience. I took it very seriously, if nothing else, because Garry Kasparov had lost the last major match against the machine in 1997. The match should actually have taken place in 2001, but was delayed on account of the terrorist attacks of the 11th September. At least that was the official reason.

As usual, I had done extensive preparation, played over a hundred training games and tried out various openings. That caused me a few problems at the time, since it took me out of my normal rhythm. Against the computer you need to play differently, since the algorithm for thought is a different one. It is hard to go back to playing in a human way afterwards.

The match was delayed by a year and when, during my preparation, a few weeks before the event, I received the chess program without opening books, I was obliged to realize that I had to deal with a quite different, much stronger opponent. They had advance the program immensely during that year. It was considerably stronger than Deep Blue, which Kasparov played in 1997. But compared to the top programs of today, there were still odd weak points; especially in the endgame.

So I tried to approach the match strategically; to get the most positional endgames, where understanding rather than concrete calculation was important. I succeeded in that twice in the match, and was able to outplay and defeat the machine in those endings.

In the second game, a Queen's Gambit Accepted, I found 9.♔f1.

Objectively this innovation makes little sense. It achieves nothing for White, but fulfilled its purpose. I wanted to exit the opening theory in its database and succeeded. From an early stage the computer was relying on its own resources. Immediately it made dubious decisions. 9...b5 is already not the best move. It allows me to harass the b-pawn and obtain play on the queenside. Then 12...♗f8 was very curious, though not quite as mad as it looked, as the logical move 12...♗e7 would also have faced tactical problems.

After 13.a4 and 14.♘fd2 I managed to advance with my pawns on the queenside, opening up the possibility of 18.♘c4. At this point it was clear that I had a serious positional advantage and had correctly diagnosed the weaknesses of the machine. The computer calculates tremendously well, with precision and stubbornness no human can attain. So I had to handle the technical phase in a very precise manner. I am still proud of this game, since it only required one moment of negligence for the win to slip away.

I forced myself to work very hard during the game. I kept on calculating the variations.

Let us take for example 27.♗c6. When playing such a tactical move against the machine, you are never quite at ease. There is always the danger that you have overlooked something. But I decided on this move because there is hardly any other option for turning the advantage into a win. On playing 27.♗c6 I calculated all the variations up to move 35.

The computer had an inactive rook on a8. I set up something similar to a triangulation. In doing so, I saw that probably after 43.h5 Black is in zugzwang.

That means that every move available to Black contributes to worsening his position. The machine, however, continued to think that its position was defensible because, unlike a human being, it did not really understand the weakness of the rook on a8.

So I played 44.♖c5† and after 44...♔b6 45.♖b5† ♔c6 46.♖d5 the computer quite suddenly had the problem that it can no longer move its king because then my king invades. Also it can no longer move the rook on a8 because then it would lose the a-pawn or, if the rook goes to a7, I can penetrate to the eighth rank with my rook. It had to play the king to c7 and my king forced its way in with 47.♔b5.

The rest was just a matter of technique.

This was the way to defeat the machine at that time, nothing spectacular: almost perfect positional play and precise technique. This was how I won the third game. But against the computer you have to pay full attention at all times, and that is precisely what went wrong during the fifth game. In the sixth game I decided to play "like a man" and lost in the tactical series of exchanges.

But the problem was Game 5. The machine never tires, while you need a great deal of energy to keep a high level of concentration. The slightest slip leads immediately to a loss, as happened in the fifth game.

All in all, I was very satisfied with the final result of 4–4. It was an interesting experiment and basically I controlled the play – and the machine. In 2002 I was able to prove that the world champion was still the better player.

Nowadays, such a statement is unfortunately no longer possible on account of the meteoric development of the technology."

Passion and Suffering

♚28

The world championship deal with Dannemann was all sewn up by the middle of January 2004. I travelled from Zürich to the Netherlands with the players' contracts in my luggage. We were hugely relieved. The world championship match between my two protégés was for a prize fund of a million Swiss francs, but more important was that we had been able to bring about this world championship, even against hostility from FIDE and Kasparov.

The world federation either could not or would not produce anything. However, we had taken a major step forward and that filled us with unbelievable satisfaction; Kramnik felt the same as me. He was the one under the greatest pressure and now he had demonstrated the ability to act. His challenger, Peter Leko, was also happy. 14 games were scheduled from September 25th to October 18th 2004. The Hungarian would get his chance at the world championship.

Firstly, however, we had to make sure we were covered. Months before, I had agreed with Dannemann to hold a spectacular match for Kramnik. On 29th January 2004, he played a simultaneous in the Centro Dannemann against the German national team. He defeated a team of strong grandmasters, Dr Robert Hübner, Christopher Lutz, Rustam Dautov and Klaus Bischoff, by 2½–1½. That was a sensational performance, but it was only lightly reported on. The great news on this occasion was the announcement of the world championship match, which was then spread worldwide by all the big press agencies.

As Christian Burger told me, FIDE was still trying, even after this announcement, to prevent the world championship through the personal representative of its president. He had advanced financial demands in the name of FIDE in order to authorize the event, and had even threatened Dannemann with legal measures. Additionally, they would all like to have important jobs with high fees. Christian and I spoke briefly about these things and that was all that was needed. He had made a contract with us and would honour it; Christian Burger was an honourable man.

FIDE's behaviour of course was quite different. Outwardly, the representatives of the world federation always expressed in high-flown language their interest in reunifying the chess world. The reality, however, was that it was not the interests of the chess world and its professional players which they concentrated on, but rather the personal interests of individual officials. I understood better and better why Garry Kasparov had separated from these people in 1993.

Corruption was obviously widespread in the chess world, not only in FIFA. For quite some time, it had been clear to Kramnik and me that some FIDE officials in key positions were absolutely not interested in a reunification match and having a strong world champion. Especially not if he were called Vladimir Kramnik, since he is an independent thinker and would not dance to their tune. There was no other way to explain certain behaviour.

One of those who suffered from this underhand manoeuvring was Garry Kasparov. He was, as it were, being 'starved out' of chess. For whatever reasons, FIDE apparently did not want to organize the match between Kasparov and the FIDE titleholder Ruslan Ponomariov. In the summer of 2004, Ponomariov lost the title – without ever having got a duel with Kasparov – when Rustam Kasimdzhanov (Uzbekistan) won the FIDE tournament in Tripoli, Libya.

The money for this event came from state president Muammar Gaddafi, and his eldest son Muhammad was president of the organizing committee. But things were no different for FIDE's new titleholder. The match between Garry and one of the FIDE World Champions was announced four times. Each time it failed to take place for different, highly strange, reasons. In truth, it was clear to everyone that Kasparov would win the said match. That was presumably the exact reason behind FIDE's behaviour. Giving Kasparov this chance was obviously not in the interest of important FIDE officials, and accordingly it was prevented.

At first, however, we remained unaffected by all these evasions. After Kramnik's simultaneous victory over the German team, we were invited by the Burger family to St. Moritz. In the most splendid winter weather, we had a wonderful time in the world-famous luxury hotel Suvretta House. Winter sports and sightseeing with horse-drawn sleighs were on our programme, as well as celebrations with the Burger family in a ski lodge. The deal with Dannemann laid the foundation for a fantastic partnership. These were people we could work with!

Full of energy and wellbeing, we left Switzerland. For Vladimir too, developments were discernibly positive. His critics were silenced. We treated ourselves to some good whiskies, before getting down to further preparations. At the end of February we flew to Spain, where Kramnik majestically won, for the third time, the traditionally strongest tournament of the year in Linares in Andalusia, leaving the world's elite trailing in his wake.

After that, he also won again in Monaco. There we were always collected by helicopter from Nice airport in order to be brought to the principality "in a fitting manner". But that year there was such violent turbulence along the coast that the pilot had some trouble keeping the chopper on an even keel, and I decided that in future I would turn down this dubious honour.

Before more chess was to be played, Vladimir had first of all an important private event to attend to. He had taken a flat near the Paris Opera House and moved in there with Marie-Laure. So he no longer lived in Germany, but that did not represent a break in our cooperation. We phoned each other daily and I was very happy for the couple who were in love.

And as the saying goes in my home area, the Ruhrgebiet: if it's working then it's working! Kramnik was much in demand. Big firms were showing interest; above all Deutsche Bank. They organized a simultaneous with the World Champion in the Arts and Exhibition Hall of the Federal Republic of Germany in Bonn. That was more than just another exhibition event; it brought Vladimir a lot of recognition and popularity.

Publicity for the simultaneous ran for weeks on all the TV stations, and with full-page adverts in the major German daily newspapers under the headline "Check to the World Champion". On eBay it was possible to bid for one of the coveted 20 places. Players were prepared to come up with 3,000 euros for this opportunity. Each participant who defeated Kramnik was to receive 50,000 euros. All the proceeds from the event went to SOS-Kinderdorf. In addition to the twenty who paid to take part, there was also the German women's team and the well-known actor Mathieu Carrière. For about four hours, Kramnik cruised from board to board. In the end he won all the games except for a single draw. SOS-Kinderdorf received from this, as well as other donations, a sum in the high five figures.

The Bonn simultaneous was a milestone for Kramnik as far as his marketing opportunities in the West were concerned. After the advertising campaign by Deutsche Bank, everyone knew him in Germany. In addition, it turned out that the German Art and Exhibition Hall was very interested in the subject of chess in general and Kramnik in particular. In the years to come, there would follow some major events with this famous partner.

In world championship years as a rule the finalists are cautious about taking on other commitments. With Kramnik, however, the opposite was the case. He took on numerous commitments and played a lot. As well as the events already mentioned, in 2004 he played in Belfort for his club NAO Chess Paris, who once again became French champions. In Dortmund he did not win this time, but was an undefeated second. His preparations for the world championship match against Peter Leko could begin.

For me, there was also a lot of work to be done in advance. Dannemann was of course rather inexperienced in the organization of high-level chess events; I had to promise to look after it. This commitment was a central condition to ensure the staging of the match. That was okay with me, because in any case I was obliged to be neutral and could thus, for example, ensure both teams had the same general conditions.

As well as committing myself, I brought into the organization the tried and trusted organizing team of the Dortmund Chess Days, tournament director Stefan Koth, Guido Kohlen (technology) and Rolf Behovits (press officer). The Association of Chess Professionals (ACP) with its president Joel Lautier meant that the event had a worthy framework. The arbiters were Dr Markus Angst (Switzerland), Dr Andrzej Filipowicz (Poland) and Albert Vasse (Netherlands). The German grandmasters Artur Yusupov and Dr Helmut Pfleger commented on the games onsite and on the internet.

Brissago is a sleepy little place. Apart from the beauty of the countryside and the islands with their exotic gardens, the Centro Dannemann is the big point of interest. Our hotels were in Ascona, known worldwide for its sophisticated Mediterranean atmosphere, and only a few kilometres from where the games were played. The Hotel Ascona, picturesquely situated on the side of the famous Monte Verità, offered a fantastic view over Lago Maggiore. So it was on the "Mountain of Truth", where for over 100 years great artists and thinkers had found inspiration – including Hermann Hesse, Paul Klee and Carl Gustav Jung – that Kramnik and Leko would now seek the truth in their chess variations.

♔30

When, in Brissago on 25th September 2004, Peter Leko, in the presence of the twelfth World Chess Champion Anatoly Karpov, moved the king's pawn to e4, an enormous weight fell from my shoulders. After all the toing and froing with various incompetent rights holders, as well as the constant strife with FIDE, we could finally get started. It was to be a dramatic match.

Despite the out-of-the-way venue, there were a fantastic number of visitors to the world championship. The internet figures brought tears of joy to the eyes of the Dannemann marketing people. During the course of the match, more and more servers had to be rented. The decisive 14th game was being followed by more than 750,000 people from all over the world on the Dannemann homepage alone. During the world championship, 300 journalists from 47 countries reported from where it was happening.

Kramnik's core team consisted of Evgeny Bareev (Russia) and Miguel Illescas (Spain), who had also been there in London, as had the Russian physiotherapist Dr Valery Krylov. The French grandmaster Joel Lautier, now present as president of the players' organization the ACP, was replaced on the team by Peter Svidler from St Petersburg, who is of course an elite player. The team's preparations had essentially been done in the South of France.

In Peter Leko's team, which had prepared in Hungary, there were also three grandmasters: Vladimir Akopian (Armenia), Vladislav Tkachiev (Russia) and Leko's father-in-law Arshak Petrosian (Armenia).

After the players had moved into their quarters, I principally looked after their communications and also questions of organization for the promoters. Apart from small talk, in principle I left Kramnik and Leko in peace during the match. For good reasons, I wanted to know nothing at all about their strategy or specific chess preparation.

Game 1

The match began with a drumroll, rather unusually for the start of a world championship match. Kramnik was Black and had decided on the Petroff Defence, followed by a rare continuation. After his 17...♘a5, Leko thought for 40 minutes.

Kramnik had done something which no computer would do; he played a move based on the idea that Leko would *not* answer with the complicated 18.♘e5. Game 1 is a textbook example of how psychology works in chess. At the very highest level, players do not always go for objectively the best move, as in this case perhaps 17...♖cd8 or 17...h6 would have been, but now and then one which does not suit their opponent. Leko thought that with 18.c4 he was in a safe haven, and was hoping for a slight advantage in the endgame; completely in line with his style.

In the subsequent variation, Kramnik gave up his queen, but obtained in return a rook, bishop and pawn, and also an isolated pawn of Leko's as a potentially weak target to attack. The position was now anything but balanced. Kramnik felt at home; this imbalance was not Leko's world.

In such games, the decisive mistake is frequently made by the one who feels the greater mental burden; in this case by Leko on move 44 with 44.♕f4??. After that, as he so often does, Peter demonstrated immense defensive resolution. But Kramnik played precisely and increased his advantage move by move. After six hours and 65 moves, he logged the full point.

Score: 1–0

Games 2-5

That Leko was no fly-by-night, and that he had every right to be fighting for the chess throne, can be seen from the following games. In his situation, Leko adopted the completely correct strategy. First of all, he tried to avoid any struggle and to consolidate. In the second game, a line of the Ruy Lopez with Black, this succeeded perfectly. In the third game, the Petroff Defence was played; a quick draw. With Black, Kramnik employed a strong innovation with 17...♛c2, which neutralized the position. To the disappointment of chess fans, Leko had to offer a draw after only 23 moves. In the fourth game, Kramnik tried hard for an advantage, but Peter Leko equalized relatively easily with Black and drew after 43 moves.

From then on, one thing was clear to the Hungarian: he would not achieve much with 1.e4 as his opening move. The World Champion's preparation in the Petroff Defence was too strong; Leko and his team would not be able to crack it during the match. Consequently, Game 3 was the last one in this world championship match in which Leko opened with 1.e4. In Game 5 he did something which hardly anyone would have expected of him. His own Ruy Lopez with the black pieces was holding up well, so he took a risk with White. Never before had Peter Leko opened a serious tournament game with 1.d4, but that was precisely what he now did. The Queen's Gambit, Slav Defence, Queen's Indian, Modern Benoni – all these would appear on the board.

Kramnik sat at the board, visibly surprised; this had practically undermined his preparation. Vladimir's uncertainty was surely one of the reasons for his remaining passive all through the game. In a Queen's Gambit, Leko achieved a slight advantage with 16.♗xa6, which he carried forward into a promising endgame.

(After 26.♔g2)

Under powerful positional and time pressure, on move 59 Kramnik missed a chance for a draw (59...f5?! instead of 59...♗h4!).

Then with a blunder three moves later (62...♗g3? instead of 62...♗e1!) practically gave the game away and resigned after six and a half hours. The World Champion had been jolted.

Score: 2½–2½

Games 6-8

Games 6 and 7 ended in short draws. It was the calm before the storm. Before the eighth game, Kramnik decided to give up his Anti-Marshall: "Three times I had been unable to get any play, anything of a struggle with this opening. For two whole days my entire team had worked on a very sharp variation in the Marshall, an idea I had already had a long time before the match."

A queen sacrifice lies at the heart of the variation. Leko, as he assured me later, solved all the problems at the board, and in doing so found an enormous hole in Kramnik's preparation. This can also be seen from the time management of the players. Kramnik had only used 20 minutes, Leko on the other hand over 100.

This supposed advantage made Vladimir more careless; he wanted to step up the pressure on Leko in the latter's time trouble, only to then make the decisive mistake with 23.♕f2? (instead of 23.♕d1). He played this move, which came from his preparation, *a tempo*. And he did so although he absolutely suspected it was dangerous. This all-or-nothing play by the Russian was exploited in ice-cold fashion by Leko, and after a further nine moves Kramnik had to resign.

Kramnik's team was nominally a fantastically strong one, nevertheless it was not so powerful as in London. But the eighth game clearly showed up one of Vladimir's weaknesses, which was seen against Shirov back in 1998. It is not easy to describe this failing, but nevertheless I shall try: Kramnik, externally calm, a man who thinks and acts very logically, displayed, in certain situations during his great matches, strong emotions, even a certain impatience. He then at times showed a stubbornness, which his grandmaster team now also began to feel in this match against Leko.

In such a mood, whenever Vladimir had considered something to be correct, there was practically nothing which could make him change his opinion. He was hardly open to argument. First of all, this stubbornness embodies a major strength. Namely, Kramnik is always prepared to accept complete responsibility for his chess and his mistakes. And this also held true for mistakes of his teams, without any ifs and buts. This important characteristic and the fact that he could not be influenced made him World Champion. At the same time, in extreme situations he had some problems keeping his emotions under control. Therefore, sometimes this emotional state turned against him and influenced his ability to remain objective – the consequence of which was a lack of flexibility.

Concerning the eighth game against Leko, Peter Svidler expressed it like this: "We told Kramnik that the Marshall had not been sufficiently well prepared and that he should hold it back until the tenth game. By then we would be finished." But he replied: "No, I can no longer do that. Enough!" Thus, the team was not yet ready and warned him. Despite that, Vladimir wanted to fight at last, to play; blood had to flow. In principle, he was perhaps even correct in this case. In any case, by doing so he broke the dynamics of the match. So possibly the loss in Game 8 was the decisive key to his later defence of the title. Who knows?

However, it was clear that the whole situation was weighing heavily on the World Champion. How heavily could be seen immediately after the game. Kramnik suffered a physical and psychological collapse. His physiotherapist did his best, but finally he too could do no more. It was not only the defeat or the match situation which led to severe panic attacks. It was so severe that Christian Burger, Dr Helmut Pfleger and I took him to the Accident & Emergency department of the local clinic in Locarno. From time to time Kramnik would exhibit the symptoms of chronic illness. This diffuse feeling of physical insecurity, paired with the high demands made on him by the match, led on this occasion to even greater problems.

He had sensed that something was not quite right now and then over the years; even before the world championship match against Kasparov. But Kramnik had never received a concrete diagnosis. A few months later, his illness would break out again violently, and a year later force him into a longish pause. The option to postpone the next games for health reasons was not foreseen in the match regulations. On October 7th and 8th, the match was close to being terminated.

Score: 3½–4½

Games 9-11

Kramnik was unbelievably lucky. The eighth game was followed by a rest day. Another doctor was consulted, and Vladimir was able to relax a little. But he only took the decision to continue at midday on October 9th.

When he arrived for the game, Kramnik was under the influence of strong tranquilizers. His circulation was rather irregular, and he was swaying as he went up the long staircase to the playing hall. Neither Leko nor anyone else in his team noticed the desperate condition of the World Champion. To this day I cannot explain this, since if they had looked Vladimir in the eye, everything would have been clear. In this game Leko had White, was leading by 4½–3½, and what did he do? After 16 moves he accepted the offer of a draw from Kramnik, whose position was worse.

Despite the short draw, Vladimir was unable to appear at the press conference after the game. At this point, at the latest, Peter and his people should have noticed.

If Leko had simply played this game out to a finish, then I am sure that the match would practically have been decided. Whether a subsequent resignation from Kramnik came on health grounds or at the board would have mattered little. In his form at the time, Peter would not have surrendered a two-point lead.

In Game 10, Leko declined the Marshall Variation in the Ruy Lopez. For the first time Kramnik had an advantage out of the opening, but played extremely weakly in the endgame and after 35 moves conceded a draw. This was understandable, since he was still not in top form. A further rest day followed; Vladimir was still plagued by dizzy spells. His partner Marie-Laure called me and asked whether she should come. "Yes," was my answer.

In the eleventh game, play developed along the same lines as in Game 9. Leko and his team had still not realized the way things were with Kramnik. Peter had the white pieces and agreed a draw after 16 moves.

And he did so in a situation in which all the pieces were still on the board and the struggle had just begun. This pragmatism by Leko earned him harsh criticism in the chess world. His hitherto perfect image as the "Marathon Man", which appositely defined a young player of incredible resilience and fighting spirit, started to crumble.

Score: 5–6

Games 12-14

Peter obviously thought he could win the title with his safety-first strategy. He was counting on the fact that Kramnik would have to take ever more risks, and that he could then counter-punch. Whether this strategy was his own or advised by his team is still not quite clear today. But I am sure that the World Championship was finally lost for Leko in the twelfth game. Kramnik played well and at first caused him problems. However, in time trouble the World Champion lost the thread. After 34...♕g6 Leko offered a draw.

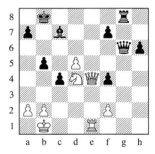

At that moment I was in the playing room, and it was clear Kramnik was surprised – he wrinkled his brow and a few seconds later shot out his right hand to accept. No wonder, since at that point he was two pawns down. In all variations, Peter had the advantage in the endgame, and Kramnik would have had to fight hard for the draw. That day when I returned to the hotel with Vladimir, his future wife Marie-Laure had arrived.

In Game 13, Kramnik had Black. As usual we sat in the SUV on the way to the venue, and on that day I found him completely transformed. Suddenly the body language was totally different and, despite being behind, he even cracked a few little jokes. Marie-Laure, who had wanted to visit for just one day, was now remaining, after consulting with her boss at *Le Figaro,* till the end of the match. Her presence was clearly very helpful to Kramnik.

He had Black, chose the Modern Benoni and was active. At times he outplayed Leko, who was only saved that day by his magnificent tenacity. Peter absolutely lived up to his reputation as the world's best defensive artist. He had to find a series of only-moves to keep the position more or less balanced; he was really skating on thin ice. Despite missing his chance, Kramnik was not so disappointed. He had finally overcome his mental and physical crisis.

By the time of the memorable final game on 18th October 2004, Vladimir had already lost more than 10 kilos. That is astonishing, but a match for the chess crown requires spending huge energy, intellectually and physically. Chess is a mind sport and at first sight has little to do with the physique of the players. Nevertheless, no other sport demands, over such a long period of time, so much concentration and nervous energy as a match for the world chess championship.

All the members of Kramnik's team appeared at the venue. Prominent chess fans from Paris, such as the world-famous violinist Vadim Repin, Dominique Strauss-Kahn, at that time once again on his way to the head of France's Socialist Party, the supermodel Natalia Vodianova, and the former Dior model Carmen Kass, along with the German grandmaster Eric Lobron, were all present. The playing hall, the press centre and all the side-rooms in the Centro Dannemann were bursting at the seams. Never before, and never again afterwards, did the modest little town of Brissago attract such attention.

You could feel the tension everywhere, especially among the Hungarian fans and journalists, who wanted to see one of their own as World Chess Champion for the first time. Despite such great players as Gyula Breyer, Geza Maroczy, Lajos Portisch, Zoltan Ribli and Judit Polgar, no one had ever won the ultimate title. All that Peter Leko required was a single draw. In Hungary, chess has always enjoyed high status. The papers there were even making comparisons with the football World Cup final of 1954. In the Miracle of Bern, the strongly fancied Hungarian team, with its superstar Ferenc Puskas, sensationally lost 2–3 to West Germany. Leko would now wipe that shame, once again in Switzerland, from his country's memory. Things worked out differently.

Kramnik had to win the game. That would be enough since, like in boxing, chess kept the rule that in the event of a tie, the World Champion retained his crown. Thereafter, this rule was changed in favour of a tiebreak. Kramnik opened, as he had done all match, with 1.e4. As in the twelfth game, Leko went into the Caro-Kann Defence. Kramnik had looked at this and chose a variation which was rarely played at that time. Leko at first reacted quickly and accurately. After the opening phase, I asked Bareev how he evaluated the situation. His opinion was that it all looked like a draw and he would now go and treat himself to another little glass of wine.

But then Leko played 22...♔d8 instead of the correct 22...♔e7, where White is only a little better. This slight but subtle difference of having an exposed king on the queenside changed the situation fundamentally. Kramnik hurried out of his restroom and sat down bolt upright. He scratched the back of his head, held his thumb, index and ring fingers over the piece three times. He kept pulling his hand back. This is precisely the body language which Kramnik displays at decisive moments. Then he moved the knight to g5 – the optimal continuation and to a certain extent already the decisive move. According to some experts, the 39th World Championship match in chess history was decided by that simple, inconspicuous king move. After the time control, Leko resigned on move 41, two moves before the mate.

Final score: 7–7

♔31

Immediately after his title defence, Kramnik compared the Hungarian grandmaster with Garry Kasparov: "For me, and I am not just saying that, the match against Peter was more difficult than the World Championship match I won against Kasparov. In this form Leko is tremendously hard to beat; above all in a match. I have never come up against such strong defence as his. In the future, Peter will certainly get another chance to play for the title in a World Championship final."

But Kramnik would turn out to be wrong in this prediction. At first Peter Leko struck back in Wijk aan Zee, where in January 2005 he won the tournament in great style. Off and on in his later career there were successes, such as at the Tal Memorial in Moscow 2006, and the Candidates matches in Elista 2007. But basically he never got over the 14th game in Brissago. His career gradually went downhill. It was and remains a tragedy for the one-time youngest grandmaster in chess history. He came so close to the world title, only to fail by a hair's breadth at the last minute.

In my opinion, what prevented Peter Leko from becoming World Champion was the lack of a "certain something". Perhaps it was simply his lack of a killer instinct or just the failure to take into account what was happening outside the 64 squares; weaknesses which could not be picked up by his team in Brissago. Peter Leko's career was nevertheless a great one – not least because of the dramatic events of the 2004 World Championship match – and will remain a permanent part of chess history.

Before and after the world championship, I was often asked whom I wanted or would have wanted to see as the winner of the match. Quite honestly, I did not know the answer. I met Leko when he was twelve years old. One might say he was in and out of my family all the time. Other things formed my connection to Kramnik. One thing was clear in any case: with his title defence, Vladimir had earned even more recognition in chess world. The path to a reunion would be a stony one for him, but now it had to be taken.

Vladimir Kramnik had convinced me in another respect. The problems which were kept hidden from the public during the match were massive. He displayed, however, an ability I had not seen in him before. It was incredible how he was able to pull himself together and not give up. In doing so he went over and beyond his physical and mental limits on some occasions. He was able to manage a feat beyond comparison and free himself from a serious crisis and continue the match. Not every top player would have been capable of such behaviour under these conditions. To this day, the fact that over and above this he managed, despite the greatest of pressure, to win to order the final game against such a man as Leko, commands the greatest possible respect.

In the days after the match Kramnik gave interviews without end. When asked about some short draws and the criticism they had attracted during the match, he said in an interview with *New In Chess*: "A painter never asks people what he should paint. He paints!" In doing so he gave himself a new nickname and a new image. From then on, Kramnik was "the painter".

This was no coincidence. Communicating an authentic image is an incomprehensibly complex business. As a chess player, Kramnik sees himself first and foremost as an artist, and we often discussed this. With a single utterance he managed to communicate this authentic image. After the world championship match no one used the terms "iceman" or "rock" any more. In the years to come all the major media platforms took on the image of the chess artist. We did not need to indulge in a costly image campaign after the match.

By the end of the year, however, we could realize how unimportant all our affairs were. On 26th December 2004, over 200,000 died as a result of a great tsunami in the Indian Ocean, caused by an earthquake close to Sumatra. But we did not have time for more than a short pause.

♔32

2005 followed: the Einstein year. Albert Einstein (1879-1955) once said: "Chess is the fastest game in the world, because thousands of thoughts have to be organized every second." Einstein the thinker absolutely loved chess, but in a certain way he pitied the great players, including his friend the World Champion Emanuel Lasker, when he said: "Chess holds its masters in its own chains and fetters; in many ways it moulds their spirit with the result that the inner freedom of even the strongest among them is influenced."

Apropos Einstein: when Vladimir was once asked by the chess journalist Dagobert Kohlmeyer whether he was able to explain the theory of relativity, he answered with a smile: "Let me answer as follows. What is the difference between football and chess? It consists of the fact that many people understand football, but none of them can play it well. And many play chess, but nobody understands it. Everything is relative."

Right at the start of 2005, my travels took me quite close to where Einstein once lived. In the Zürich law firm Baker McKenzie, contracts were lying ready to be signed. They concerned the organization of world chess championships for the subsequent years. Dannemann was highly satisfied with the media coverage from the Kramnik – Leko match, and ready to invest a lot of money. Future title matches, candidates tournaments and more pre-qualification events for the next three cycles within six years would be happening under the management of this sponsor, and under the aegis of the players' union, the ACP. FIDE continued to want nothing to do with Kramnik, and as far as we were concerned had long since been discredited as a serious partner. Also because they continued to agitate against a final match for the world championship and against classical time controls.

When I met Christian Burger in the offices of the law firm, he was as white as a sheet. "Carsten, we can't make the deal," he said. In front of me lay a fax from a Cologne media firm, which urgently advised Dannemann against the agreements. The reason was the new prohibition against tobacco advertising in the European Union, which was to come into force during 2005. Even for events staged outside the EU, Dannemann could have been exposed to claims from its commercial rivals in the range of tens of millions. I took advice from Dr Reinhard Rauball. The president of Borussia Dortmund, and since 2007 president of the German football league, had been Kramnik's legal adviser for a number of years. Rauball, himself a passionate chess player, confirmed the legal opinion of his colleagues from Cologne.

That finally killed off the business, and we were pretty frustrated. In Dannemann we had lost a good and extraordinarily reliable partner. Okay, they produce cigars. That has always been strongly criticized in certain circles, but from my point of view they suited us ideally. After all, the royal game has always been to do with lifestyle, art and enjoyment. As, however, is often the case in this fast-moving business, once again we had to completely change direction. But we remained closely linked to Christian Burger until his death.

The failure of the negotiations because of the tobacco legislation had, however, a good side. As we know now, it would otherwise have been difficult to bring about the reunification of the chess world and the world championship match between Vladimir Kramnik and Veselin Topalov in 2006. But there was still a long road in front of us before we could get there.

Kramnik and I already had strong networks, even outside the world federation. However, an important piece of the puzzle was missing. For that reason, we founded the events-organizing firm Universal Event Promotion (UEP). Proprietor and president was Josef Resch. The Dortmund tournament director Stefan Koth was managing director and I was an adviser. We had a tried and trusted team: Olaf Heinzel, Rolf Behovits and Guido Kohlen. Through the firm, we were now in a position to bid for major chess events, all the way up to the world championships, and then to organize them.

Barely a year after the simultaneous with Deutsche Bank, we again took up an invitation to Bonn in the Art and Exhibition Hall of the Federal Republic of Germany. On 5th March 2005, we had an exhibition game of a very special sort in front of the assembled German media. The opponent of the World Chess Champion was the then minister-president of Nordrhein-Westfalen, Peer Steinbrück, who had the white pieces and acquitted himself more than honourably in their encounter. In a Ruy Lopez, the head of the regional government aimed for a closed position and held out for 37 moves before resigning. "I had been having a lot of meetings. Nevertheless I managed to look at a few Kramnik games," Steinbrück remembered. He said he had been happy to see a variation appear on the board with which he was familiar.

Steinbrück: "I simply did not want to embarrass myself by surviving for only 18-20 moves. But my initial nerves disappeared as time went past and I held out for longer that I had previously thought possible." He said he had found Kramnik to be a "normal" and therefore authentic human being, and had learned that nowadays chess was a high-performance sport, different from the days of the old champions such as Lasker, Alekhine or Botvinnik, who had remained right at the top until an advanced age.

Vladimir told me afterwards that he had been quite impressed by Steinbrück's play, above all by his strategic understanding. Peer Steinbrück, whom I already knew before this game, remained a chess enthusiast. He lives in Bonn-Bad Godesberg and would in the future support important chess events in the Art and Exhibition Hall in his role as German finance minister. To this day, his personal relationship with Kramnik and myself remains a good one. We met a few times socially and always had interesting conversations about sport and politics. Peer Steinbrück was nominated by his party in 2013 as candidate for the chancellorship of the German parliament. But on this occasion, all his strategic abilities were of no use to him. The Social Democrats, whom he led, had no chance against Federal Chancellor Angela Merkel.

On 10th March 2005, the 13th World Chess Champion Garry Kasparov officially withdrew from active chess at the age of 42. In recent years he had not played much anyway. The match against one of the FIDE champions, which had been agreed in Prague in 2002, was never organized by the world federation. A victory in such a match would have been the only chance for him to face Kramnik again. After his defeat in 2000, Garry had put too much reliance on FIDE, against which he had once battled so violently. From the point of view of Kramnik, it was perhaps Kasparov's greatest mistake, and certainly the greatest inconsistency in his otherwise brilliant career. Undoubtedly taking part in the Candidates tournament of 2002, as stated in his Braingames contract, would have been for Kasparov the more honourable and easier option.

♚33

In February 2005, I received a call from Iceland. It was from Gardar Sverrisson, closest confidant, neighbour and best friend of Bobby Fischer during his final years in Reykjavik. Apparently Bobby was interested in playing a match against Vladimir Kramnik at Fischer Random chess. In this variety of chess, which was invented by Fischer himself, the set-up of the pieces on the back rank is randomized. So modern opening theory has no role to play.

I checked out the circumstances and spoke several times with, among others, Einar S. Einarsson, the head of the Icelandic federation, and with ChessBase co-founder Frederic Friedel, who had some chess contacts in Reykjavik. Everything appeared serious. According to Gardar Sverrisson, the ex-world champion considered that Kramnik was at that time the best player in the world. "Whenever Bobby evaluated other chess champions, he set a very specific standard," Sverrisson was able to report. In doing so, he was not so impressed by those who rolled over their opponents with aggressive attacking chess, even if that was sufficient to win the game. Fischer did not especially admire the chess of a Kasparov. The way the latter played was, according to Sverrisson, not greatly to Bobby's taste, because the correctness of the games had not stood up to more precise checking by Fischer. He preferred, on the other hand, the more subtle and precise play of a Vladimir Kramnik.

As Sverrisson further explained, Bobby Fischer's self-confidence was as great as it had even been. Because he had not played for a long time, he was of course aware that most people would regard him as an outsider against Kramnik. Hardly anybody would give Fischer a chance in such a duel, even in Fischer Random chess. Even his closest friend Sverrisson was convinced that Fischer's winning chances would have been extremely slight. Gardar had naturally discussed that with Fischer, who had told him he could get into shape with swimming training.

To the remark that nobody would believe this was possible, he replied that you couldn't say that. "You mean that there is at least one person who thinks that you would have a chance?" asked Sverrisson. "Yeah," Bobby replied quite coolly and calmly. In later conversations, Fischer, however, showed himself to be in touch with reality, and would have been content with not too big a defeat. First and foremost, he was interested in raising the popularity of his idea of Fischer Random chess.

I could have found as many potential sponsors for such a duel as there are grains of sand on a beach, and not only from Russia or the Arab world. That could quickly be seen after some telephone calls I made. The purse would have beaten all records in professional chess: ten million US dollars and more is not an exaggeration. Nevertheless, the event never took place. Even today, neither Gardar nor I can say with any certainty why not. In any case, I requested from Fischer a written memorandum of understanding in order to get the authorization to go looking for sponsors. It never came. So my hands were tied and for me the whole business was over.

A few weeks later, Dr Alex Titomirov, an exiled Russian living in America, contacted Kramnik and me. We met him in Paris. He wanted to organize the match between Fischer and Kramnik, and had disposed of all the difficulties with Bobby. At some point, Titomirov set out for Reykjavik with a delegation, which included Boris Spassky and the French grandmaster Joel Lautier. According to Sverrisson, there was indeed a conversation with Fischer, but it was not a constructive one. Whether the reason for the failure was the unpredictability of Fischer, or the way the delegation handled the negotiations, is unclear. In any case, at some point after this meeting, Fischer finally withdrew from the project. A later attempt by the management team of Veselin Topalov also achieved nothing, and we never heard any more about this business.

Of course, a match between Bobby Fischer and Vladimir Kramnik, of whatever sort, would have been a worldwide sensation. However, all the fuss probably demanded too much of Kramnik, who in the spring of 2005 was already at the limits of his strength. The illness he had been carrying for years, and which every now and then made itself felt, finally broke out. When, in May 2005, I came for the second half of the tournament in the Bulgarian capital of Sofia, I found Vladimir in a desperate condition. He was taking strong painkillers and could hardly get out of his chair without help. He was plagued by bouts of rheumatism. A few weeks later in Paris, a particular form of ankylosing spondylitis (a severe rheumatic illness) was diagnosed. Consequently, in Sofia Vladimir had the worst tournament of his career and came last.

2005 was for this reason the worst year of his career. Against Leko he had once again summoned all his energies. That, however, was followed by the collapse. In Wijk aan Zee he nevertheless managed fourth place, then came the disaster of Sofia, sixth place in "his" tournament in Dortmund, and only seventh place in the Russian Championship in Moscow. When there, he gave another simultaneous for his personal sponsor, the watchmakers Blancpain, although he could hardly walk and was pumped full of medication. His lowest point had been reached.

"I could no longer think for the pain," says Kramnik now. The whole business had started somewhere towards the end of the 1990s. "At the start I did not want to admit it. But as the years went by, it kept getting worse." Vladimir looked so ill and emaciated that rumours began to circulate about his condition, that he had cancer or AIDS. And he was really very low, physically totally done. It was high time to do something.

On 5th January 2006, I issued a press statement in which Kramnik announced he was taking a break of several months. I cancelled all engagements for the first six months of the year. He was late, almost too late, in taking this vital decision which his inner circle had pushed for after the Leko match and during the whole of 2005. But as things would turn out, he was just in time.

Marie-Laure accompanied him from one doctor's appointment to the next. Vladimir finally got the precise diagnosis, and then specialists to look after him. The medicines prescribed gradually improved and became better targeted. He remained ill for a few months, but then he was noticeably better. Nowadays, he is to a great extent free of problems and medication, though his illness is chronic; it can sometimes be seen and can break out again at any time.

In the meantime, the world federation had decided to bring to an end the knock-out roulette for its own world championship. After ten years they had probably recognized that they would never find acceptance for a world championship contested in this format. Instead, however, of forcing through the reunification of the chess world, they announced out of nowhere a FIDE World Championship in the form of a tournament with eight players. Everyone could see that the Prague Agreement between the world federation and the classical World Champion, Vladimir Kramnik, had been broken. Although Kramnik was regarded by the public at large as well as by many grandmasters as the man to beat, that is to say, as the "real" World Champion, the officials were again negotiating in defiance of the overwhelming convictions of the chess world.

♚34

Before Kramnik was obliged to take a break due to his illness, FIDE had staged in October 2005 in San Luis (Argentina) a world championship tournament. The epicentre of this was occupied by one man, the Bulgarian grandmaster Veselin Topalov. Or we would do better to say: Topalov and Silvio Danailov, his compatriot and manager. But let's proceed in order. I arrived there for the sixth round, during the first half of the tournament. A 30-hour journey via Dortmund, Frankfurt, Madrid, São Paulo and Buenos Aires lay behind me. The jetlag caused me, as it usually does, severe headaches. I was exhausted, but I did not have the opportunity to rest because of events at the venue in San Luis. Some people told me of possible irregularities on the part of Veselin Topalov.

After getting my accreditation, I went into the playing hall. In it Topalov happened to have Black against Judit Polgar. His manager Danailov stood less than three metres away from him. What I saw was deeply concerning. Danailov left the playing hall after almost every move by Polgar, returned and when Topalov then looked towards him, made what could have been signs with his right hand: his fist under his chin, three fingers on his right cheek, one finger against his neck, tapping once or twice against his artery, etc.

I am not able to say for sure whether Danailov's gestures were code for specific moves. Perhaps he simply wanted to unsettle each of the opponents, but the fears expressed were justified from the point of view of those players and their support team. The games were transmitted live on the internet without time delay and even back in 2005 there would have been no problems having computer moves sent to you in order to communicate them to a player with pre-agreed signs.

Judit Polgar lost the game with White. Peter Leko told me after the round that something extraordinary was happening. He and other participants were completely surprised by the behaviour because nothing like that had ever happened before. He thought people were unsure about how to go about it. Afterwards I spoke to Gusztav Font, Judit Polgar's husband, Peter Svidler, Alexander Morozevich, Michael Adams and Anand's wife Aruna. Judit Polgar and Mickey Adams were reticent, but others – above all Morozevich, Kasimdzhanov and Leko – had noticed the behaviour of Topalov and Danailov.

Why the players affected did not protest officially remains to me veiled in mystery till this very day. On the day of my arrival Topalov had won five of the first six games. This was an outlier, but we should remember that such things have happened before in the history of chess – think of the series of wins by Bobby Fischer on his way to the world championship.

On the next day the Bulgarian was playing against FIDE title defender Rustam Kasimdzhanov from Uzbekistan. I asked two Germans who had been there for some time to keep an eye on things, International Master Olaf Heinzel and Dortmund tournament director Stefan Koth. We all took up positions in various places in the tournament hall and in the hotel, which was directly next to the venue. Olaf Heinzel looked after the hotel, since Danailov did not know him. Heinzel describes his observations as follows: "Danailov took the lift several times to go to a hotel room. The hotel and arena were only a few metres apart. After a few minutes he came out of the room and I was able to look in through the open door. In the room sat the Bulgarian grandmaster Cheparinov in front of at least two monitors, on which you could recognize chess positions."

Heinzel went on to report that he had also seen Danailov and Cheparinov occasionally meeting in the hotel lobby and having a short conversation. "After that Danailov immediately went into the playing hall, while Cheparinov went back towards the room," says Heinzel. In some phases of the game against Kasimdzhanov he had seen Topalov's manager quite close to the board. Heinzel: "Danailov's fingers were always touching his face. This also happened during previous games."

Stefan Koth observed what was happening during Game 7 partly in the playing hall and partly in the foyer. Koth: "After the opening Danailov left the playing hall after almost every move. From time to time I followed him, as discreetly as possible. He went into the foyer, sometimes he also used the lift. As the game became more hectic, he would telephone briefly out in the foyer or stand in front of the playing hall with Ivan Cheparinov. Each time after their conversation he quickly went back into the playing hall and stood in front of Topalov's table. Then he fiddled about with his fingers next to his face or neck. As he did so Topalov looked at him more or less furtively. For me it definitely looked as if Danailov were giving signs. Shortly thereafter Topalov played his move."

Topalov, who always sat at the same table during the whole tournament, due to being player number 8 in the pre-event drawing of lots, also won this game in the Closed Ruy Lopez after a complicated rook ending.

It is always difficult to interpret events of this sort correctly, let alone prove a feared fraud. In any case nothing was done on the side of the world federation, the appeals committee or the arbiter who could not have missed the abnormal behaviour.

Halfway through the tournament Topalov had the incredible score of 6½ points from seven games.

I confronted Danailov with the allegations on the rest day after Game 7. He vehemently denied any attempts at manipulation. In the second half of the tournament there was no repetition of the behaviour. Topalov had a large lead over Anand (who finished second) and drew all his games in the second half of the tournament. Thanks to his enormous lead he was the clear winner of the tournament, by 1½ points at the end.

Whether everything had been above board in Argentina or not: the grandmasters were in uproar and Kramnik too was warned. Topalov and Danailov acted in any case from our standpoint with a ruthlessness never before seen in professional chess.

With their new titleholder, FIDE continued to try to avoid Vladimir Kramnik. They would not succeed!

Vladimir Kramnik – Peter Leko

World Championship, Brissago (14) 2004

1.e4 c6 2.d4 d5 3.e5 &f5 4.h4 h6 5.g4 &d7 6.♘d2 c5 7.dxc5 e6?! 8.♘b3 &xc5 9.♘xc5 ♕a5† 10.c3 ♕xc5 11.♘f3 ♘e7 12.&d3 ♘bc6 13.&e3 ♕a5 14.♕d2!

14...♘g6 15.&d4! ♘xd4 16.cxd4 ♕xd2† 17.♔xd2 ♘f4? 18.♖ac1! h5 19.♖hg1 &c6 20.gxh5 ♘xh5 21.b4! a6 22.a4! ♔d8? 23.♘g5 &e8 24.b5 ♘f4? 25.b6!+– ♘xd3 26.♔xd3 ♖c8 27.♖xc8† ♔xc8 28.♖c1† &c6 29.♘xf7 ♖xh4 30.♘d6† ♔d8 31.♖g1 ♖h3† 32.♔e2 ♖a3 33.♖xg7 ♖xa4 34.f4 ♖a2† 35.♔f3 ♖a3† 36.♔g4 ♖d3 37.f5! ♖xd4† 38.♔g5 exf5 39.♔f6 ♖g4 40.♖c7 ♖h4

41.♘f7† 1–0 (41...♚e8 42.♖c8† ♚d7 43.♖d8#)

Vladimir Kramnik:

"I found myself in the position of absolutely having to win this game. People always say that something like that is nearly impossible, above all when you need such a win in the final game of a world championship against an opponent such as Leko, who only needs a draw. But when you consider the matter from another perspective, it was not so simple for him either. There is always this thought that only one single draw will realize the dream of winning the title. Such thoughts certainly influence specific decisions, whether you want them to or not. So it was not all so hopeless for me as it appeared.

The opening went perfectly for me. Not in in the sense that I had any concrete advantage, but the position became rather complicated, not a standard one. We left theory at a very early stage. All that is the maximum which one may expect of an opening in such a situation.

I decided on 3.e5 ♗f5 4.h4, at that time a rare, aggressive variation. There was not yet a lot of theory about it, and the play cannot be simplified so quickly. It was exactly what I wanted of this game.

And then I came out with an innovation, 6.♘d2, which had been suggested by my second Evgeny Bareev. We had not analysed it so very deeply, and it does not promise a great advantage either. But, as I said, my main concern was to deviate from known theory. Peter reacted very well at first and we simply played out an unknown, unclear position.

Then, however, the psychological aspect mentioned at the beginning played its part in the game. Peter even confirmed to me afterwards that Black might have played 14...d4 instead of 14...g6. This pawn sacrifice would have led to very strong positional compensation for

Leko. At least in that case he would not have been worse. To be honest, during the game I was quite worried about the idea that he would play 14...d4. Peter had seen this move and also thought that it was good. But mentally he was simply in no position to play like that; his mind was set on simple and above all safe chess.

After 14...♘g6 I decided on 15.♗d4.

Peter was immediately prepared to transition to an endgame with an exchange of queens. That was the next dubious decision of his. Okay, such an endgame can possibly be held, but it is not pleasant. Of course, at that time Leko was very strong in the successful defence of slightly worse endings. But on account of his weak light-squared bishop, I already had strategic advantages and I was quite happy with this turn of events.

Then an unpleasant blow for him was 21.b4.

The idea behind it is to open a second front. Normally it is very difficult to break down an opponent in such a position on a single flank. You have to be attacking on both flanks, which I did with 21.b4. Additionally, it suited me that his knight on h5 was slightly out of play. After 21...a6 I played the important 22.a4 and here too he remained passive, although his position was already becoming dangerous.

Leko may no longer have had many options, but now at the latest, the time had arrived for him to calculate and seek active counterplay. But he was probably hoping to be able to draw with this passivity. I tried to keep on provoking him into playing sharply because I could really feel that he was not ready to do so.

That was also the reason why I played 24.b5, not the optimal move, and one which normally would also not have been needed. But this move then led to 24...♘f4, a really serious mistake on his part.

He could have played, for example, 24...b6, which would have been a last practical chance for him. Then I myself played 25.b6 and with that move White was winning. I began to invade down the c-file and I had pressure on the g-file. The position could no longer be held, even if that was not immediately apparent.

Now was the time for me to calculate concrete variations. After 34.f4 everything worked out in my favour.

There were several routes to the win, but I very much liked the king march to f6, though I had to sacrifice two pawns. But my pieces were simply so incredibly active that he no longer had a defence. After the time control and his 40th move, 40...♖h4, I actually first intended to play 41.e6. Then, however, to my joy I saw 41.♘f7† with mate in three moves. Now I could see how hard it hit Peter to lose, not to win the title of World Champion. Normally after 41.♘f7† he would see in a few seconds that the game was finally lost, and would resign at once. But this time Leko needed a whole ten minutes before he could force himself to do so.

It was a terribly painful defeat for him. On one hand I felt sorry for him, because of all the challengers in the history of chess, no other one had been closer than he was to winning the world championship title; only at the very finish not to manage it. On the other hand, it was really an outstanding game on my part. Not only from the point of view of chess, but also as far as my psychological strength and willpower were concerned. Peter, for his part, simply wanted the draw too much, and at the end paid a very high price for that. I, however, was prepared to fight and took advantage of my last chance."

The Unification of the Chess World

♚35

2006 should go down as one of the most turbulent yet important years in the history of the royal game. The split in the chess world caused by Garry Kasparov in 1993 had lasted for 13 years. By the end of 2006, there would be only one World Champion, recognized by all, and under the aegis of FIDE.

Before this, however, in the football World Cup, Germany experienced the so-called Summer Fairytale. Our country had never previously seen a sporting event which galvanized the whole nation in such a way. It was unimportant that the German team finished in third place. We sincerely enjoyed the visit by our numerous foreign guests; we were joyful and we celebrated. During these four weeks, we hardly saw a single cloud in the sky. Our glasses were suddenly no longer half empty, but half full. The whole nation was like a street party, people were as exuberant as though they were in the Rigoletto area of Buenos Aires, or on the Copacabana beach in Rio. A single event should not permanently change the mentality of a whole people, but we Germans like to remember these days, even with a little nostalgia.

The chess year began for me in January with the traditional visit to Wijk aan Zee. I had been travelling to this tournament since the start of the 1990s. This event on the Dutch North Sea coast had for many years been one of the top three tournaments in the annual chess calendar, along with Linares and Dortmund. On one hand, the elite grandmasters met there, on the other you could enjoy that very special wonderful ambiance that can only be found in the chess world. I have never felt it so intensively in any other sport, be it football, boxing or table tennis.

The core of the elite scene in professional chess involves around 80 to 100 people. It is a wonderful mixture of grandmasters, event organizers, officials, sponsors and representatives of the media. This circus travels around the world, and over the years you become close to many of these people; some remain lifelong friends. It was a marvellous time, above all in the 1990s. For me, many stories and positive memories are linked to these events. And there was no better place to get a feel for the chess world in all its facets than the quiet town of Wijk aan Zee, with its cobbled alleys and cosy pubs.

Despite the natural rivalry between us, within that core scene we respected one another. When I was in Wijk aan Zee in 2006, however, things looked somewhat different. It was the first tournament from which Kramnik had to withdraw due to his illness. Our events-management firm UEP and I had, immediately after the tournament in San Luis, already negotiated with Topalov's manager, Silvio Danailov, in order to bring about a possible reunification match. By mutual agreement, we at first left the world federation out of the negotiations. We wanted to first sound out whether agreement could be reached between Kramnik and Topalov. That had absolutely top priority. At the beginning of November 2005, Danailov came to the Bonn Art and Exhibition Hall. After several hours of conversation, all parties had reached an agreement; that is, the sponsor UEP, the venue Bonn and the management of both players. The match between the two titleholders was to take place from 25th November to 17th December 2006, in Bonn.

We all expressed the desire to reunify the chess world, and we had a contract ready for signing with prizemoney of 1.4 million dollars; we shook hands and drank to it. Topalov's manager now wanted to bring in FIDE in order to involve them after our verbal agreement. The world federation was to receive a licensing fee of $280,000. We were all convinced we had found the royal road, since now the much-desired reunification was lying on the table in front of the officials of FIDE, like a present.

Only two days later, however, Danailov called and announced that he would not sign the agreements. He said FIDE had other plans and that was the end of the matter. The whole previous process of negotiations had not been made public. Nevertheless, for no reason the Topalov side then put out a totally unnecessary press statement in which it impolitely attacked Kramnik and disputed that he had any right to a match with Topalov. The FIDE president went one step further and insulted his possible sponsor, the UEP.

I instantly assumed that the Bulgarians had gone completely mad. After all, following our first conversation in Argentina we had negotiated for six weeks. But after a few days it became clear that there was a real background to the 180 degree turn by the FIDE Champion. In professional chess there is a lot of money at stake, and now he was turning down a fantastic offer. It was the first time in Topalov's career that he was able to aim for such prizemoney. He and Danailov would hardly be rejecting it for personal reasons unless they were getting compensation from some other source.

And that was correct. During the tournament in Wijk in January 2006, I received reliable information from FIDE circles. They wanted to finally manoeuvre Kramnik out of the way. His illness, and the weak results associated with it during 2005, allegedly gave them the opportunity to do so. Topalov was, on the other hand, offered the prospect of a match against the Azerbaijani Teimour Radjabov. That is to say, the chance for a voluntary defence of his title before he might once more be able to take part officially in a tournament for the FIDE World Championship. FIDE vice-president Zurab Azmaiparashvili (Georgia) was a close friend of the Radjabov clan, and one of those who were pulling the strings for this deal.

So that was the real reason. It was possible that big money could be made against an inexperienced player and not against World Champion Kramnik. The published opinion of some so-called insiders that Topalov still wanted to appear against Kramnik, but had started a war outside of the chess board, belongs in the realm of fairy tales. The Topalov side and FIDE were in agreement: they wanted to push Kramnik out!

A final working meeting between Topalov's manager, UEP owner Josef Resch and me, then took place in Wijk aan Zee in January 2006. The Bulgarian appeared arrogant and even claimed that Kramnik's illness was only a pretext. He could bring his career to an end right away, because he was dead from the point of view of chess. They would not face him under any circumstances. "Kramnik is so weak that it makes no sense for Veselin to play against him," was their line.

Everything was unbelievably complicated, the situation once again totally muddled. The overwhelming majority of the chess world accepted Kramnik as the conqueror of Kasparov and World Champion in the classical line. But that no longer seemed of interest to anyone in FIDE. Of course, we had to accept that the position of Topalov was stronger than that of all the other previous FIDE titleholders. To the joy of the spectators, the man played "aggressive" chess and his results in the past year had been fantastic.

♔36

Thus the reunification, which Kramnik was still striving for, had disappeared into the distance. But in this situation he still had some aces up his sleeve, and in February and March 2006 we played them all, one after the other. First there was the question of showing strength. That aim was served by a second version of the duel against the chess computer Deep Fritz, which had been scheduled for the end of 2006 in the Bonn Federal Art and Exhibitions Hall. The struggle of man against machine still attracted great international attention, even outside the chess scene, especially since the first duel between Deep Fritz and Kramnik in Bahrain had ended 4-4, and thus without a decision.

As main sponsor we acquired the German firm RAG, and had at our disposal a seven-digit budget. Suddenly our opponent had to take note that, despite his illness and forced break, Kramnik was still able to attract major sponsors. From his difficult situation, he was preparing, outside FIDE, a world stage on which he could excellently continue to present himself as the 14th World Chess Champion.

Over and above that, we began to have the Prague Agreement legally checked, and we confronted the world federation with this. The breakthrough to reunifying the chess world followed at the start of March 2006 in Moscow. Alexander Zhukov now became involved. Zhukov was at that time Deputy Prime Minister of Russia and President of the Russian Chess Federation. In Russia he is one of the most influential politicians and nowadays president of the National Olympic Committee.

Zhukov probably made it clear to Kirsan Ilyumzhinov that all the little games of his people could not continue. For Ilyumzhinov too, a lot was resting on this – he wanted to be re-elected at the forthcoming presidential elections, for the Russian Federal Republic of Kalmykia as well as at the FIDE congress at the start of June in Turin. So after the intervention of Zhukov, FIDE changed its mind. Topalov was then "convinced" and the way was at last clear. In any case, the renewed change of opinion of the Bulgarians was made especially tasty for him. After the unification match against Kramnik, Topalov was in addition to have, in April 2007, the already-promised match against Teimour Radjabov, in Baku, Azerbaijan. A double jackpot was quite to their taste.

I suppose that another important point, which moved Topalov and FIDE to a completely different view of matters within a few weeks, was Kramnik's presumed weakness. As a result of his illness, his performances in 2005 had been abysmal compared to his ability. Before the match in September, he would hardly get any playing practice, since it was known that Kramnik had had to withdraw from all tournaments in the first half of the year. On the other hand, Topalov saw himself at the height of his powers. Over and above that, he enjoyed the goodwill of some FIDE officials, who wanted to see their titleholder win and were also following their own personal interests.

So they were quite certain of winning the duel against Kramnik. How certain can be seen from the following detail. FIDE had already set up for September 2007 a world championship tournament in Mexico City. Danailov vehemently demanded in the negotiations for the Kramnik – Topalov match that the loser should not take part in the said tournament. Kramnik was not particularly bothered and agreed. Thus in the event of a defeat, Topalov and Danailov would harm themselves. No sensible person would demand something like that unless he was 100% sure of his position.

From this moment on, at the latest, Kramnik was well aware that what was awaiting him was more than just a chess duel. In addition, in May 2006 the Azerbaijanis, with the agreement of Topalov and in the presence of FIDE vice-president Zurab Azmaiparashvili, announced the match against Radjabov for April 2007. Here too, they were delivering a clear message: the World Championship match against Kramnik was only a stopover on their journey, purely a matter of form. Their behaviour towards Kramnik, who was still suffering from his illness, was simply arrogant and lacking in respect. It did backfire a little, since in the chess world the number of critical voices was growing; they were losing sympathy.

I handed in the first drafts of the World Championship contracts, flew to FIDE headquarters in Athens, and then the negotiations started. Both players should receive a fixed sum of 500,000 dollars net after tax, and at the same time have a share of any further income from sponsorship. In the contract, the term "World Champion" was totally avoided. For Kramnik, however, I had come to an additional agreement with the FIDE president, so that he could continue to describe himself as classical World Champion.

The World Championship match was to be over twelve games with classical time controls, and would be played from 21st September to 13th October 2006, in the Kalmykian capital Elista (Russia). In the event of a drawn match, a tiebreak of four rapid games would decide the World Championship. Essentially, all the conditions were identical to those which had been on the table a few months previously in Bonn, after having been negotiated by the two camps. FIDE announced the match on 13th April 2006 in a press statement accompanied by euphoric words from its president. How little trust Kramnik had in the officials of the world federation, however, can be seen from the fact that he insisted on being the last to sign. He did so on 23rd April 2006, ten days after this press release.

♚37

In Elista, the FIDE president ruled in the fullest sense of the term. Kirsan Ilyumzhinov was President of the Russian Federal Republic of Kalmykia, and some years ago had had a district of villas built there called 'Chess City'. Despite my many previous journeys, Kalmykia was for me a rather exotic place, which I only knew from hearsay in the chess world. I would soon get to know it. My first thought was: just how do I get there?

At that time one flew to Elista via Moscow. There was no alternative, unless you wanted to drive from Volgograd, the former Stalingrad, a good 400 kilometres south through the steppes. I went to Elista from 16th to 18th August 2006, in order to inspect the playing hall and our conditions on site. I was accompanied by Alexander Bakh, the director of the Russian Chess Federation.

Departure was from the Moscow airport, Sheremetyevo II. Over the years I had grown accustomed to air travel within Russia, which at that time was known to be associated with higher risks. But when I saw this aircraft, I became really queasy. Patched outside and inside hundreds of times, the aircraft was of the Yak type with rear entry, from the early 1960s. It took far more than half an hour for us to finally reach our cruising altitude. The aircraft was groaning at the seams, but the Russians remained calm: always a good sign. At some point all we could see was the steppes and shortly afterwards were happy to land at Elista airport.

The first things to catch my eye were two discarded JU-52 planes of the German army, whose swastikas were insufficiently covered with paint. We were received by a committee. An exotic girl then handed me a bowl full of camel milk. This is a traditional gesture to important guests, I was told. I looked at Alexander Bakh; here there was no way out. We had to go through with it, and even the assurance that this drink strengthened one's virility could not hide what was for Western tongues the very strong taste of cold sweat.

In total I was in Elista three times: after the three-day inspection before the World Championship, there was a whole month during the reunification match, and another three-week visit in 2007 with Peter Leko for the World Championship Candidates matches. Quite independently from what happened during the match against Topalov,

I have really positive memories of the Kalmyks. They are a hospitable people of Mongolian origin. They are Buddhists and, from their history, used to a frugal life on the steppes. Their loving nature is something we all remember.

Who can understand why so much suffering was inflicted on this modest people in the former Soviet Union? Under Stalin in 1943, more than 300,000 Kalmyks, that is almost the whole nation, were deported to Siberia. Allegedly they had been on the side of the Germans and had collaborated with them. Only half of the population was able to return ten years later after the death of Stalin; the other half perished in the work camps of the gulag.

On account of the numerous rumours about the abnormal behaviour in San Luis, Kramnik had demanded checks. "I received warnings from grandmaster colleagues who accused Topalov of manipulation. These were massive accusations which did not exactly make it easy to concentrate on such an important match", is how Vladimir describes the situation at the time. The Russian Chess Federation and its director Alexander Bakh assured they would support the application of these controls.

They included: searches carried out on both players and all restrooms including toilets in the presence of a member of the opposing team, a ban on mobile telephones in the playing hall and the prevention of wireless transmission of information in the playing hall by signal jammers. In addition, a glass wall was erected in front of the playing table; its reflections should prevent the players from distinguishing gestures from the playing hall. Finally, special areas were set up in the playing hall for team members making visual contact with the players impossible.

Whether there had actually been cheating there and on other occasions was never investigated, but Vladimir wanted to be as well protected as possible from such an eventuality. The appropriate measures were the responsibility of the world federation FIDE and their local organizers.

♔38

In the meantime, from a purely sporting point of view, the Bulgarians could no longer be so sure of themselves. Vladimir Kramnik's results, following his comeback at the Chess Olympiad in Turin at the end of May 2006, were outstanding. Russia may have taken a disappointing sixth place, but Kramnik had overcome the deepest troughs of his illness. On first board he played like a man set free, and was awarded the gold medal for being the best player in the whole Olympiad.

After that he again won the tournament in Dortmund, for the seventh time. The therapy had taken effect: Vladimir had put on some weight, and in the summer of 2006 I found him as full of energy as he had been in 2000 before the match against Kasparov. Moreover, he was not opening, as in previous years, with 1.e4, but going back to his original systems with d2-d4. So Topalov could no longer rely on a specific opening move from Kramnik, which made his preparations more difficult.

For the players and teams, even months before the event the pressure was incredibly high. It was not only a prestige match of the highest level. For Kramnik it was more about the fulfilment of the reunification. He wanted, at the latest after the subsequent world championship tournament in Mexico, to ensure a world championship system with serious time controls and to guarantee the maintenance of the classic world championships in the form of a final match. He could only achieve this if he was the winner.

Should Topalov lose, he would miss out on the lucrative match against Radjabov. In addition, his reputation was at stake. He had not defeated Kasparov; in the event of a defeat, the FIDE title from San Luis would remain a footnote in chess history and be of no importance whatsoever. In order to get the recognition he craved and to earn the big money, he would have to defeat Kramnik. There was a lot at stake.

Personally, from the start I had a good feeling. Vladimir's score against Topalov was positive. In addition, I was helped a little, as so often, by superstition. I had begun in sports management between 1987 and 1989 in the organizational team for the 40th World Table Tennis Championships. That event was in every respect a complete success. Why should things be any different for the 40th world championship match in the history of chess?

♚39

Our team consisted, besides Vladimir Kramnik and me, of five other people: grandmasters Miguel Illescas (Spain), Alexander Motylev and Sergei Rublevsky, the physiotherapist Dr Valery Krylov, and the cook Viktor Bobylev (all from Russia). Kramnik and I were already in Moscow when we met the rest of the team on September 15th. Of the personnel from the London match against Kasparov, only Illescas remained. Compared to the world championship against Leko, Bareev and Svidler had been replaced by Rublevsky and Motylev. The change from Svidler, especially, made it clear that Vladimir Kramnik would no longer be opening with 1.e4, but would be going back to 1.d4, as in 2000 against Kasparov. It was important to keep this secret until the very last moment, which we managed to do.

It had been agreed in the contracts that the teams should consist of a maximum of seven people. We met the Bulgarians at Moscow's Vnukovo airport. Veselin Topalov's team consisted of grandmasters Alexander Onischuk (USA), Ivan Cheparinov (Bulgaria), Paco Vallejo Pons (Spain), Silvio Danailov and other Bulgarians who were unknown to us: these were allegedly a press attaché, a so-called attaché from the Bulgarian embassy, a supposed expert in satellite technology, and a physiotherapist. And in addition, a cook would also be coming. So the whole team consisted of ten people – obviously more than the agreed maximum. It was the first violation of the agreements, which, despite our enquiries, FIDE simply waved through. They pretended to be surprised, but of course they already had all the names on their list.

We assumed that agents of the Bulgarian secret service would pop up in Topalov's team, and were reckoning on a lot happening, though we did not know exactly what to expect. I remember the first meeting with Topalov, Danailov and his people at the airport. Kramnik and I went over to them to shake hands. We had known each other well for many years, but at this point they were already creating a repellent atmosphere. Topalov was taken to one side, and during the handshake Danailov looked past us with an expression of disgust.

At first, however, Vladimir, tried not to be affected by all the negativity. Externally he looked as usual quite cool. On the flight to Elista we were in very good humour. The ambiance was perfect, especially as Miguel Illescas was in the mood for jokes. Vladimir laughed a lot, and everything seemed good.

When we landed in Elista, whose airport was to remain closed from 25th September 2006 for reasons of security, we were greeted by an ostentatious reception, which seemed never-ending. Kirsan Ilyumzhinov was unbelievably cordial and energetic. We were taken into the steppe to a camel race. Then we went into the capital. There we saw a lovely Asian-style park and visited the central square where the parliament was located. In the coming weeks, the games were to be played there in the auditorium of the parliament which had been newly built especially for the world championship. We met some members of the government of the federal republic, and after we had seen the just-finished playing hall, off we went to the Buddhist temple of Kalmykia, the biggest on European soil.

Towards 16:00, we were at last able to move into our lodgings in Elista's Chess City. Vladimir was satisfied with the accommodation. There were still a lot of minor things to be sorted; the internet did not work and there was nothing provided for our cook in the kitchen. But we could set up home for the next four weeks in this villa, with its 16 living rooms and bedrooms, five bathrooms and five kitchens. The final preparations could begin.

On 19th September I had to, in the fullest sense of the term, "stand by my man". Kirsan's head of organization, Valery Bovaev, had announced he would visit us. He wanted to get to know me a little with some welcoming drinks. That naturally consisted of vodka. We learned that Bovaev could drink a lot of alcohol, but you could not refuse such an invitation. I had a word with our cook – Viktor gave good advice and prepared for me a hearty soup as a foundation. After each little glass I was to eat something substantial immediately, above all olives marinated in oil, and to drink a lot of water. I did as he said and was lucky.

To my good fortune, Bovaev, who did not consider drinking with namby-pamby Westerners to be a serious business, was already slightly merry when he reached our accommodation. A woman interpreter, his driver and a security official were present too. They were not allowed to drink, but were condemned to observe the whole performance. We ended up drinking two bottles of vodka. Valery Bovaev lost:

completely unexpectedly, he collapsed to the floor and his people had quite enough to do to get him safely back. When I saw him the following day, I had earned his respect. "Only a man who can hold his drink is a real man," is what they say in Kalmykia.

The next day I had a few hours to myself. Vyacheslav Namruev, the director of Chess City, is a very spiritual man. He proposed to me a meeting with a Buddhist monk, who could predict the future. I agreed and was driven to the temple. There I had to give some information about Vladimir. When the monk had all the information, he shook some objects in a little box and let them drop on to the table.

After searching in some paper scrolls and finding what he was looking for, he said: "Vladimir Kramnik will win the match. But it will be a very close-run thing, and really decided only at the very last moment. Everything can, however, also go wrong. On the way to victory, he will have to survive a very serious crisis and that will have nothing to do with chess. Only if he takes the correct decision will he triumph at the end."

Whenever I think back to it today, I get goose bumps. Every detail of this prediction came true. A year later, I met the monk again. In my presence he foretold to Peter Leko the exact (!) results of his Candidates matches on the way to the world championship: against Mikhail Gurevich (3½–½) and Evgeny Bareev (3½–1½). There are several witnesses to both meetings. If in the past I laughed at the supernatural, nowadays I am certain that it exists. In the Buddhist temple I saw people who were writhing in pain. Neither doctor nor medicine could help them. They went to so-called healing monks. It sounds incredible, but they came back out pain-free, completely relaxed and with smiles on their faces.

As a rule, the Kalmyks radiate contentment and peace; Buddhism certainly plays a great part in this. The large Elista temple constitutes a 60-metre-high symbol of this. Despite the financial problems in this impoverished part of Russia, what one saw in the streets was decent. There was very little advertising in public spaces.

♔40

On 21st September, there was the traditional inspection of the playing conditions. Vladimir wanted a few changes made to the lighting. Russian television wanted the removal of the glass wall. On site we saw the chief arbiter Geurt Gijssen (Netherlands) and his deputy Panagiotis Nikolopoulos (Greece). Kirsan Ilyumzhinov and his head of organization, Valery Bovaev, were also present. Actually the only one missing was Veselin Topalov. He did not come and was represented by his manager. With expansive gestures, Danailov checked the placing of the chair, the chess board and the light. Just as if he was appearing against Kramnik himself. In the presence of the officials he declared himself satisfied with the playing conditions.

But on the very same evening, a first protest rumbled in from Topalov's team. In the players' restrooms there were monitors on which the up-to-date position could be seen. The Bulgarians suspected evil-doing here, and requested the use of conventional demonstration boards. Every time a move was made, specially trained youngsters should update the position on the demo boards. We found it mysterious how one could manipulate things on a free-standing monitor without a computer, but this change did not bother Kramnik.

By now, Vladimir had settled in well in our quarters. We were all slightly tense, but there was no trace of nerves. Viktor was a really great cook; we nicknamed him "Potato King", because he was able to conjure up all sorts of tasty dishes from potatoes with only a few herbs and spices. He had bought an enormous sturgeon, and day by day he produced high-energy meals from it. Everyone made his own breakfast, but whenever possible the team came together for lunch and dinner.

Our building was under 24-hour police protection for the whole four weeks of our stay. Not even a mouse could get in or out. One of the most stubborn at trying to do so was the German journalist Dagobert Kohlmeyer. But even he failed. We felt sorry for the officers who had to do this boring job, and regularly supplied them with tea, fruit and cigarettes.

In order to get a little physical activity, we had ordered a table tennis table. At the start, it was used frequently. The internet was only available in my quarters, and could be used there by my colleagues whenever they needed to. Vladimir went walking a lot. Now and then his rheumatism caused him some discomfort. He needed a special mattress, which Valery Bovaev immediately organized for him. Organizationally there could be no complaints about how things worked.

On the evening of 21st September 2006, the world championship was opened ceremonially in the football stadium of Elista, in front of more than 5,000 spectators. The show was organized with great effort and much love, and presented the typical traditions of the Kalmyks. The choosing of colours for the first game was carried out with black and white doves. In two days' time, Vladimir would begin with White. At the end of the ceremony we all needed a little luck when embers from the mighty closing fireworks fell down on the stand for honoured guests. Fortunately, nobody was injured.

A day later, a second protest from the Topalov camp reached us. The shower booths in the bathrooms and the glass wall protecting the view from the stage should be demolished. We had nothing against the removal of the shower booths. However, we refused the removal of the illuminated glass wall which we had demanded as protection against possible attempts at manipulation by means of body language.

Our standpoint was in any case clear: the playing conditions had been defined by contract and finally agreed with the site inspection of 21st September. Extensive security measures against possible attempts at cheating had been implemented. Nobody from Topalov's team had mentioned anything during the inspection. This should actually have been an end of all this nonsense, but they simply did not stop their protests. In principle it was about unimportant details, but we became more and more convinced that the composition of the opposing team was essentially directed at causing trouble.

The fact that the tension was rising was further brought to my notice when Vladimir spoke to me about a parapsychologist. In the opinion of the Russian media, one of these was working in Topalov's team and was capable of disturbing Kramnik's concentration. There had already been a question of parapsychologists during the scandal-ridden 1978 match between Anatoly Karpov and Viktor Korchnoi in the Philippines. I was, however, certain that here quite specific rumours were being circulated, and that there was no parapsychologist in Topalov's team at all. But I had no difficulty in believing officials from the Bulgarian secret service were present. Topalov's people, in any case, were creating uncertainty just through the unclear roles of some members of their team, and the Russian media were joining in.

I again talked through all the protective measures with Vladimir, and afterwards phoned Alexander Bakh, the director of the Russian chess federation. The latter travelled to the opening game with his president, Alexander Zhukov. Bakh assured me that organizationally everything had been done to forestall any attempts at manipulation. I informed Vladimir, but I noticed that his doubts could never be totally swept away. It was really time that things got going.

♔41

Games 1-4

Vladimir and I drove to the first round in a black SUV under police escort. Kramnik had sweaty palms, which is seldom the case before a game. This time, however, the tension was extremely high, because of the years of background to the match. Chess history was being written, and that could almost be felt physically. I wished Vladimir luck and said to him: "Enjoy the match!" In the presence of the FIDE president, and of Alexander Zhukov and his sports minister, the ice-hockey legend, Vyacheslav Fetisov, opened the decisive match for a unified chess throne. 13 years of split caused by the 13th World Chess Champion were being overcome: a really defining moment in the history of the game.

Vladimir began with 1.d4 and aimed for positional play in the Catalan. In that first game, we experienced all the highs and lows that chess has to offer. Topalov, who was the first to deviate from current theory, took the initiative at first. In the endgame, it did not look at all good for Kramnik; his position was paralysed. But Topalov let him escape, and then we were counting on sharing the point.

But the Bulgarian not only missed gaining the full point, in what followed a bad mistake with 57...f5 even cost him the draw. Kramnik was winning and the technical liquidation didn't raise any problems for him. As in his previous world championship matches, he had struck early and taken a 1–0 lead. Only Illescas joined us for dinner. Rublevsky and Motylev wanted to work through the night, and got some sleep beforehand. We rejoiced only briefly over the fortunate start.

In his career as World Champion and Challenger, Vladimir made 67 world championship appearances, playing a total of 69 games. I accompanied him to the venue 52 times. In principle, we always had the same ritual. When everything was ready, the limousine's air-conditioning on and security matters checked over, I would knock at his door, and after a little delay we would then set off. I had already factored in his tendency to be late, and regularly turned up a few minutes earlier. We never arrived late for a world championship game. On the way there, we talked mostly about politics, sport or anything else from the news. When we reached our destination, I wished him luck. Although the procedure was always similar, the tension was so intense that I can remember every single one of these world championship days; sometimes even the content of the conversations we had on the way there. Going to a world championship game was always something quite special, but psychologically never easy to manage.

On the drive to the second game, Vladimir was a little less tense than on the previous day. Topalov, on the other hand, still came across to us as something like a puppet. Until then, our relationship with him had always been basically rather neutral, even friendly. In any case, until 2006 there had never been any personal problems. I can well remember his defeat at the hands of Peter Leko in the 2002 Candidates final. After all, this was about the qualification for the world championship match against Kramnik. Despite his disappointment, he congratulated Peter and me fairly on the win. Of course, he was then already under the strong influence of Danailov, but he was still friendly. That had changed dramatically. His manager and all these people around him, who were quite out of place in a chess team, were visibly changing him.

Topalov also opened with 1.d4, and the Slav Defence appeared on the board. The game may have been full of tension but, for a world championship, the level was abysmal. One blunder followed another.

By the end, Topalov had overlooked a clear win three times, missing above all 32.♖xg4† instead of 32.♕g6†, and then overlooking two winning continuations in time trouble. Things did not go much better for Kramnik, except that in the decisive phases he made fewer mistakes than the Bulgarian. In the playing hall, you could feel the nervousness during this game.

It affected the players, their teams and the spectators. Yes, even organizers and journalists looked as though they were infected by it. Topalov had the initiative, but was obviously less able than Kramnik to stand up to this unbelievable pressure, and resigned after 63 moves. In the subsequent joint press conference, both players were washed out, as if they had run a marathon. After seven hours, we returned to our quarters with a fortunate 2–0 in our knapsack.

On the rest day, Veselin Topalov visited an Orthodox church, and he appeared less tense during the third game.

In the Catalan Opening, Kramnik worked up some pressure with White and with 32.exd5, instead of 32.cxd5 as he played, he might have been able to achieve more than a draw. After his two opening wins, however, sharing the point was a perfectly normal result. Topalov was also pleased; he had first of all to consolidate, since 3–0 for Kramnik would have been more than just an early lead.

With hindsight, Vladimir was worried about the variation he had played. During the game he had obviously wanted to play 17.♘e4, but was not sure of his ground and at the board chose the unspectacular 17.♗xe7.

That evening, our cook excelled himself: fish, meat, poultry and fresh salads stood on the table. The highlight, however, was fresh crayfish from a nearby lake. Food was of central importance for us, since during the match we were all consuming lots of energy. Of course, Vladimir above all had to take care of himself: the nervous breakdown of Brissago was still a clear memory. Later he went for a walk with Rublevsky and Motylev. Illescas was dead tired and told us he had to sleep. But half an hour later I saw him back at work.

Immediately before the fourth game, Vladimir consulted his seconds. Firstly he consulted briefly with Motylev, then with Rublevsky. During the drive, we spoke a little about football; CSKA Moscow had beaten Hamburg in the Champions League by 1–0.

In the opening phase Vladimir fell behind on time – a good half an hour. On move twelve the lights went out in the playing hall; the game had to be interrupted. After that a fly kept circling around Kramnik's nose, and the air conditioning in the playing hall temporarily failed. All in all, it was a remarkable day. The game was at first complicated, but then it was a dead draw. Nevertheless, Topalov played 54 moves and far more than five hours before sharing the point. Another strategy of our opponents became clear: Topalov wanted to tire Vladimir out.

Score: 3–1

On the morning of the rest day, we at last played a series of games of table tennis. From the team, Alexander Motylev especially was very adept. But Vladimir too got on outstandingly well with his long arms. However, he played his table tennis almost exclusively with the backhand, which severely limited his options. As a former ranking player, I did the honourable thing and played a purely defensive game. It was to be the last time during this match that we would really have fun.

♔42

Game 5

The rest day ended abruptly for me in the early evening. Danailov had handed in a third protest: Topalov would decline to continue the match if the toilets in the players' restrooms remained available. A little later I saw it was already on the internet; they had immediately involved the media. This was a serious business. "Toiletgate" – as the subsequent scandal was titled in the world press – was underway.

Late in the evening, after 22:00, I was officially confronted with the issue. Opposite me sat the appeals committee: Zurab Azmaiparashvili (Georgia), Georgios Makropoulos (Greece) and Jorge Vega (Guatemala), who had in the meantime replaced Israel Gelfer. Even before the world championship, Kramnik had been anything but enthusiastic about this combination. Unlike with the choice of arbiters, FIDE – despite numerous interventions – had given us no opportunity to discuss the choice of these committee members.

The three put on serious and weighty expressions. Topalov's camp had monitored the number of Kramnik's toilet visits. Danailov had been given the videotapes by the organizers, and he claimed that Kramnik had been in the toilet more than 50 times. They said they had checked that. It was quite an exaggeration; in reality there were between 16 and 18 toilet visits, but whatever. They would now consider closing the toilets completely. The players could be accompanied and make use of a common toilet. And I was asked what I might have to say about the toilet visits.

I guessed where all this would be going and said to them: "What Kramnik does in the toilet is his business. Perhaps he needs a little more space, he likes to walk up and down, perhaps he washes his face frequently. No matter, that is his business." Makropoulos spoke for them: "That is not a good enough justification for us." The other two members said as good as nothing. Azmaiparashvili grinned at me several times. Vega, whom they had in their pocket in any case, didn't understand much: he was almost exclusively occupied with severe bouts of coughing.

I replied: "Okay, we have a contract and the playing conditions are clarified in it. Kramnik has the right to his own restroom with a toilet. In addition, we had an inspection before the match. That was the last chance to change anything. What is this all about? This is now their third protest. It has got to stop some time. We are in favour of you checking the rooms, the players and everything else more strictly. But if you change the playing conditions and accept this protest, it can only mean that you believe Kramnik is cheating. If you close the toilet, then you have a real scandal on your hands."

As I left, I met the chief arbiter. I asked him: "What is all this about? Do you think that Kramnik is cheating?" His answer was: "No, of course not. But they are not on your side. This is not a simple situation." I then said to him that he should take some action against it, after all he was the chief arbiter. But he only shook his head. For the first time I became aware that this world championship was on the edge. The score was 3–1 for Kramnik and some people wanted to avoid the threat of a defeat, no matter what the cost. On the way back to our quarters, I saw FIDE vice-president Azmaiparashvili going into Topalov's house.

The fact that recordings from Kramnik's restrooms had been passed to Topalov's team and from there on to the press capped it all. In doing so, they had clearly infringed on Vladimir's privacy and his personal rights. They were quite sure that they could do anything they wanted. Our team only learned about these actions after Topalov's protest, that is to say some days after the handing over of the tapes.

I possess a document from the head of the organization in which he logs the fact and confirms that the videos were passed on several occasions, specifically on the 25th, 27th and 28th September 2006, from him to Topalov's team. In it he indicates that on each occasion he had been required to pass over the tapes by FIDE and its representatives, Makropoulos and Azmaiparashvili.

The action of team Topalov was quite obviously the start of a scandal which they had planned to launch against Kramnik, should anything go wrong on the sporting side. And that had happened; Topalov had lost the first two games. In our opinion, this 'Plan B' was now in full swing. They were very cunning, since they never directly accused Kramnik of cheating, but suggested that there was a possibility of it. The fact that both players had made mistakes in the first games, and that alone precluded any sort of outside assistance, was completely ignored. Even the meticulous checking of the players and the restrooms, including the toilets, before the games did not play any part in their argument. Everything which endangered Plan B was deliberately ignored.

It was after 23:00 when I returned from the session with the appeals committee. I met Vladimir, who had already been informed by me early in the evening about the hearing and the reason for it. He had already taken his decision: "If this protest is accepted, they will never give us peace. If they close my toilet, I will not continue the match. I am not putting up with this nonsense any longer. It is beneath me."

As we feared, Topalov's protest was essentially accepted. This decision was absurd, since in giving the reasons they certified that all the controls were working perfectly – including the searching of players, restrooms and toilets – and that was the case before each game. Cheating was neither proven nor possible in practice. So why in God's name did they accept such a protest? I was informed of the decision at 11 a.m. – only four hours before the fifth game. After I had contacted Alexander Bakh in Moscow, I wrote an open letter to the FIDE president, in which Kramnik's central demands were stated.

This included replacing the appeals committee. And as long as his toilet was not made available to him again, Kramnik would no longer be taking part. Vladimir did not want to make a formal protest to the then appeals committee. His trust in FIDE vice-presidents Zurab Azmaiparashvili and Georgios Makropoulos was totally gone. He would reserve the possibility of legal action regarding Topalov's team having been given access to tapes from his restrooms, which made it possible for them to have them published in print media and on the internet, which represented a violation of his personal rights.

After receiving the decision of the appeals committee I had to inform Vladimir. I did this as quickly as possible, within 30 minutes. We had only a little more than three hours before Game 5 to cope with the situation. Vlad had expected it and at first remained astonishingly calm, at least on the outside. I once again tried to persuade him to play the fifth game, though under protest. He said quite calmly: "Carsten, there is no way I will play if they do not take that back. That's enough. If I agree to a neutral toilet, they can easily blame something on me. I would have to leave the stage and walk through rows of spectators. Outside the supervised restrooms, it would be easy to make up some sort of evidence to accuse me of cheating." He instructed me to enter into no further communication, either with Topalov's people or with the appeals committee.

From the very beginning, Kramnik had been fearful that an attempt would be made to construct some allegation of cheating against him. That was not so easy to do with the security measures which had been agreed, but he was correct: with a neutral toilet, such "proof" would be easy to arrange. To outsiders, this way of looking at things may appear paranoid, but his fears had some justification. Vladimir's standpoint was therefore understandable, but all of us in the team were resistant to the idea that Topalov would now get the present of a full point without having to fight for it; a reward, as it were, for the aggressive and dishonourable behaviour of his team. In addition, I could not see the match being continued. We could feel from our opponents a lack of scruples such as we had never known. It obviously did not matter to them whether chess or their image was damaged. The only thing which counted for them was not to lose this match, whatever the cost.

Though he appeared calm on the outside, Vladimir was unbelievably emotional. His feelings told him that he had to act exactly in this way. He listened to his inner voice, and during the match I became more and more convinced that he had been absolutely correct in his decision. These first protests and "Toiletgate" were possibly just the start of a diabolical plan, the real point of which we fortunately never learned. Team Topalov could not have reckoned with Vladimir's reaction, and with his uncontested loss of the fifth game, Vladimir won back his ability to act.

When we came to the playing hall, Kramnik's toilet was closed. Kramnik did not start the fifth game, though the chief arbiter Geurt Gijssen several times called on him to do so. On the request of the vice-president Georgios Makropoulos, Gijssen delayed the start by a good 20 minutes. In our view this was another breach of the rules, since according to those rules a game may only be delayed with the agreement of the president of FIDE. But Kirsan was not even in Elista.

A few days later I found out why they had started the clocks so late. When the members of the appeals committee noticed that Kramnik was serious, they got cold feet. On one hand it suited them that Ilyumzhinov was not even in the city, but on the other hand they did not want to attack before having their decision confirmed by the FIDE president.

Kirsan knew nothing about all this; he was in Sochi in a meeting with Vladimir Putin and could not be reached. They solved this problem "creatively" and quite in their style. The leader of Chess City Elista drove rapidly to the local FIDE office in order to have the signature of Kirsan put on a document which confirmed the decision of the committee. Only it was not the original signature of the president. They used a facsimile stamp!

When the forgery, which was not recognizable as such at first, was present, the game was set in motion at 15:22. At 16:22 Geurt Gijssen declared it a win for Topalov. At that point Topalov lost almost all sympathy in the chess world. Especially since he and Danailov beamed over the scoresheet which they held in their hands and on which the unplayed game was marked as 0–1 for Topalov. A great number of prominent chess players expressed themselves in public and sided with Kramnik. Danailov allowed himself to be feted by representatives of the Bulgarian media. Outside there was already a press conference being given hectically by FIDE under the leadership of Makropoulos. Vladimir and I were joined by Miguel Illescas and we simply burst in.

Vladimir interrupted Makropoulos: "Do you believe I am cheating?" Makropoulos answered: "No!" So what is this all about then? The Greek did not let him say any more, endlessly saying something about wanting to be fair to all sides, until Vladimir turned to the Russian journalists in his mother tongue, with the famous sentence: "I did not sign a contract to appear in a reality show." After that we left the building.

In Sochi, all the presidents of the Russian federal republics had gathered on the invitation of the national president. Vladimir Putin had already heard about the scandal. He asked the surprised Ilyumzhinov whether his people were not capable of organizing a game of chess. Kirsan was ordered to leave at once and to deal with the matter. His first decision was to postpone the sixth game. There were two additional rest days and endless meetings. In the end, Kramnik prevailed on all points. Azmaiparashvili and Makropoulos officially resigned their posts; in reality they were forced to do so.

The role of Azmaiparashvili was so suspect to the FIDE president that he ordered the former to leave the country within 24 hours. Playing conditions were to be as they had been before Game 5, and Kramnik was also allowed to use his toilet. The walkover point, however, remained with Topalov. From Ilyumzhinov's point of view, this was the only possibility of saving the match. Anything else would have landed him with great political difficulties. The Bulgarians would have left and had the best of prospects at the Court of Arbitration for Sport in Lausanne. The chief arbiter had declared the game won for Topalov, and that was the decisive problem.

Speaking to the Russian media, Kirsan's crafty secretary, Berik Balgabaev, had suggested that under certain circumstances the fifth game could have been replayed. The lack of a written protest to the appeals committee – within two hours after Game 5 – meant that for legal reasons that would not be possible. Of course, that was a pretty uninspired statement to protect themselves, but it was gratefully accepted by some Russians. In this way it was possible to cast a little of the blame onto the shoulders of the German manager. In this case, however, no management in the world could have influenced events or been able to achieve any other result.

Kramnik no longer recognized the authority of the appeals committee. He was simply no longer prepared to communicate with these people. He had good reason to fear that otherwise the whole drama would have dragged on endlessly, and he dealt with the whole business logically and rigorously. As for the realities of the situation, we had of course made our protest against the scoring of the fifth game – in the public press conference immediately after the game, and again immediately after the setting up of the new appeals committee, consisting of Boris Kutin, Faik Gasanov, and Jorge Vega who remained. This protest was turned down for the reason that all decisions of the original committee were absolutely final; not, for example, because a protest from our team had not been delivered within the time allowed. According to the statutes of FIDE, even the old committee could not have reversed its own decision any more.

Despite the deduction of the point, Vladimir finally decided to continue playing. Previously, during the crisis, we sat together for a long time and discussed many alternatives and their possible consequences. Marie-Laure and Dr Reinhard Rauball also spoke at length with Kramnik on several occasions. But nobody tried to persuade him to do anything specific; that would, in any case, have been pointless. Whatever he would now do, he had maintained his dignity and at the same time established boundaries for Topalov and the latter's supporters in FIDE.

At some point Vladimir made his decision. After the match he told me: "I suddenly understood that these people should not get the title. I simply had to win in order to prevent this. Everything had suddenly become a matter of principle." Playing on in this situation was certainly the most difficult, but also the most important, decision in a long career in chess.

Further actions and protests by Topalov's team during the subsequent course of the match were ineffective. For example, publishing statistics on those moves of Kramnik which were supposed to correspond with those of the chess program Fritz. Basically their procedure was always the same – they wanted to hint at the possibility of cheating by Kramnik without directly accusing him of it. Topalov's real problem lay hidden behind all these actions. As far as the match was concerned, he was trailing by 1–3 and defeat was looming. But as well as the theft of a point, however, they had achieved two things: powerful media interest and shifting many sympathies to Kramnik's side. The world championship match now had the attention of the whole world. The world's big press agencies set out on the complicated route to Elista. Reporting in the print media was so huge for a chess event that the only comparison which could be made was with the world championship match between Bobby Fischer and Boris Spassky in 1972. After all this time, chess had made it back to the front page of the *New York Times*.

Public opinion was pretty clearly on our side. Not least because Kramnik was supported by the overwhelming majority of grandmasters. A good example of the atmosphere on the chess scene was the evaluation of Grandmaster John Nunn, who on 30th September 2006 on the ChessBase website very clearly took Kramnik's side. He sharply reprimanded the one-sided procedure of FIDE, which was taking action against Kramnik without any specific allegation or proof. The composition of the appeals committee, the handing over of the surveillance tapes to Topalov's team, and also the decision of the appeals committee on the Topalov protest, were clear indications of this one-sidedness. Dr Nunn wrote about the handing over of the video of Kramnik in his restroom to Topalov's team: "This act was so obviously wrong that one can hardly imagine it being committed by an unbiased person." He described the scheduling of the fifth game before the resolution of the conflict as against the rules.

After the match, there were discussions on the chess scene: it was considered that Topalov was not the driving force behind these events and that the responsibility lay with his manager. I see things completely differently. Veselin Topalov was a very strong chess player, the public loved his games, and he was now playing in a world championship match. He bore sole responsibility for his team and its actions. His manager Silvio Danailov was not playing for the world championship and nor were the other members of his team. In this sense, Danailov was a nobody, no more than an agent of the FIDE champion. Only one person was responsible for the activities of his manager: Veselin Topalov himself!

Months later, the ethics commission of FIDE reprimanded the behaviour of Topalov and Danailov during the match. But in our opinion, this judgement was neither fish nor fowl. There was for Topalov a strict reprimand and the threat of a playing ban in the event of a recurrence. This was because during an interview with the Spanish journalist Frederico Marin Bellon, he got carried away and directly claimed that Kramnik had cheated. The barrier Team Topalov had at first meticulously respected, namely to "only" suggest this possibility, had now been clearly over-stepped by him.

The fact that Veselin Topalov had left the field free for his manager meant that for many chess lovers he had sacrificed his own character in the restrooms of Elista. Kramnik said on this point: "The world of chess has a very negative opinion of Topalov, and there are certain tournaments to which he is no longer invited. His behaviour is like a blot on his entire life. In 2006 he risked everything – honour, decency – because he so desperately wanted to win. Morally, it was important for me to win, so that in the final resort he did not get to lead the life of his dreams."

So for Vladimir there was only one thing left to do: win! The tendency of the Bulgarian to give his manager a free hand in all important affairs would turn out to be an advantage for Kramnik in the decisive phase of the match. But that was still a very, very long way away. At first, Topalov gained an impetus because the scandal had an effect on Vladimir. He had been too much engaged in senseless negotiations during these days.

Never before or since have I seen him in such a state. The substantial loss of energy and concentration it caused was one of the reasons he would later be on the edge of defeat. The scandal had a considerable effect. They had knocked Vladimir completely off his emotional balance. The match was open once more. It was officially 3–2 for Kramnik, although Vladimir never accepted the decision to deduct the point, and only played on under protest.

Score: 3–2 (FIDE); 3–1 (games actually played)

♔43

Games 6-9

The good mood in our team was gone. From the start, I had consulted with Miguel Illescas among all the grandmasters. We did not see what we could have done differently. Miguel had a problem, as we all did, with the fact that Vladimir had not played the fifth game and that Topalov had received such a present. The Russians in the team, however, began to look for a guilty party and to reproach me.

Right at the beginning of the scandal, Kramnik had for good reasons banned interviews with anyone from the team until the end of the match. That was respected, but there were continual phone calls with Ilya Levitov, Evgeny Bareev and other people in Moscow. Levitov, who was always trying to get involved in our business, probably saw this as his big chance to score points with Vladimir; basically this had been going on for some years. During the match and afterwards he agitated through various publications. His actions helped neither Vladimir Kramnik nor the team.

So via certain circles in Moscow, some internal matters and criticism reached the Russian public, and these were also quite specifically aimed at journalists present in Elista, with whom I now had to battle. At least we managed to keep these things away from Vladimir. He was to some extent diverted by a visit from his mother and his brother.

Towards midday, two hours before Game 6, Vladimir made a public statement. He would continue the match, though only "under protest". That meant quite simply that he did not accept the walkover accorded to the Bulgarian, and reserved the right to take legal steps to contest it. Neither FIDE nor Topalov knew for sure until this point whether Kramnik would actually appear again.

In order to leave Topalov in uncertainty for as long as possible, I informed the FIDE president at the same time as the public statement, that is to say just two hours before the game. That was certainly a weight off Kirsan's shoulders, since he was under considerable pressure. There were definitely times during those days when we felt sorry for him. He had tried everything, had not been personally responsible for this scandal, but at the same time he was heavily compromised by the actions of his officials.

Miguel Illescas drove to the game with us. At this time I met Evgeny Bareev and Peter Svidler, who were visiting Kramnik. Vladimir easily held a draw in the Slav Defence. For the first time in the match, his opening preparation paid off. That would tend to be the exception in the further course of the match.

On 3rd October, before the seventh game, we had the next rest day, and the mud-slinging continued merrily on its way. All the time we feared that Team Topalov would somehow work up some "proof of cheating", to take Kramnik right out of the match. To our way of thinking, that would have been their only chance to justify their behaviour which had up till then been unacceptable. To forestall such a possibility, I wrote an open letter to the head of the organization.

Before Game 7, Topalov's team published some statistics. They contained no comments, but they "proved" a high correlation between the moves played by Kramnik and those which the chess program Fritz would play. They did not mention that a certain correlation is totally normal at the level of an elite player. Above all, when you allow the machine to run for so long as to render such a correlation inevitable. They also failed to mention that Topalov's correlation ratio was at times even higher. It was simply laughable. Vladimir was hardened against such attacks; they fell flat and had no effect.

Our lawyer, Dr Reinhard Rauball, had meanwhile examined the facts more closely. From the start, he had advised continuing the match "under protest". The FIDE appeals committee had broken the contract, and in this regard we could always bring in the Court of Arbitration for Sport (CAS) in the event of a defeat, especially with respect to the violation of personal rights connected with the handing over of the video tapes.

In Rauball's opinion, however, Vladimir would have little chance of recovering the point lost to a walkover in Game 5. Not on account of decisions of any appeals committee or officials, not even on account of whether a protest had been filed or not, but solely because of the factual decision of the chief arbiter. His official evaluation was the only one which the court would find relevant when all was said and done. After the clocks had been started and the uncontested win had been confirmed on the scoresheet, neither the FIDE president nor a court could reverse the result. This, however, did not affect possible suits for damages against the world federation. In order for an emotionally-troubled Kramnik to hold onto the hope of future justice, I did not tell him of this evaluation during the match.

In the seventh game, Vladimir chose the Slav Defence. Once again, the Bulgarian had the advantage in the opening and created pressure. According to the commentators, both sides committed some inaccuracies. After 60 moves Topalov offered a draw. After the game the Bulgarian refused to do the contractually-agreed joint press conference. That suited us, since each time he now had to wait until Vladimir was finished. Some commentators claimed that the players refused to shake hands before and after the game. These commentators were not there. The refusal to shake hands happened for a time *after* the world championship match, but during the match they continued to shake hands. After Game 7, Vladimir looked rather drained. He was above all frustrated that he was getting the worse of the opening phase in almost every game.

On account of the scandal, its psychological effects, and above all on account of his suboptimal opening preparation, a dynamic had set in which was clearly working against Kramnik. Vladimir lost the eighth game, and that was with White. In this match, it was his first defeat over the board. When I fetched him for the press conference, he was sitting slumped on the sofa in the restroom. He was not at all annoyed, but was frustrated and completely drained.

Once again he had been surprised in the opening by Topalov. For the first time, Topalov carried his advantage to its logical conclusion and seized his chance. Immediately after the game, Vladimir told me he had deliberately aimed for this endgame: he believed it was good for him. When we sat in the car he explained that during the game he had not felt well. He may have been prepared, but he had totally forgotten the variation and after that simply played badly.

Hardly anybody had a word to say during dinner. After it, Vladimir came up to my room and asked for a cigarette. Before the match he had given up smoking and now he was starting again. We spoke together for a long time. He felt let down by his compatriots, the political elite in Moscow, and also by the chess federation. I said to him: "Vlad, see that you get the scandal out of your head. The point is gone. You will lose the match if you continue wasting your energy on it."

I told Kramnik about the prediction of the Buddhist monk, and brought him together with Vyacheslav Namruev. The two of them had a short conversation. On the subsequent rest day, they drove to the Buddhist temple. There Vladimir met the lama, Telo Rinpoche. When he returned all he said was: "It was impressive. They are praying for me." After the match he wanted to visit the temple one more time, which we did.

Silvio Danailov had fallen ill. All the stress had its effect on him too. In the days which followed, I rarely saw him in the playing hall. He had a terrible rash in association with a serious intestinal infection. Peter Leko, Kramnik's challenger only two years previously, phoned me on the evening before the ninth game, wished us all the best, and said that he could no longer bear the tension.

In the ninth game, Vladimir completely collapsed. He had Black and on move 39, just before the first time control, he had to resign in a hopeless position. All over the world, chess fans discussed what could have gone wrong in this game. But it was not so difficult: Kramnik had reached his nadir in the world championship duel. On the way back, he again spoke about his preparation not being okay. When I was in my rooms I phoned Peter Leko. He said: "Topalov's innovation 10.f4 was nothing. Vlad is simply not playing chess, he is much too passive, too hesitant." He advised us not to immediately bet everything on a single card in the tenth game. In the eleventh and twelfth games, Vladimir could still take risks. He knew from his own experience that now all the pressure was on Topalov. After that I let Peter speak with Kramnik.

Score: 4–5 (FIDE); 4–4 (games actually played)

Games 10-12

Every morning, after I had made myself some coffee, my routine was to log on to the internet to deal with my emails. On days we had been successful, we received on average far more than a hundred messages, congratulations and requests. After the defeats, there were only two: from Sebastian, my son, and from Stefan Koth, tournament director of Dortmund Chess Days – they wished us luck. But that was it. The old adage that you are quite alone in defeat was confirmed once more.

I met Josef Resch about 11:30. On the previous day, his nerve had completely gone and he wanted to leave. The fact that he nevertheless remained during the dark days says a lot about him. Right to the end, he was a loyal companion to us. Remarkably, despite the two defeats, the mood in our team had improved considerably and the grandmasters were working on the attack with great concentration.

"There's life in the old dog yet." This old saying came true on 8th October. Kramnik won Game 10 after 43 moves. Everything was open again, and many doubts assuaged. Topalov had committed a major blunder in the Catalan Opening with 24...f6.

He had been known to make such blunders now and again in the past, but that had not been the case in the previous two years. For Kramnik, the Bulgarian's blackout came at just the right moment. At the board, Kramnik's reactions were perfect (25.♘d7!) and he was back on his game! The talisman of the day was our cook, Viktor Bobylev. It was his first visit to the playing hall.

The interest in the world championship took on huge proportions. More and more major internet platforms broadcast the games live. The organizers in Elista reported that on their server alone, more than a million people had followed the tenth game. These were fantastic numbers and would rise even further. If you took into account all chess servers worldwide, other internet live tickers of the mass media, TV and teletext, then according to a survey by a Moscow agency, there were on average 30 million people watching a game live. In the playing hall, the mood had finally turned in Vladimir's favour. After his win in the tenth game, there was intense applause from the spectators. Even in the subsequent press conference there was applause from the professional representatives of the media – a highly unusual event.

The eleventh game ended after 66 moves as a draw. Topalov again had an advantage from the opening, which Vladimir was able to cancel out in the endgame. After the game, the two players had the doping control. Danailov and I were supposed to wait for the players in a tiny ante-room. Not a word was said. Danailov became very uneasy in this situation, kept flipping open his mobile and staring at the floor. It did not take long until he fled the room.

Topalov came out of his booth because he was unable to provide a sample. He asked for warm water. But instead of clarifying that with the people from NADA (National Anti Doping Agency), he looked for his manager, who, however, was no longer there. A NADA employee had to catch him. Veselin's face was as red as a turkey-cock; he looked quite despairing and downcast. In any case, there was no longer any trace of inexhaustible energy. Vladimir for his part had done the business in five minutes. In the press conference he again pointed out that he would never accept the result of the fifth game: "The score is not 5½–5½, but 5½–4½ for me."

In the twelfth and last game of the regular match, Vladimir had White. In order to win this match at classical time controls in the purely sporting sense, a draw would suffice. The players agreed one after 47 moves. At the board, Kramnik had won the world championship match by 6–5, and with the additional handicap of having one White game less. Our congratulations, however, counted for nothing. The public would soon forget this if Topalov should win the subsequent tiebreak. In that case, people would recognize him as the united World Champion of the approximately billion chess players on our planet.

Score: 6–6 (FIDE); 6–5 (games actually played)

♔44

Friday 13th October, the 13th match day: a day which in popular belief is unlucky. Our team had now been at the venue for exactly four weeks. The decision by FIDE to award Game 5 as a walkover to Topalov, and thus set the score at 6–6, forced Kramnik into the tiebreak, just as had been agreed in the event of a draw after twelve games. Four rapid chess games lay before us. For each game, each player had 25 minutes plus ten seconds increment for every move made.

For Vladimir, heightened tension was not an unusual experience. He had experienced it in the decisive games in his world championship matches against Kasparov and Leko. This time, however, it was almost unendurable. I consoled myself with the thought that "my man" was always able to concentrate completely on the game at the decisive moments. This quality was one of his great advantages, and he kept on prevailing because of it. A victory in the tiebreak in this extraordinary world championship would answer all the questions and kill three birds with one stone: victory in classical chess, victory in rapid chess and victory in an unprecedented PR battle.

We drove to the playing venue with the whole team. The building was bursting at the seams with people. The drama could begin. Vladimir was playing Black in the first game. Three grandmasters sat next to me, but the hope that their evaluations could help me proved to be a misapprehension. The information varied from "perhaps a win" via "is worse" all the way to "level". Chess is so complicated; it was an emotional see-saw. In the end it was a draw.

In the second game, Kramnik was in his element. He had White and played quickly, in crystal-clear fashion; simply a virtuoso performance.

This immense pressure, a bad position and time trouble led to the collapse of Topalov, which manifested itself in the move 31...b4.

There was a short break, but in principle the players had little time to think. Also they were not allowed to make contact in any way with their teams, something we had insistently hammered home before the tiebreak with the world federation, the organization and the arbiters.

In the third tiebreak game, Topalov achieved a big advantage from the opening phase, which this time he exploited without any problem. In three rapid chess games, the Slav Defence had appeared on the board. And the final game would be no exception. That finally established a record. In the history of chess, there had never before been a world championship in which every game opened with the same move – in this case 1.d4.

Before the final rapid chess game of the tiebreak, the score was thus 1½–1½. The tension of this play-off could not be outdone. The servers of many internet platforms collapsed; too many fans had logged on to follow the decisive games live. A draw in the fourth tiebreak game would have been followed by blitz games; that was what was in the rules. Nobody wanted to see the classical world championship decided by blitz games. Especially not this important unification match.

Topalov placed his light-squared bishop on a dubious diagonal; it was rather ineffective there. Some inaccuracies followed, the position was practically won for Vladimir, and then on move 44 Topalov put his rook on the c5-square, and in doing so put the major piece en prise.

Kramnik's posture changed to bolt upright. Miguel Illescas pinched my leg and whispered: "We've done it, that loses!" Kramnik seized his chance and on move 45 put his rook on b7 – check! Topalov stared for a moment at the board, shook his head several times, and resigned. Kramnik raised his fist in a sign of triumph, just as he did after his epic world championship victories over Garry Kasparov and Peter Leko.

The Kalmykian chess public erupted and turned the playing hall into a madhouse: cries of hooray, stamping feet, and staccato clapping went on for several minutes. We leapt up and hugged each other. I could not stay in my place any longer. Vladimir was still standing somewhat bemused by the playing table, and trying to clip his pen into the inside pocket of his jacket. I rushed onto the stage. We hugged each other.

I gave vent to the pressure built up within me in several cries of joy and could not resist brandishing my fist in the direction of Team Topalov. Kramnik's first words were: "Crazy, that was really massive!"

Vladimir had won everything; Topalov had lost everything. Any legal action against FIDE had become unnecessary. After endless intrigues and 13 years, there was again a World Champion recognized by everyone in the chess world: the chess genius Vladimir Kramnik, now 31 years old, born on 25th June 1975 in Tuapse on the Black Sea, had finally reached the goal of all his dreams.

Kramnik had not been able to show his very best chess against Topalov, not like he had when winning the title six years previously against Garry Kasparov in London. There were reasons for that: the opening preparation, the superiority of Topalov's chess team in this respect, and last but not least the shameful scandal which hit him hard mentally. But the fact that he nevertheless completed the task under these circumstances made the match the most emotional and important of his great victories. It also brought him worldwide recognition, and in retrospect considerably enhanced the value of his world championship successes against Kasparov and Leko outwith the world federation FIDE.

It was typical that only after this win was Kramnik's photo hung next to that of Kasparov in the famous Moscow Chess Club with the caption "Vladimir Kramnik, 14th World Chess Champion". All of the champions produced by FIDE during the 13 years of the division were at a stroke rendered meaningless, and their photos were taken down. Order had been restored by Vladimir Kramnik to the history of chess world champions, which at that point stretched back 120 years.

♔45

A good ten years after these events, Vladimir still sees things as he did then. In an interview with the Moscow *Sport-Express*, he expressed himself as follows: "When I decided to play on I was taking risks. I could have lost since I fell behind during the match, but I equalized and managed to get the upper hand in the tiebreaks. I think that with respect to my capacity for resistance and willpower, this was the greatest performance of my career."

After what Topalov and his manager had said and done, Vladimir really did not want to lose. Kramnik: "It was a matter of principle, since they had attacked my honour. I was illegally robbed of a whole point. The behaviour of Topalov's team during the match was simply outrageous, a case of real chicanery. I had never experienced such aggressive behaviour during a chess event previously, and I hope that I will never do so again."

Vladimir was very happy after the match, much more so than after his win over Kasparov. And this despite the fact that although Topalov may well be a very strong chess player, he was inferior to Garry. Elista had clearly been more emotional than London.

"It was important to me to punish the Bulgarian for his behaviour. People love winners and forgive them almost everything. I am well aware that everybody would quickly have forgotten how Topalov had behaved during the match if he had won – he would have become a hero. I really did not want to allow that!"

Alongside endless interviews, ceremonies and presentations, we somehow managed to phone our families. We had not been allowed to have mobiles with us, so we borrowed some. The then president of the Turkish chess federation, Ali Nihat Yazici, gave us his. At some point, Vladimir also reached Marie-Laure, who had played an important role in the background. She had supported Vladimir at difficult moments, as she had already done in Switzerland against Leko.

We did not get back to our accommodation until late in the evening. Viktor brought out the beluga caviar, and for the first time there was also vodka, champagne and beer. Only Alexander Motylev could not enjoy all that. For the last few days he had been working so hard without rest that his circulation almost collapsed, and he had to rest. We were not far from calling a doctor.

In the days which followed, the swirl of congratulations did not let up. On the first day after the match alone, I received 187 texts and 284 emails. Hundreds of chess fans logged on to Vladimir's website and expressed their congratulations. Vladimir Putin, Alexander Zhukov, Peer Steinbrück, Natalia Vodianova, Carmen Kass, Vitaly and Vladimir Klitschko, Vadim Repin, Christian Burger and Dr Reinhard Rauball; they were among those offering congratulations. In the two days which remained to us before our departure to Moscow, Vladimir gave 44 exclusive interviews on-site and over the telephone. Everything was represented from small chess magazines to the *New York Times*. Kramnik signed thousands of autographs for those Kalmyks who wanted one.

The international chess press paid tribute to Vladimir Kramnik. After having received some harsh criticism at times during the previous year, he now received his second chess Oscar in recognition of his performance. Those who had been criticizing him severely a year ago, were now amongst those patting him on the back. We experienced this afresh and with greater intensity. When Vladimir and I got back to Moscow, we stayed in the Hotel Arbat. That was exactly where, eight months previously, the decisive phase in the negotiations with FIDE had begun for me, as we agreed our contracts for the world championship match which would unify the chess world. We celebrated with Josef Resch in his Moscow office, and took our leave one by one from our comrades on the team.

On 16th October 2006, in the Moscow Chess Club, there was a final obligatory event. There Vladimir and I took part in a press conference to which Alexander Zhukov had invited us. On the following day we sat together for a while in Moscow's Sheremetyevo airport, before travelling back to our families. A professional team of film-makers accompanied us the whole time and filmed certain occasions both then and two years later. This gave rise, amongst other things, to the well-known production *Fighting for the Crown*.

Topalov vehemently demanded a rematch. In the Bulgarian capital Sofia, 1.5 million euros in prizemoney was available for it. That Vladimir Kramnik declined, after the scandalous events, hardly came as a surprise to anyone, probably not even to the Bulgarians.

The final word on the reunification of the chess world would belong to the president of the world federation. In an interview, which was published on 25th October 2006 on the popular chess platform ChessBase, he himself admitted that the recognized title of World Chess Champion had not been in the hands of FIDE for 13 years: "The chess crown has come back home," was Kirsan Ilyumzhinov's brief conclusion.

Vladimir Kramnik – Veselin Topalov

World Championship, Elista (rapid tiebreak – 4) 2006

1.d4 d5 2.c4 c6 3.♘f3 ♘f6 4.♘c3 e6 5.e3 ♘bd7 6.♗d3 dxc4 7.♗xc4 b5 8.♗e2 ♗b7 9.0–0 ♗e7 10.e4 b4 11.e5 bxc3 12.exf6 ♗xf6 13.bxc3 c5 14.dxc5 ♘xc5! 15.♗b5†?! ♔f8 16.♕xd8† ♖xd8 17.♗a3 ♖c8 18.♘d4 ♗e7 19.♖fd1

19...a6?! 20.♗f1 ♘a4 21.♖ab1 ♗e4 22.♖b3 ♗xa3 23.♖xa3 ♘c5 24.♘b3 ♔e7 25.♖d4 ♗g6 26.c4 ♖c6 27.♘xc5 ♖xc5 28.♖xa6 ♖b8

29.♖d1 ♖b2 30.♖a7† ♔f6 31.♖a1 ♖f5 32.f3 ♖e5 33.♖a3! ♖c2 34.♖b3 ♖a5 35.a4 ♔e7 36.♖b5 ♖a7 37.a5 ♔d6 38.a6 ♔c7 39.c5 ♖c3 40.♖aa5 ♖c1 41.♖b3 ♔c6 42.♖b6† ♔c7 43.♔f2 ♖c2† 44.♔e3 ♖xc5?? 45.♖b7†

1–0

Vladimir Kramnik:

"This was the first rapid chess tiebreak in a classical world championship match. I was always strong in games with rapid time controls, and certainly also the favourite against Topalov. But such a situation after a scandalous and difficult match has its own laws. Much depends on one's form on the day, and the players are under enormous pressure.

In the first game I had some slight difficulties after the opening. But I was able to trick him and take over the initiative. At times I even worked up significant winning chances as Black, but then I missed a few tactical possibilities, so that a draw was the final result. I played very well in the second game with White, almost perfectly. Above all when you take into account that it was rapid chess. I found it easy to slowly outplay him. In the endgame I then found a lovely clear route to the win. That made me quite optimistic with regard to my chances. I was leading 1½–½ and there were only two games left to play. In the third game, however, my opponent produced a strong performance. He gradually improved his position after the opening phase and deservedly won.

With the scores level at 1½–1½, we met for the decisive fourth game. Basically of course anything can happen under these circumstances. But despite the loss of the third game, I remained confident. I was not at all nervous and did not think about the result either. I was able to concentrate all my attention on the game itself and avoided thinking about the consequences a possible error might entail. This ability, to concentrate entirely on chess and to forget everything else around me, is moreover one of my strong points. It brings me a decisive advantage over my opponent, especially at the most important moments.

Basically I can say that during the whole world championship match, Topalov was incredibly well prepared and generally a bit ahead of me. He was the one coming up with innovations and interesting plans. This tendency also continued in the final tiebreak game. He came up with 14...♘xc5, which to this day is still considered correct. In principle it has put to an end to any thought White might have of winning in the whole variation. Naturally it was painful to have to deal with this in the most important game of this match, perhaps even the most important in my whole career. And it just had to be in rapid chess where you only have a little time to react correctly.

It was good that I very quickly understood that 14...♘xc5 could have very serious consequences. Pondering for a long time achieves nothing in this case. In such a situation you simply have to carry on and make an attempt to find the best moves at the board. I played 15.♗b5†, which is a normal reaction. It does let me prevent him permanently from castling, but objectively speaking White has nothing at all.

However, after 15...♔f8 I played 16.♕xd8†. Exchanging queens at such a point is a somewhat unusual decision, because the black king is in the centre. But unfortunately in this position, nothing constructive occurred to me. Something like 16.♗a3 is followed by 16...♕c7, when he has the better pawn structure and a powerful knight on c5. If he manages to get his king out of the danger zone and to connect his rooks, he will simply be better.

For that reason, I decided on the exchange of queens, although my basic problem in this position remained: his structure was simply stronger. For the moment I did have the initiative and the better development, but if he warded off my threats, Black would be better and would begin to exert serious pressure. In order to prevent this, I had to be very quick. And after I had played 19.♖fd1, there came from my point of view the historic moment which decided the tiebreak.

After 19.♖fd1 he had the opportunity to play 19...♘e4, a move which would have given Black a significant advantage. But once again, we were playing rapid chess and we had only 25 minutes plus ten seconds increment per player for the whole game. We saw the move 19...♘e4, but we both probably thought that after it White would be better. After 20.♘e6† fxe6 21.♗xe7† ♔xe7 22.♖d7† ♔f6 23.♖xb7 we overlooked in this forced variation the tactic 23...♘d6. After this Topalov would have won the exchange. There still would have been reasonable chances of a draw, but I would have had to fight for it very hard and with precise defence.

Fortunately, however, Topalov played the natural 19...a6, which also looked good. But here he had overlooked 21.♖ab1, a very strong move which is not so easy to find. I was just in time to secure everything. His rooks were not connected, his king was exposed on f8 – both of these became increasingly unpleasant factors for Black.

White was now better, and with 24.♘b3 I won a pawn and his position became problematic. But there was still a long way to go before the win.

After 28...♖b8 he had active rooks and we both had only a few minutes on the clock. It was far from clear whether the extra pawn would suffice for me. In a classical game with sufficient thinking time, it surely would, but like this it was not clear. In this phase of the game, however, my play was technically outstanding. I had 31.♖a1 and Topalov desperately sought for counterplay with 31...♖f5 and 32...♖e5.

I was able to avert that with 33.♖a3, which I logically followed up with 34.♖b3. That meant that my a-pawn could get going.

In principle, my position after move 40 was already a relatively simple win. But we had perhaps only two minutes left on the clock and in time trouble like that, victory is never certain. When he then played 44...♖xc5, I almost had a heart attack. In chess terms it was a collapse. This bad blunder of Topalov's, which admittedly he made in a bad position, showed in any case that his nerves had simply given out. He had simply overlooked 45.♖b7†, and in doing so effectively conceded the game.

He shook his head, and I knew that the game would not be continued and that he would resign. I can still remember the frenetic applause from the spectators. But I was so focused on chess that for a moment I did not realize that this battle, which had been in so many respects complicated, had ended in my favour. It was the most difficult situation I had to overcome during my chess career. I survived it successfully and, six years after my world championship victory over Kasparov, I was now the uncontested World Chess Champion. In an instant, the 13 years of the split were history. The position after 45.♖b7† will remain the most defining and unforgettable of my entire career."

The Loss of the Chess Crown

♔46

The life of World Chess Champions is subject to scheduling problems. Especially after big matches, they are very much in demand and have to take on a host of social obligations. Nor did Vladimir Kramnik seek to escape this after his match against Topalov; after all the popularity of the World Champion serves the game. All classical world chess champions become in a certain sense immortal. After their matches, they have been asked to give something back to the world of chess. Of the 16 titleholders so far, each one has felt this responsibility.

After the reunification match, Vladimir had to fulfil a host of obligations, many of which were not public. He was at the absolute high point of his career. In Elista he had come closer than ever before to the edge of his physical, and above all psychological, capacities. Once again, he had lost several kilos. Now and again his rheumatic illness made itself felt with minor outbreaks. Actually he urgently needed a break, time to regenerate.

But there was no way that was going to happen. The match against Deep Fritz in Bonn was fixed for 25th November to 5th December. Targeted thorough preparation, like before the 2002 duel in Bahrain, was not possible in 2006 due to lack of time. I organized for Vladimir and his little team, consisting of Grandmaster Christopher Lutz and computer expert Stefan Meyer-Kahlen, our traditional training camp in Weiskirchen. But on this occasion, it could only be for two weeks. Of course that was much too little against the computer. There was nothing we could do to change things; the organization in Bonn was far advanced and the contracts had to be respected.

First of all, the positive aspects: the event in Bonn's Art and Exhibition Hall of the Federal Republic of Germany was fantastically well organized. Josef Resch and the Dortmund organizational team with Stefan Koth, Guido Kohlen and Rolf Behovits had put in a lot of work. The media reported with an intensity never before experienced. More than 300 journalists took accreditation for the Man versus Machine match. Vladimir Kramnik was a much sought-after man; his popularity had reached a peak after the scandalous world championship match against Topalov. All the games were sold out. And finally, Vladimir Kramnik would be richer by 500,000 euros, no matter what the result of the duel.

Vladimir lost by 2–4. He gave everything he had. The first game ended in a draw, but in the second game he experienced a severe blackout: he was a little better, and in any case could have easily aimed for a draw, when he overlooked a mate-in-one against him. With that, the match was over. It was the most extreme case of chess blindness in Kramnik's entire career. There followed three more draws. In the sixth and final game, Vladimir risked everything with the black pieces and consequently also lost this game.

The great duels there had been against chess computers since the start of the 1980s came to an end with this encounter in 2006. After Kramnik's defeat, humanity was obliged to realize that against the machine there would no longer be any prospect of victory. In the best case, Vladimir could have drawn all the games, but there was practically no chance of winning a game.

We live in an age of digitization, where the goal is the creation of machines that can perform better and better. Machines are taking away from us humans more and more of the chores of everyday life. To me, this logically means that the process will inevitably continue until humanity will leave to the computers even the most important decisions.

We are still at the start of this development, but it is already happening. You just have to look at certain dynamics on the stock exchanges, in trade, in the areas of energy and supply, in road, rail and air traffic, or even in the military. For reasons of safety or efficiency, computers are "authorized", and hardly anyone is in a position to stop the processes they set in motion – even when they involve dangerous exaggerations.

So we will more and more leave the decisions to the computers in structural, political or even quite personal spheres. As time goes by, this employment of the machines will inevitably be considered totally normal. That is in my opinion the point at which artificial intelligence will begin to turn against us, not actively but through omissions on the part of humanity itself. We human beings, unlike the computer – whatever the form in which it may come – have available to us qualities such as creativity, the feeling for beauty, empathy and inspiration.

Intuition still speaks to us and we hear its voice. We are still capable of listening to the little voice deep within us, and of feeling whether something is right or wrong, good or bad, beautiful or ugly. The assistance of the machines will lead us at some point to seek these answers outwith ourselves and then, gradually but inescapably, we will lose our natural intuition. If the process which has already begun is naively pushed forward by us, then one day, along with the loss of our intuition, we will even lose our humanity and lose all control over the process itself.

Chess against or between computers clarifies my thesis. If two computers play chess against each other, the resulting games scarcely move the observers. At most one is impressed by the precision and the plethora of "objectively correct" moves. What is objectively correct is in turn decided by the computer. When a human plays against the machine, things are similar. He tries to adapt the algorithm of his thinking so as not to lose at once. It is a "mechanical" dance, to use Vladimir Kramnik's language.

But even when humans play against each other, the first tendencies towards this "correct" emotionless way of playing have been observed for some years among grandmasters. Adjusting one's thinking may be the way which at first sight promises the modern professional player the greatest success. But is that really the case? For many years grandmasters have been studying predominantly with their best friend, the equalizer called "Computer". And it can already be noticed that inspiration and above all the individual's intuition are becoming the victims. The players are shifting more into their computer's way of thinking and playing, more and more neutralizing each other, and in the meantime are playing a completely different type of chess from 20 years ago. This process, which got going so strongly at the beginning of the millennium, is accelerating.

Vladimir Kramnik, and also the present World Champion Magnus Carlsen, have proved often enough that in a game between two humans, one's intuition can be just as important as good opening preparation with the computer. Quite deliberately they now and then throw in moves which, according to the calculations of the computer, are only the third or fourth choice, or sometimes not even that. But by doing so they challenge their opponents, surprise them and obtain free play. In addition, they are no longer so easily neutralized, and in most cases they nevertheless win through, thanks to their strength and creativity.

So let's forget computers; they are not so important. No human needs, in the truest sense of the word, a chess duel against the computer. In this respect, it is only logical that since Kramnik's defeat against Deep Fritz in 2006, no serious match has been organized against the machine. Such an event simply no longer makes any sense, not only on account of the fact that now the human has no chance. We humans would do best to simply hang on to our humanity. Even in chess!

Vladimir, when struck by chess blindness in missing the mate-in-one against Deep Fritz, would be able to confirm the statement by Isaac Asimov. The great science-fiction author, who dealt as few others have done with the subject of "man and machine", once wrote: "In life, unlike chess, the game continues after checkmate."

♔47

Vladimir's life also continued. On 31st December 2006, he married Marie-Laure, née Germon, in a civil ceremony in Paris. The Russian Orthodox ceremony followed a few weeks later in the Alexander Nevsky cathedral in Paris.

At the start of 2007, Steve Jobs introduced the new iPhone from US giant Apple. It is significant that the two richest men in the world at that time possessed more wealth than the 45 poorest countries were able to show as their GDP for the whole of 2007. This last example may be extreme, but it is a symbol of a fatal development which to this day is advancing unchecked, as globalization increases.

When Vladimir Kramnik lost to the machine in Bonn, many of his fans feared that he would fall into a similar hole to that of 2001, after his struggle against Kasparov. The opposite was the case, however. The successful world championship match against Topalov this time gave him as much of a boost as did his happiness in the private sphere. More than ever before, Vladimir was ready for commitments.

He gave lectures at important business meetings; he was just as active for the German firm Siemens IT Solutions as for Ernst & Young and Bain & Company. Vladimir was taken under contract by Celebrity Speakers, he advertised products of the firm DGT, and produced, under the title *My Path to the Top*, a very instructive and successful DVD for ChessBase in Hamburg. We followed up on countless invitations from the worlds of politics, sport and the economy.

But even more importantly, Kramnik felt in the mood to play chess again. He was undefeated in Wijk aan Zee with three wins and eight draws, he won the tournaments in Dortmund, Monaco and Moscow. In his rapid chess match in Miskolc in Hungary against Peter Leko, he won 4½–3½. At the end of 2007, he was again triumphant at the Tal Memorial in Moscow, this time in great style. At this high-profile event, he turned in possibly the best tournament performance of his career. Consequently, Vladimir Kramnik was once more in first place in the world ranking list on 1st January 2008.

In 2007 Vladimir played 38 games at classical time controls and lost only one, but that just happened to be in Mexico City against his compatriot Alexander Morozevich. This defeat was fatal – it cost Kramnik his world championship title and Viswanathan Anand became the 15th World Champion in the history of chess. But let's consider things in order...

FIDE had in two respects broken the contract agreed with Kramnik before the match in Elista: by its decisions during the scandal-ridden match against Topalov, and above all by not sticking to an important clause. It was duty-bound to inform Kramnik about revenue from sponsors, which did not happen within a specified time period. In such a case, Kramnik had the right to cancel the contract, which I then arranged.

The termination became final and effective. From then on, Vladimir was therefore in no way obliged to play in the previously-agreed world championship tournament in Mexico City. Actually, the tournament was in any case a thorn in his flesh, because he wanted to maintain the tradition of the final world championship match between titleholder and challenger. To play or not to play? That was the question here! Vladimir decided to take part in Mexico City.

It was one of the very few situations during our cooperation in which, to this day, our opinions are diametrically opposed. Vladimir Kramnik was already very tired of chess politics, the never-ending wrangling about world championships and their formats, spiced up with plots and corruption by brazen officials who wanted to push their own personal interests. No world champion, before or after him, had to deal with such complex problems. I advised him, several times and insistently, to retire undefeated.

Even today, I still believe that withdrawing would have been the correct decision. I saw that he no longer had sufficient motivation to come up with his best chess for world championships. That flame no longer burned as it once had. Nothing could top the drama of the reunification and the match against Topalov, and I am certain that the whole subject of the world championship had been put to bed for Vladimir after that great duel, though only subconsciously.

The real reason which moved him to participate in Mexico City is, however, a perfectly honourable one. Quite independently of any legal niceties, Vladimir had at one point declared himself prepared to play in this tournament. He had given his word and above all did not want to harm the interests of his grandmaster colleagues, who had qualified for this world championship in Mexico. Had he withdrawn, then the world championship tournament in Mexico City would never have taken place. That was made quite clear by the Mexican organizer, Jorge Saggiante.

The world federation, on the other hand, had continually broken its word over the past years. From my point of view, morally speaking Kramnik would have had every right to withdraw, but he saw things differently. In any case, our termination of the contract had left us in a strong position vis-à-vis FIDE, who could never be quite sure that he would take part in Mexico. So in January 2007, I negotiated a new contract with FIDE.

This contract included a so-called rematch clause. Should Vladimir not win the tournament in Mexico, then in 2008 he would get a match against the victor of the tournament. That was naturally a great privilege for the World Champion, and was accordingly criticized by parts of the chess world. However, a second important agreement was being overlooked, one which finally guaranteed for Vladimir Kramnik the realization of an important goal. From 2008 on, the title of World Champion would again be contested in a final match between a challenger and the titleholder.

Kramnik would therefore in any case deliver to the future the most important tradition of the classical line of world chess champions. The successful duels for the chess crown would be maintained. Next to his great matches and brilliant games, this result, against the strongest resistance from the top officials of the world federation, can be looked upon as the greatest historical achievement of his career. Vladimir had thus lived up to his responsibilities in every respect. It was a final step in the patching up of the split which had originally opened up between Kasparov and FIDE. He could achieve no more than this in the sport or its politics. Anything else would now come as a bonus.

♚48

The world championship tournament took place from 12th to 30th September 2007, in Mexico City. In order to acclimatize, we arrived a week before the start. The capital of Mexico was then far and away the most dangerous city in the world. Nowhere else were there so many murders, muggings and corruption. I too was not to be spared this. The organizer of the Mainz Chess Classic, Hans-Walter Schmitt, was attacked from behind by several men who set about choking him. Apart from the fact that he was robbed of his mobile telephone and his watch, he got off quite lightly thanks to strong resistance.

We were lodged in the Hotel Sheraton Centro Historico, one of the best addresses in the city. Vladimir wanted to tip the staff from time to time, but had only high-denomination notes. So I set out for a nearby bank, some 400 to 500 metres away from the hotel. When I came out of the bank, I was accosted by a young man with a knife in his right hand who said: "Vamos, dollars!" I hit him hard on the arm and shoved him away. He fell onto a mobile newspaper stand, which immediately collapsed. Only then did I see behind me a second Mexican who was moving towards me. I turned round and shouted at him, whereupon he ran away.

The shock had caused me to make a big mistake, and I had been quite unbelievably fortunate. But somehow at that moment there was nothing else I could do. I was overcome by naked rage and any safety valve was over-ridden. It happened in broad daylight, right in front of a bank in the centre of town. Hardly 30 metres away, at a big crossroads there were several policemen. During and after the incident, they just stood around there and the whole business did not bother them in the least. One must suppose that such attacks were the order of the day, and that the forces of order were involved in them.

The world championship tournament took place in the Sheraton Hotel, where we were lodged. Jorge Saggiante, the Mexican organizer, did his very best, but he was let down by his compatriots. The organization was absolutely chaotic. Only a few hours before the start of the first round, it looked as if there would not be any broadcasting of the games within the playing hall and over the internet. There were no toilets near the stage; there was a shortage of personnel and experience. Somehow the tournament did get going and was completed. Presentation and organization, however, were not worthy of a world championship.

Parallel to this, FIDE managed once more to have its own worries. The vice-president well-known to us all from the Kramnik – Topalov scandal, Zurab Azmaiparashvili, was again the talk of the town. A chambermaid confronted him with an accusation of sexual harassment. He had to leave the hotel and from then on was obliged to follow a predetermined route through the hotel to the playing hall in order to carry out his duties during the tournament.

Instead of giving some thought to its own reputation, FIDE covered up the incident at first. Back at the 2004 Chess Olympiad on Mallorca, Azmaiparashvili had been involved in a physical confrontation with police officers, his role in the scandalous match of 2006 in Elista was also well remembered, and now this. But even this scandal did not harm him permanently. He still occupies a high position on the board of the world federation to this day. Since 2014, he has also been president of the European Chess Union.

Vladimir Kramnik had engaged as his second the Dutch grandmaster Loek van Wely. But that was as far as he had gone with respect to specific preparation. He was motivated, but not much more so than for one of the classic tournaments which fitted into his normal calendar; perhaps it had to do with the local conditions, perhaps because even after a defeat he would appear in a match for the world championship in the coming year. Although Kramnik played outstandingly and his openings were full of inspiration, nevertheless at the decisive moments he lacked the necessary tenacity. In any case, he was too relaxed and far from as focused as he had been in his world championship matches.

♔49

Games 1-7

Vladimir had White in the opening game against his friend Peter Svidler. The game soon petered out and after 24 moves Kramnik offered a draw. In the second game he sat opposite the fourth Russian in the tournament of eight grandmasters, Alexander Morozevich. The Catalan appeared on their board and Vladimir lit some fireworks. Somewhat in the style of his creative opponent, he played aggressively and tactically. He sacrificed a knight with 13.exd5. After only 27 moves of a complicated game Morozevich had to resign in a hopeless position.

In the third game Kramnik had Black against his greatest rival, Viswanathan Anand. It was a fantastic, enormously precise performance by the World Champion. In the Petroff Defence, he outplayed the Indian and liquidated to a rook ending in which he was a pawn up. However, it was as if bewitched. Anand defended prudently, and Vladimir could not find a way to win. The Indian saved the day with a stalemate, and thus put down the first marker on his way to winning the title.

Until then, everything was running according to plan for Vladimir. In the next game against his compatriot Alexander Grischuk, however, he ran into a severe setback with White.

He held a big advantage and stood to win, only to falter in time trouble with 38.罝xa7?? and let Grischuk escape with a draw.

In the next three games of the first half of the tournament – against Peter Leko, Levon Aronian and Boris Gelfand – Vladimir in each case achieved an advantage. His openings were full of ideas, but there was always some tiny thing lacking for victory. After his performances in the first cycle, Vladimir could actually have been leading the tournament. But with only one win and six draws, he had to content himself at half-time with third place. Viswanathan Anand, on the other hand, had seized every chance on offer. The Indian profited from some bad mistakes by his opponents and survived his game against Kramnik. It was incredible, but Anand was already leading the field by a whole point.

Games 8-14

In the second half of the tournament, Vladimir was obliged to take more risks. After an opening draw against Peter Svidler with the black pieces, he had to face Morozevich, again with Black, in the ninth game, and had to accept a bad defeat. Thereafter he had White against Anand, and only a win might still have offered him some chances in the tournament. In a Queen's Gambit, Kramnik again exerted pressure for the whole time and was better placed. Anand, however, again defended very strongly and held the draw. In practice, that buried all hopes of the 14th World Chess Champion defending his title. It is to Vladimir Kramnik's credit that he did not give up after this, but fought on.

He won two more games with White, against Peter Leko and Levon Aronian. At the finish, he occupied second place behind the new World Champion Viswanathan Anand, ahead of Boris Gelfand according to the tiebreak system. After seven years on the chess throne, Vladimir Kramnik had lost his title. It may sound unbelievable, but the mood in our small team was not bad. The loss of his title was in no way emotional. Vladimir was not sad, on the contrary; he appeared as though freed. This relaxed attitude may also have been the main reason for his second place. According to the opinion of some experts, based on his play and his many chances, the World Champion would have totally deserved to win the tournament in Mexico City.

But from our point of view, none of that mattered. It is hard to describe, but after the three big World Championship matches against Garry Kasparov, Peter Leko and Veselin Topalov, the tournament in Mexico City did not feel like a world championship to us. Vladimir heartily congratulated Anand on a well-deserved success, but we all felt that Kramnik would have to be defeated in a classical duel. Vishy was always reticent on such matters, but to this day I think that deep inside, he saw things no differently. From now on, only one event was the focus of all interest: the return match between the new titleholder Viswanathan Anand and his predecessor Vladimir Kramnik, a match which was to be played a year later in Bonn.

World Championship Tournament Mexico City 2007: Final results

	Player	Rating	1		2		3		4		5		6		7		8		Points
1	Viswanathan Anand (IND)	2792			½	½	½	½	½	½	1	½	1	½	½	1	1	½	9
2	Vladimir Kramnik (RUS)	2769	½	½			½	½	1	½	½	½	1	0	1	½	½	½	8
3	Boris Gelfand (ISR)	2733	½	½	½	½			½	½	½	½	1	½	1	1	½	0	8
4	Peter Leko (HUN)	2751	½	½	½	0	½	½			½	½	1	½	½	0	1	½	7
5	Peter Svidler (RUS)	2735	½	0	½	½	½	½	½	½			½	0	½	½	1	½	6½
6	Alexander Morozevich (RUS)	2758	½	0	1	0	½	0	½	0	1	½			½	½	1	0	6
7	Levon Aronian (ARM)	2750	0	½	½	0	0	0	1	½	½	½	½	½			1	½	6
8	Alexander Grischuk (RUS)	2726	½	0	½	½	1	½	½	0	½	0	1	0	½	0			5½

Vladimir Kramnik – Alexander Morozevich

World Championship, Mexico City 2007

1.♘f3 ♘f6 2.c4 e6 3.g3 d5 4.d4 dxc4 5.♗g2 a6 6.♘e5 ♗b4† 7.♘c3 ♘d5 8.0–0 0–0 9.♕c2 b5 10.♘xd5 exd5 11.b3 c6 12.e4 f6?! 13.exd5! fxe5 14.bxc4 exd4 15.dxc6 ♗e6 16.cxb5 d3 17.c7 ♕d4?

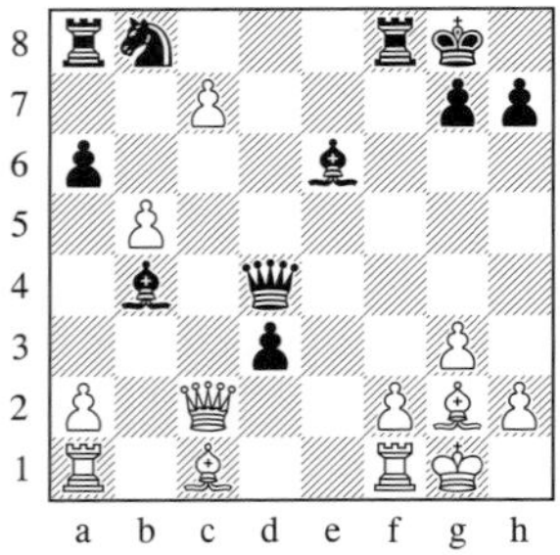

18.♕a4! ♘d7 19.♗e3 ♕d6 20.♗xa8 ♖xa8 21.♗f4? ♕f8? 22.b6! ♘e5 23.♗xe5 ♕f3 24.♕d1 ♕e4 25.b7 ♖f8 26.c8=♕ ♗d5 27.f3 1–0

Vladimir Kramnik:

"For the tournament in Mexico City, I had done some quite serious preparation. I also played good chess, but after the world championship match against Topalov it was not easy to motivate myself. The match had taken place not even a year before, and after it I found it psychologically very difficult to focus on new goals. In the end, my second place was a decent result and I would like to state that Anand absolutely deserved to win this tournament.

In the second round against Alexander Morozevich, I played the Catalan: the opening which had served me so well in recent years. During my career, I invested a great deal of work in these systems. In general, the Catalan demands active positional play, which is in keeping with my playing style. That is probably why in this opening I can look back on an outstanding rate of success.

In 8.0–0 I played an innovation, though at that point my analyses were not very deep. Nowadays, this is an established move. In playing it, I did not worry about my c3-pawn. My opponent also castled short, and I must admit that I had not had that on my screen at all, and thus had not analysed it. The game is open and somewhat untypical of the Catalan. White has good play, while Black has an extra pawn and no obvious weaknesses.

We began to study the position on the board, and I had an unusual idea: 10.♘xd5 That was absolutely not the way the world's top players treated this opening, but I had a tactical justification for it. Of course the piece sacrifice was very risky, but at the beginning of the tournament I really wanted to get off to a good start. I could have won the pawn back with 12.bxc4, but I decided on 12.e4. He now had various possible ways in which to react, but the most critical is 12...f6, which Morozevich played.

With 13.exd5 and the subsequent ...fxe5, I sacrificed my knight for a pawn. But in return I got a powerful initiative, whilst Black was badly developed. My opponent's pieces were almost exclusively on the eighth rank. Despite that, it was hard to evaluate the position objectively or to play it perfectly. There were simply too many options with uncertain outcomes. Here we were actually dealing with a type of position which Alexander Morozevich seems predestined to handle; of all the top players such unclear patterns suit him best.

So the whole undertaking was doubly risky, but I was feeling good and was ready for it. After 15.dxc6 we both began to use up a great deal of time, because the position was terribly complicated. Our play was perhaps not perfect, but the game was highly interesting.

After 16...d3 for example, 17.♕a4 would probably have been better instead of 17.c7. But naturally it is more human to play 17.c7, linked with the double attack on queen and rook. It is difficult to resist such a move.

The same can be said about his reply 17...♕d4, which was an inaccuracy. But this move too was completely natural. He was freeing his queen from the attack and at the same time attacking my rook on a1. But as you know, chess can be infinitely complex. Later analyses proved that in this case 17...♕d6 would have been the better reply. For some reasons which are hard to understand, this move is more precise, although it does not attack the rook on a1.

I now finally got the upper hand, and when in this complicated position we had 20 moves behind us, we had already played for over three and a half hours. Each of us had only about ten minutes on the clock for a further 20 moves.

I played 21.♗f4 and thought that was the most accurate move. Alexander thought the same – 21.♖ac1 would have been better according to the computer – and replied with 21...♕f8.

In doing so he overlooked 22.b6, after which Black no longer has any defence at all against 23.♕c6.

Be that as it may, I had played a very nice game and made only one single mistake with 21.♗f4. When you take the complexity of the positions in this game as a benchmark, that was an excellent performance. However, what impressed me most was the course of the game. For a Catalan, it was extremely unexpected and interesting. It is quite special to win such a game against an opponent who is uncannily good at playing exactly that sort of chess.

Personally I did not have the feeling that the tournament in Mexico City was a world championship. In saying that, I have no wish to insult anyone or to be too forthright, but only the overall situation and already existing contracts had brought about this compromise after the reunification. Please do not get me wrong: I lost my world championship title in Mexico City, where Vishy deserved to be the victor, and I recognize that. But deep within me, I considered this competition to be a Candidates tournament in which, for specific reasons, the world champion was obliged to take part.

After Mexico City, Anand was fully justified in seeing himself as World Champion, and I had no other claims. But for me personally, the true world championship was the match against Anand, which took place a year later in Germany. This traditional match, in which the challenger must defeat the titleholder, has helped chess to gain the importance which it enjoys nowadays. In my opinion, this tradition should be maintained for any number of good reasons."

The Last Great Duel and the Future

♔50

Vladimir Kramnik may have lost the title in Mexico City, but nevertheless was in good humour. At the start of 2008, he led the world ranking list. In any case, this year would be marked by the world championship match between him and the new official titleholder, Viswanathan Anand. The running to host the world championship was made by Bonn. Peer Steinbrück, now federal minister of finance, was strongly committed to this cause. This top politician, who was so enthusiastic about chess, wanted after a 74-year gap to bring back to Germany a final match for the chess crown.

As well as Steinbrück and myself, the Art and Exhibition Hall of the Federal Republic of Germany in Bonn was strongly involved. The rights to this major event were secured by Universal Event Promotion (UEP) with its president and owner Josef Resch. UEP's efforts to stage the reunification match between Kramnik and Topalov in Bonn had been in vain – it had failed at the level of the world federation. This time it would finally work out.

With Evonik Industries and Gazprom – ironically the main sponsors of the great football rivals Borussia Dortmund and FC Schalke 04 – we were able to win powerful sponsors. The prize money was 1.5 million euros. The world federation FIDE would receive 300,000 euros for licensing, and the players were each guaranteed 600,000 euros before tax. In addition, there was enough cash at our disposal to set up an excellent organization. The world championship in the Bundeskunsthalle was to be the best organized one to date. Standards were set in many respects which have unfortunately not been equalled even to the present day.

Stephan Andreae of the Bundeskunsthalle had organized around the event an attractive program called "Behind the Mirrors". Chess and art were presented in perfect symbiosis. There was live commentary on the games on the internet in several languages. Despite what were, for the chess scene, relatively high ticket prices of 35 euros, the playing hall was always full. Chess was booming in Germany in a way it had not for decades.

The organizing team of the UEP with Stefan Koth, Olaf Heinzel, Kema Goryaeva and Rolf Behovits, could not have performed their tasks any better. Everything went perfectly including Foidos, a new technology for the presentation of the games live on the internet. For this, UEP had joined forces with the Dutch firm DGT, which produces electronic chess products. For a relatively low fee, it was possible to choose between commentators in several languages and different video streams. The fans became de facto their own director, and could choose different camera positions and thus follow the games in a way that was exclusive to them.

It was one of the great innovations of this world championship, but unfortunately found far too few subscribers. Chess lovers are used to getting chess broadcasts free of charge and were not prepared to pay approximately five euros per day for the wonderful extra service. Professional chess suffers from these side issues. No successful business model has yet been developed for a pay-per-view setup for broadcasting the moves. Amongst other reasons, courts in the USA and Russia have ruled that chess moves are purely news and not the protectable property of the organizers and players. As a result, this fantastic technology had to be shelved after the Bonn world championship, because the costs were too high. From the professional point of view this was fatal, and to this day prevents professional chess from becoming a multi-million dollar business.

The ones to be pitied are not the world chess champions or the top-ten players; financially they have no problems. Things are quite different for the hundreds of grandmasters who dedicate their entire life to chess and achieve great things. These players earn barely enough to keep body and soul together. Countless chess firms, however, profit from their intellectual property.

But apart from Foidos, there was nothing to complain about. During the match, which was took place from 14th October to 2nd November 2008, 427 journalists took out accreditation. Free internet broadcasting on the world championship website was accessed by an audience of millions. There was praise from all sides; the event was a financial success and in the end almost all the participants were satisfied. Only Vladimir Kramnik, who had for the first time accepted a personal sponsor in the form of the Russian construction company Eurocement, could not be satisfied. He never quite came to terms with Anand and lost by the clear score of 6½–4½. No matter how unambiguous this result may appear, the way his defeat came about really frustrated him.

To the public, Kramnik appeared to have had no chances at all. At the halfway mark of the match, Anand was already leading 4½–1½. In wins it was 3–0 for the Indian. Nobody had expected that. Probably least of all Kramnik himself, who before the match had a clearly better score against Anand in their long tournament games. Different things had gone terribly wrong and they all came together during this match. But let's take it from the start...

♔51

Vladimir's preparation began seven months before the match. We visited the Sport University in Cologne for advice on questions of physical preparation and diet. With his background of chronic illness, he underwent lengthy examinations of his bones, joints and musculoskeletal system in the Cologne University Clinic.

Six months before the match, a psychological profile of Anand was compiled. Vladimir Kramnik did all that was humanly possible; nothing was left to chance and never before had he been as professional as he was at that time. One of the key conclusions in the profile was the belief that in order to maximize his chances, Anand would have to open with 1.d4. Kramnik, however, immediately rejected this possibility. The Indian, unlike Kramnik, employed d4-systems extremely rarely, and therefore ought not to feel at home in them. But Vladimir was deceiving himself, since Anand actually did play 1.d4 in the match. Although he may have been unable to do much damage to Kramnik with White, at least Vishy had undermined all of Vladimir's preparation in the Petroff Defence, which was at that time regarded as unbeatable in his hands. To this day, Kramnik describes Anand's choice of 1.d4 as a mistake. What is true, at any rate, is that during the match Vladimir would have problems with White and not with Black.

Vladimir and his chess team allowed themselves plenty of time, but in their preparation they found themselves in a "creative crisis". They would never find a way out of it, neither before nor during the match. Months before the world championship, Kramnik had already made some unfortunate decisions, especially with respect to the composition of his team of seconds. Vladimir has hardly ever said a word on this subject, but it is a fact that in the early months of 2008 he spoke with several other grandmasters, who all turned him down for different reasons.

So his 'dream team' was not available for Bonn. In my view, this was one of the reasons why during the match things just did not work out. In the team there were Laurent Fressinet (France), Peter Leko (Hungary) and Sergei Rublevsky (Russia). Even in the training camp in Weiskirchen in the early summer of 2008, I had the impression that things were not working as well as they might. It would get much worse during the match.

Now, it is not the case that weak opening preparation should mean a Vladimir Kramnik will inevitably lose such a match. His success against Topalov is proof of that. But since he and his team now found themselves in this creative hole, he was once more robbed of his greatest strength, namely creativity. In addition, a lot of time and energy had been spent to no avail before the match. Anand had sidestepped the Petroff Defence by playing 1.d4, and Kramnik basically did not know before the first game what he should play with White. There was a lack of fresh ideas in the 1.d4 main variations, and none would occur to him or to his team during the contest. The chess world believed that Anand had anticipated his opponent's strategy and out-prepared him. In truth, however, Vladimir and his chess team were wide of the mark.

The whole business became temporarily rather emotional, since there was a heavy burden on Kramnik's shoulders. In this connection, a great role was also played by the fact that Vladimir loved the whole framework of this world championship. Those close to him had financed and organized everything. In this match, chess was presented as harmoniously linked to art and creativity. That fitted exactly with his ideal. In contrast to his usual attitude, this time he was extremely results-orientated. Vladimir tried to plan every aspect in minute detail. He put himself under enormous pressure, determined to win the match, and seized up. Probably because – consciously or unconsciously – he felt indebted to 'his people'.

For Viswanathan Anand, on the other hand, things were rather relaxed. He mustered a strong and harmonious chess team. As well as his permanent second, Peter Heine Nielsen (Denmark), the grandmasters Rustam Kasimdzhanov (Uzbekistan), Radoslaw Wojtaszek (Poland) and Anand's compatriot Surya Shekhar Ganguly, were working for him on-site.

However, before the chess world championship could get going, the financial crisis exploded. In the summer of 2007, the US real estate crisis had already begun as a consequence of an overheated market in the USA. The bursting of the bubble put pressure on the banks. Losses and insolvencies piled up, the climax being the failure of the major American bank Lehman Brothers on 15th September 2008. At that moment, and in the weeks afterwards, the world was on the edge of the abyss. Only the courageous intervention of states to save countless banks, by raising the equity deposits, avoided a meltdown.

For Germany, it was federal finance minister Peer Steinbrück who managed the financial crisis. The way he did so will never be forgotten as his outstanding political achievement. As a patron, he had really hoped to enjoy "his" chess world championship, for which he had made such efforts. But although it was taking place close to where he lived, that was denied him. He was not even able, as had been arranged, to make the opening move of the first game on 14th October 2008; circumstances were keeping him so busy. He would later have just one single opportunity to visit the event.

♚52

That something was not right with Vladimir Kramnik could be seen in the very first game. Kramnik had White and with 4.cxd5 steered into the Exchange Variation of the Slav Defence. At the highest level, that is almost always a dead draw, which was agreed on move 32. In the second game, Vladimir tried with Black to surprise Anand with 9...♘d7 in a rare continuation of the Sämisch Variation of the Nimzo-Indian Defence.

His attack ran out of steam, however, after the exchange of queens, and once again there was a draw after 32 moves.

If you look at matters objectively, it must be admitted that in this match Kramnik lacked chances from the very start because of his failed opening preparation. The unambitious draw in the opening game was followed in Game 3 by the Meran Variation in the Semi-Slav. He lost with White – an extremely rare event. In this variation Vladimir had no trump cards, no ideas and was insecure. In his analysis Anand points out that with 29.♖a3 Kramnik made a decisive mistake, but that was almost incidental. He was given another chance, but did not find it.

White could play 32.♖d3!! ♗f5 33.♔b3 with a wild game ahead, but after 32.f3? the game was lost.

When we got back to the hotel, Vladimir told his grandmasters to work out some ideas for him in the main lines of the Meran System. That was easier said than done: including the next game and the rest day, all that remained were 65 hours. In contrast, it was clear that during his preparation Anand had had the Meran on his board for weeks. With Black in Game 4, Kramnik once again had no trouble and easily equalized.

Kramnik's next game with White was now looming. The match was due to last only twelve games and he had already lost one game as White. Now, almost at the halfway point of the match, Vladimir had to come up with something in Game 5. On the rest day before the game, Kramnik had worked day and night. He had developed ideas, but all he had heard from his people was: "That is not playable!" or "I don't like that!" or "That doesn't look promising for White!"

The Meran had been analysed, but once again nothing creative had been found.

During the night, he had asked his analysis team to again check out the White move 16.♗f4 as a reply to a possible innovation for Black with 15...♖g8. When he asked them about it, at midday the next day before the game, the grandmaster responsible had forgotten about this analysis. Kramnik reacted indignantly, and after that the communication between him and his seconds was compromised.

This psychologically-difficult situation gave rise to the next faux-pas between Vladimir and his chess team. The team had checked out 15...♖g8 as well as they could in the short time available. When I fetched Vladimir for the fifth game, he walked straight past the workroom of his people. They were standing in the open doorway, but he ignored them. I had never seen Kramnik like this. His people obviously wanted to say something to him, but he simply took no notice of them. His team had in the meantime clearly established that the variation 15...♖g8 16.♗f4 could be extremely dangerous for him, and at least required deeper analysis. But instead of speaking to Vladimir and giving him some tips, they simply let him pass. They could also have reached us by my mobile telephone for 15 minutes as we made our way to the venue.

This did not happen, and so Kramnik ran into his misfortune. As already stated, he thought he needed to immediately try something in Game 5 in the Meran. So to change the flow of the match, he bluffed and played 16.♗f4 after 15...♖g8. Whether the innovation 15...♖g8 was objectively good or not, Anand knew the variation very well compared to Vladimir. After Anand's 17th move 17...f5, with which he put further pressure on the white bishop, Kramnik thought for 45 minutes. It is to his credit that, despite everything, he continued to play very actively and for a win. Despite the lack of preparation, he risked everything in this game, but in the end gave it away with 29.♘xd4. Kramnik had missed the final move in the variation:

34...♘e3! and Black won.

One day later, in Game 6, Kramnik effectively lost the match. On move 18 he played the aggressive ...c5 much too early, and in doing so opened up his position. This cost him the tiny chance he had of making a comeback. It must be considered that Vladimir already felt there was little hope and wanted to make a last desperate effort. But once again in a world championship match, strong emotions had overcome him. Perhaps a little more patience might have been appropriate, and not the sledgehammer he unsuccessfully employed in Games 5 and 6.

Mentally, Kramnik recovered from the shock relatively quickly and conducted himself totally professionally in the second half of the match. At least he managed to keep the defeat within limits. In this situation it was understandable that Anand switched more to defence and did not want to take any more risks. Games 6 to 9 were four draws, and especially in the ninth Kramnik, with Black, brought the Indian to the brink of defeat. In the tenth game, to the delight of his many fans, Vladimir won, before the match ended with a draw in Game 11. Anand had won clearly and convincingly by 6½–4½.

It was only at this point that we really felt that the title of World Champion was lost. There was a little melancholy in the air, but after all the stressful years there was also a feeling of liberation. We congratulated Viswanathan Anand sincerely. Kramnik saw him as a worthy successor as the 15th World Chess Champion. For many reasons, Vishy more than anyone else deserved this title and the recognition which went with it. In Bonn we took our leave from a great event, such as the chess world had not previously experienced.

After the defeat, our connections gradually dissolved; Vladimir and I ended our professional cooperation. Before the Bonn world championship, I had agreed to take on a position with UEP. In the first year after our professional separation, I continued to help Kramnik to settle all his affairs in an orderly fashion. Since then he has not taken on another professional manager.

A decade after these events, we still enjoy talking about the good old days. From this distance it becomes more and more clear to me what the unique achievements of the 14th World Champion were: in his big matches, in the development of chess theory, and as someone who was forced to be deeply involved in chess politics.

The years between 2001 and 2006 constituted the most difficult and complex situation a world champion ever faced. Vladimir Kramnik stood strong throughout this lengthy and opaque situation; he did not relinquish the central principles in accordance with the traditions of the classical world championship, and he united the world of chess. In addition to his great world championship duels, this will eternally earn him his place in the history of chess.

After the world championship in Bonn, Kramnik was 33 years old. But he was not considering giving up for a long time yet. He loved the royal game too deeply and the unique atmosphere of the various chess events all around the globe. Now, however, an incredible amount of pressure was taken off his shoulders; because he had never really felt free in the role of World Champion. Now he had more time for many other things which he had previously had to give up. Vladimir would soon be a father. On 28th December 2008, Marie-Laure brought their daughter Daria into the world.

After the world championship match in Bonn, we needed a decent break; the past years had left their mark on us. My time in professional chess was slowly but surely drawing to an end. But first, in Nanking in China an extremely strong tournament was to take place in 2009. At the end of September, I visited this former imperial city. Nanking is certainly worth the journey, and to my taste preferable to Beijing or Shanghai. The metropolis on the Yangtse, with its six million inhabitants, incorporates more of the old, traditional China. Nanking was for periods the capital of China and its empire under the Ming dynasty. After the First World War, this was the headquarters of the regime of Chiang Kai-shek. The Confucius temple is a special highlight.

For the chess world, the tournament in Nanking was a turning point. An unchained Magnus Carlsen played brilliant chess, as though from a different planet. With his victory in this super-tournament, at just 18 years old, the Norwegian outclassed most of the world elite. He won the tournament with eight points out of ten (six wins and four draws) – with an Elo performance of 3002 it is considered one of the most impressive tournament performances of all time. Vladimir Kramnik was not in this tournament, but nevertheless Carlsen had heralded a change. It was the beginning of a new era and the established players such as Kramnik, Anand or Topalov would be replaced at the top by the Norwegian. From then on he dominated the world of chess, although it would take another four years, until 2013, when Carlsen was able to win the world championship title from Anand.

Even before I went to China, I was negotiating for UEP with FIDE about the future of the world chess championships. The negotiations had begun immediately after the match in Bonn. The UEP would gladly have marketed the next three world championship cycles as the commercial arm of FIDE. Josef Resch was prepared to give all the financial guarantees for that. FIDE's share would be 20% of all prizemoney as licensing fees. For the federation that would have meant an income as high as a million dollars.

Vice-president Georgios Makropoulos was leading the negotiations for the federation. He came on his own to Dortmund, the headquarters of the UEP. After several days of constructive negotiations, agreement was reached. On the table lay a final version of the contract which had only to be signed by FIDE President Kirsan Ilyumzhinov. But this did not happen. At the very last moment the federation wanted, against previous agreement, to have the right to make all sponsors and patrons brought in by UEP dependent on its approval. In addition it suddenly insisted on having the right to bring in an additional main sponsor of its own

Thereupon the negotiations ended abruptly. It was crystal clear this could never work for us. An investor such as the UEP needs the ability to make its own decisions concerning commercial rights in order to market such a high-profile series of events, with a mighty financial risk to the tune of at least eight million euros. That was clear to the world federation and yet it rowed back. For me, from this moment on, the marketing of world chess championships no longer made sense, since it would have been irresponsible vis-à-vis my client, the UEP. I remained linked to many people in the world of chess, but professionally I turned to other things.

♔54

Vladimir Kramnik is through and through a political person, though he is never fixated on specific persons or a political philosophy or specific movements. I would describe him best of all as a liberal democrat. In any case he likes to maintain his independence with respect to any political questions. This is also true in respect to the situation in his homeland, and the point of view of the West about these questions. Thus, for example, he judges the West's present policy of sanctions against Russia to be poorly thought through, one-sided and counter-productive.

After the Bonn world championship, Vladimir had some well-paid offers from economics and politics. He thought about it for quite some time – whether he should pursue his career in chess or follow the siren call of the managers. The decision was not easy for him. We had built up outstanding contacts with global firms and Kramnik always impressed them with his strong and cultivated personality without a whiff of arrogance.

His deep voice and outstanding speaking, with the intensity of his charisma, would certainly have made him a successful representative for an internationally-active business. This may have been an option for him, but to the good fortune of millions of chess lovers he took a different decision; he loved and still loves the game too much. Perhaps in the years after 2008 he did not always reach the strength and stability of days past. Quite particularly when the comparison is made with his outstanding performances in 2006 and 2007. In purely chess terms these two years represent – and Kramnik does not deny it – the best in his career. But without the burden of the title of world champion, Vladimir could now enjoy chess and private life much more intensely than ever before.

This could be seen from his play: Vladimir just exploded with the joy of playing and tried out a lot of new things. From those on the chess scene he received a lot of applause for his creativity and even the loss of his title did not negatively affect his popularity. Even if he no longer finished every tournament in a top place, he was still able to achieve quite outstanding results. Financially he had long been independent in any case. In my opinion, during his professional career of almost 30 years he must have earned between 15 and 20 million dollars in starting fees and prizemoney, including all sponsorship, licensing fees and other income.

Financial independence makes life easier, above all when you live with your wife and two children in Geneva in Switzerland, one of the most expensive places in the world. After a short dip in 2014, on 1st January 2016 Kramnik was back in second place in the world ranking list, a place he still occupied in July 2017 with 2812 Elo points, right behind World Champion Magnus Carlsen.

Vladimir Kramnik, at over 40 years old, is still a powerful player. In a chess duel he can prove dangerous to anyone on this planet, even the reigning world champion Magnus Carlsen. In 2009 Vladimir won the super-tournaments in Dortmund and Moscow. In 2010 he was victor in the Grand Slam final in Bilbao and in 2011 he was on the top of the podium in Dortmund for the tenth and currently last time. In the same year he was victorious in London ahead of the assembled world elite.

When in 2013 Vladimir took part in the Candidates tournament in London, he once more came very close to a match for the title. He shared first place with Magnus Carlsen. Only the tiebreak system – in this case the number of games won – finally decided matters for the young Norwegian. Carlsen became the challenger to Viswanathan Anand, from whom he took the world title in the same year, six years after the latter's victory in Mexico City. Anand had no luck and was even outclassed in his hometown Chennai by the young Norwegian by 3½–6½.

At the end of 2013 Kramnik won the World Cup for the first time, ahead of 127 grandmasters: a competition in which he had not played for many years. He reached his best Elo rating with 2817 in October 2016. In June 2017 he shared second place in Stavanger in Norway behind the Armenian Levon Aronian, clearly ahead of Magnus Carlsen, whom he once more was able to defeat in their direct encounter. Ten players from the top twelve of the ranking list were taking part. Vladimir Kramnik is thus still an 'evergreen' in top tournaments and the rising computer generation, astonished, pay him respect.

At the 2018 Candidates, Kramnik started brilliantly, winning two of the first three games in style. In the fourth round he lost maybe the most combative game of the tournament to Fabiano Caruana. Having taken lots of chances earlier, Kramnik had a winning position after the first time control, but fell for a cunning trick, which allowed Caruana to get back into the game. After further ups and downs, Kramnik over-pressed and blundered a piece just before the second time control.

Later in the tournament he played the most interesting chess and essentially stole the show until the last few rounds, where people started to pay attention to who was actually leading the tournament! His win in round 10 against Levon Aronian was perhaps the most imaginative game of 2018 and an instant classic for sure.

Another serious run at the world title is not unthinkable for a man with the abilities of Vladimir Kramnik, even at what is an advanced age for chess players. But it would be highly unusual if he could summon the required energy and motivation yet again. The question is not whether he could do it, but whether he really sets it as a goal and does everything possible to achieve it. I find it hard to believe that, especially if one knows what efforts are required to win a world chess championship. Vladimir, who feels secure with his wonderful family, has nothing more to prove in chess. After all his successes, he is playing only for pure pleasure.

It is clear that chess is a very tough competitive sport. As I have experienced it, considerably tougher than many sports which are predominantly physically based.

Results, title and world ranking places are essential for professional players. Certainly Kramnik has less of the singleness of purpose and energy of a Garry Kasparov or Bobby Fischer. In contrast to the vast majority of elite players in history, Kramnik took part in most of his competitions without an overriding will to win. Therefore his performances and great successes should be rated all the higher.

Despite a great deal of work, which he doubtless put in, he has to thank for his triumphs a special gift from God: his talent. As far as creativity and intuition are concerned, linked to the ability to recognize the hidden subtleties of a position with precision, to integrate these into his analysis and play, there has hardly been a better player in the history of chess than Vladimir Kramnik. Many professionals and grandmaster colleagues are agreed on this.

In his career Vladimir has seen everything, played everything and won everything. He wanted to set himself a test to find what level he could reach. He climbed the highest peaks in his own way and in doing so always remained true to his principles. He was World Chess Champion three times and for seven years held the most important titles the sport has to award. He overcame the split in the world of chess under the most adverse conditions. For his many fans and friends their meetings with Vladimir Kramnik were no test. They walked along a magic road with their idol. Vladimir followed his own personal path with great dignity and authenticity. And as long as chess is still played on this planet, he will be immortal.

A considerable future now lies ahead of him, to be found perhaps in the promotion of the next generation of Russian players. With the end of the Kramnik era, Russia's hegemony in chess has been broken. That should change one of these days. But in his homeland, this nation enthused by chess, they are still short of outstandingly talented players and professional structures. So, in the presence of the president of the Russian Federation, Vladimir Putin, in the spring of 2016 Vladimir opened the "Kramnik Chess School" in Sochi, quite close to Tuapse where he was born. In the years to come this is where the future of Russian chess could lie.

But for now, it is his own offspring who enjoy the highest priority. With this in mind, the Bohemian, who enjoys life and has various interests outside of chess, has the final word. In a wonderful interview with the Brazilian filmmaker Clara Cavour, Kramnik gave an insight into his private life. He plays in many tournaments and is quite often not at home. "That," said Vladimir, "is a problem, because I have young children and they miss me." His daughter often cries when he leaves her and is overjoyed when he comes back home again. Apart from the frequent pain of separation, however, they are a very happy family.

Cavour: Are your children proud of you?
Kramnik: *Yes, they are, but not because I am a chess player.*
Cavour: ...because you are their father?
Kramnik: *Yes, exactly!*

Vladimir Kramnik – Viswanathan Anand

Bonn (10) 27.10.2008

1.d4 ♘f6 2.c4 e6 3.♘c3 ♗b4 4.♘f3 c5 5.g3 cxd4 6.♘xd4 0–0 7.♗g2 d5 8.cxd5 ♘xd5 9.♕b3 ♕a5 10.♗d2 ♘c6 11.♘xc6 bxc6 12.0–0 ♗xc3 13.bxc3 ♗a6 14.♖fd1 ♕c5 15.e4 ♗c4 16.♕a4 ♘b6 17.♕b4 ♕h5 18.♖e1 c5 19.♕a5 ♖fc8 20.♗e3 ♗e2 21.♗f4 e5 22.♗e3 ♗g4 23.♕a6 f6 24.a4 ♕f7 25.♗f1 ♗e6 26.♖ab1 c4 27.a5 ♘a4 28.♖b7 ♕e8 29.♕d6 1–0

Vladimir Kramnik:

"The world championship match against Anand was a remarkable duel. I made a mess of my opening preparation; everything went wrong. I was working in completely the wrong direction although for this match I invested more time and effort than ever before. In the variations which were important for me, neither I nor my team could find any interesting ideas. That was quite particularly true for White. The nearer the match came, the fewer weapons I had. This situation is very difficult to explain to an outsider, but from the first game on I understood very clearly that I was not well prepared. That was a really rotten feeling.

Before such significant duels I had always been very honest with myself. In order to be successful in a match at this level, everything must fit into place. This time that was absolutely not the case, since my team and I were suffering a crisis of creativity. For some reason we could not find any ideas, which played straight into my opponent's hand. For his part he came up with very interesting innovations in almost every game and bombarded me with them.

After the very unfortunate experiences in the Meran Variation, from a sporting point of view things had gone very badly for me by the middle of the match. It was of course clear to me that it would be impossible to get three wins in six games against such a strong opponent in top form. The world championship match was practically lost, but I still wanted to do a good job. There were hundreds of journalists present in Bonn, the games had been sold out and in the second half of the match I did not want to collapse but simply give of my best.

Freed from all the pressure, from Game 8 on I also began to play better. In Game 9 I was already quite close to winning with Black and I succeeded in winning the tenth game. It was the only time I was able to surprise Anand. In all the other games it was the opposite, but this time I at last got on the board the type of position which I knew and in which I was able to play to my strengths.

We played the Nimzo-Indian Defence, which, however, because of my move 7.♗g2 was very much reminiscent of a Catalan Opening.

My 18.♖e1 novelty at first sight looked slightly comical but in reality contained a lot of venom. The black position was strategically already endangered; I had the bishop pair and wanted to prevent the exchange of one bishop, to stabilize the position. After 18.♖e1 he was no longer able to achieve his aim: forcing the exchange of the light-squared bishops.

At the latest after 20.♗e3 ♗e2 and 21.♗f4 it was time for Black to take some subtle positional decisions. Vishy may well be a universal player, but his strengths do not necessarily lie in this sort of position. I tried to force him into playing 21...e5, which then happened. It all somehow looked laughable, I moved the bishop back and forward. But Anand began to sense that White had some strong points and used up time. But I do not think that he saw how great the danger really was. Because the black position looks very solid and not like something which is going to fall apart after a few moves.

But that is what actually happened. He replied to 22.♗e3 with the logical move 22...♗g4.

Logical, yes, but in fact it was a mistake. After 23.♕a6 White could simply march forward with the a-pawn. This idea was certainly underestimated by my opponent, because now he was no longer in a position to regroup his pieces in good time. I understood that I was well placed and had pressure. But to my own surprise too, the technical problems of Black's position suddenly became very critical. (Still with 23...h6 Black is not yet lost, but 23...f6? made things much worse)

164

After a few logical moves I played 26.♖ab1.

Perhaps Anand overlooked that. In any case it was a subtle and very strong move. Vishy now no longer had the time to play ...♗c4. If, for example, I had played the direct and natural 26.a5, on which Anand had probably speculated, then 26...♗c4 followed by 27.♗xc4 ♘xc4 would have been played, which would have led to equality. But this inconspicuous move 26.♖ab1 completely changed the scenario of the game. Suddenly Black was losing and he resigned after only 29 moves.

At the end it was a surprise to score such a quick and relatively simple win against him. This game was impressive because of the rapid collapse of a position. And that although Anand made no obvious mistakes and almost all the pieces were still on the board. It was a special game in which for most of the time I played prophylactic moves and nevertheless in the process found myself in the situation of destroying the position of such a strong opponent in fewer than 30 moves. For that reason, despite the overall situation in the match, this win gave me a lot of pleasure and a certain satisfaction too. With this win I showed the great public my strengths and till the finish kept the match slightly open.

If I think back to the world championship match in purely chess terms, on the other hand, then the negative memories predominate. However, my feelings as to the presentation of this world championship match are quite different. I always enjoyed playing in Germany. But this time the Germans outdid themselves. I loved the organization of this world championship. It was incredibly well received by the public and there were very many spectators. The linking of chess and art thematically in this way is something I will never forget.

The event set benchmarks and proved that even today the game of chess has lost none of its popularity. Under those circumstances it was of course regrettable to lose the match. That made me sad at first. But I did my best and found in Viswanathan Anand a worthy successor who more than any other player at that time deserved the victory and the recognition."

Grandmaster to Grandmaster

As a final treat, some renowned grandmasters of the present day give their opinion of the 14th World Chess Champion. I asked them all three questions:

How would you describe Vladimir Kramnik's playing style?
What were Vladimir's contributions to the development of chess?
What is your opinion of Vladimir Kramnik as a man?

Of course every master has a slightly different point of view on Vladimir Kramnik, be it of a professional or a personal nature. You may compare and contrast the opinions below with my own views in this book. They are presented below in alphabetical order according to the players' surnames.

♚55

Adams, Michael (England)

Michael Adams, born on 17th November 1971, has been Britain's best chess player for many years. He was awarded the title of grandmaster back in 1989. Mickey, as his friends call him, has several times been a Candidate in the race to the world championship, reaching the final match for the FIDE title in 2004, losing narrowly to Kasimdzhanov. Adams' highest placing in the world ranking list was fourth.

Michael Adams:

"Vladimir has a classical style. Normally he plays solidly with Black, while seeking to exert pressure with White without doing anything over-risky. I have always been left speechless by his very special strength in positions where he has stable control over the centre. Many of his games against the King's Indian and Grünfeld are textbook examples of this.

His belief in himself and his psychological power of resistance are key abilities, especially during hard world championship matches such as against Garry Kasparov, when he was in a position to avoid a single defeat. Another example is his win "to order" in the final game against Peter Leko, to defend his title. Or how he managed to hold out against the poisonous atmosphere which had developed in Elista. It is remarkable that he was totally able to concentrate on playing the game. Like against Kasparov, something which I and some of my colleagues have regularly missed doing.

All through his career he was a leader in the development of opening theory. The most famous example is the Berlin Defence, which he transformed from a modest side variation into a standby for every top player. Quite generally Vladimir breathed life into many variations which often became popular for some time on account of his influence. He unites both of the main qualities required for such innovative work: creativity and a great understanding of the game. Last but not least he has an impressive work ethic.

Our first game was played in a tournament in Halkidiki, in 1992, at a time when many of our present-day rivals had not even been born. Vladimir had longer hair than nowadays and brought his brother along, more as a companion than as a second, I think. It was not unusual to meet them at the pool for a drink. I remember that he easily won the tournament and was in another league from his opponents. Although nowadays you normally have to wait till the end of a tournament to meet him at the bar, he has not changed much. He is a hard fighter at the board, but always has a friendly smile and even during the tournament he is always ready for a good chat."

♔56

Anand, Viswanathan (India)

Viswanathan Anand was born on 11th December 1969 in Madras (nowadays Chennai). Anand's exceptional talent was recognized in his youth because he has an intuitive understanding of the characteristics of a position. He won many tournaments but in 1995 lost the world championship match against Garry Kasparov in the New York World Trade Center. At the world championship tournament in 2007 in Mexico City, Anand was victorious ahead of Vladimir Kramnik, whom he also defeated by 6½–4½ in the following year in their world championship duel in Bonn. He replaced Vladimir Kramnik and went down in history as the 15th classical World Chess Champion. He held the title of World Champion until 2013, when he lost it to Magnus Carlsen in the town of Anand's birth, Chennai.

Viswanathan Anand:

"Kramnik is a strategic player, someone who likes to play a game that flows perfectly. He is less fond of chaotic games in which he is restricted to reacting to events over the board. In order to play as he wishes to do, he works very hard and makes the effort to gain deep understanding of his favoured systems. In addition he is quite objective and not vulnerable to speculation or taking excessive risks. Interestingly, as is often the case with strategic players, he nevertheless plays very strong tactical chess. If he is forced into it he can also gamble quite effectively. Despite that, usually he is driven by the dictates of the position.

Vladimir is a great explorer of the secrets of the game, always at the forefront of opening theory. In doing so he brings to light many new ideas. His speciality is defensive technique. He has developed this area and shown how many defensive resources the game has to offer. It is no coincidence that his 'main bunnies' were attacking players whom he punished seriously when they had overstepped a certain mark.

Especially because he penetrates very deeply into a position, he has a host of new opening ideas. 'His' variations dominate the discussion of openings. Finally, he has adapted his style to today's computer age. Although he was once used to specializing in the main variations and classical structures, he is now contributing to the discovery of as yet unknown directions.

When I first met him, I was speechless when it came to his confidence and self-belief. He is more an honest person than one who produces shallow opinions and he has a dry sense of humour, which I greatly appreciate. I have the feeling we drew closer to each other when we became fathers. At the moment we have frequently exchanged presents for our young children. Vladimir is very accessible, never gives himself airs, and likes to surround himself with nice people during tournaments."

♔57

Bischoff, Klaus (Germany)

Klaus Bischoff is a German grandmaster who was born on 9th June 1961 in Ulm. Amongst his greatest successes are the bronze medal in the World Junior Championship of 1980, when he took third place behind Garry Kasparov and Nigel Short, and the silver medal which he won with the German national team at the Chess Olympiad of 2000 in Istanbul. He became well-known over the years through his activity as a live commentator, for example on the broadcast platform of ChessBase and at the Dortmund Chess Days.

Klaus Bischoff:

"It is at the same time simple and difficult to say something about Vladimir Kramnik's style. Of course he is an 'all-rounder'. That too is not really a surprise. It is obvious that a world champion must be able to do everything: attack, defend, positional play and tactical melees.

In any case for live commentators like me, Vladimir is almost a present. Right at the beginning of the game he hands you a red thread which, especially on his very good days, keeps on getting thicker and thicker. If, after a longish period of thought, he decides on a move, I can simply rely on the fact that he has considered every detail, be it ever so small. So I can immediately begin to explain the variations. Trusting his calculations has always saved time.

Of course, even a Kramnik has not managed to avoid working with chess computers. But in his games there is always a tremendous amount of sound common sense."

♔58

Gelfand, Boris (Belarus & Israel)

Boris Abramovich Gelfand was born on 24th June 1968 in Minsk in Belarus. Since the Chess Olympiad of 2000 in Istanbul he has played for Israel, where he has also found a new homeland. Since the start of the 1990s he has been counted among the best grandmasters in the world. He is famous/notorious for his irrepressible fighting spirit. He achieved his greatest successes at what was – for chess players – a high age. In 2007 he took the bronze medal in the world championship in Mexico City and in 2009 he won the World Cup in Khanty-Mansiysk in Siberia. Gelfand was already 44 years old when in 2012 he qualified for a world championship final match. As a total outsider, he drew 6–6 in classical games with titleholder Viswanathan Anand and narrowly lost the match in the tiebreaks by 2½–1½.

Boris Gelfand:

"Vladimir is probably the only player who with his playing style has been able to adapt frequently to the situation at that time. He has a subtle positional understanding and excellent technique. In the 1990s he won several fantastic Sicilian and Semi-Slav games by counter-attacking. In 1998 he improved his defence and adapted his style in consequence. This helped him to defeat Garry Kasparov in their world championship match without a single defeat. Five years ago he once more began to play more aggressively and that too brought him success.

His contribution to chess is immense. I believe that no other player in the history of chess has contributed so much to opening theory as Vladimir Kramnik. He was the trendsetter of the last 20 years. When he played the Sveshnikov, all the others also played the Sveshnikov; when he changed to the Petroff Defence, it became modern. And when he selected the Berlin, it became the most popular opening of the last 15 years. When he recently began to avoid opening theory as much as possible, that too became the trend.

I see Vladimir Kramnik as an intelligent and well-balanced person. I am privileged to be able to describe myself as his friend. I have learned a lot from him, both in chess and otherwise."

♔59

Illescas Córdoba, Miguel (Spain)

Miguel Illescas was born on 3rd December 1965 in Barcelona and is a well-known Spanish chess player. In 1988 he became a grandmaster and for years was the strongest player in Spain. For three of Vladimir Kramnik's world championship duels he was part of the team of seconds. Today Illescas runs the chess school "Edami", the most important and successful of its type in Spain.

Miguel Illescas:

"Kramnik has a classic-positional style which is based on strong elements from the Russian chess school as well as deep strategic understanding. When he was young he played more active variations. Since he became world champion, he has played very solidly.

I see his main contribution to the development of the game of chess as being his responsibility for the resurrection of the Berlin Defence. The Berlin led to a complete rethink among elite players and influenced their way of analysing opening systems. Within his opening preparation, Vladimir first of all does not examine only individual moves. He prefers to study the complete system and then has many new ideas such as in the King's Indian, in the Catalan Opening (with White), the Petroff or the Slav Defence.

I cannot describe Volodja objectively as a human being because he is my friend. In any case he has a balanced personality, is very cultivated and polite. But when chess is at stake, he is very demanding, even a perfectionist."

Of course, even a Kramnik has not managed to avoid working with chess computers. But in his games there is always a tremendous amount of sound common sense."

♔60

Karpov, Anatoly (Russia)

Anatoly Yevgenevich Karpov went down in the history of chess as the twelfth world champion. He was born in Zlatoust, Russia on 23rd May 1951. He is the only world champion to be awarded the title by the world federation FIDE without playing for it, when Bobby Fischer did not appear against him in 1975. Karpov went on to win every important tournament and for more than a decade was the best player in the world. He became famous, however, for his legendary world championship matches against Viktor Korchnoi and Garry Kasparov.

Anatoly Karpov:

"All in all, Kramnik's style is built upon that of other world champions. It contains profound opening preparation and is universal. As to his system of preparation he stands like Kasparov and I in line of succession to what Mikhail Botvinnik developed.

For a long time now Kramnik has stood on the peak of the Mount Olympus of chess. He began in 1992 with his triumphal entry into the elite of chess. At that time and at the age of only 17 he achieved at the Chess Olympiad on the Philippines the incredible result of 8½ points from nine games. He won many chess tournaments of the super class, with his ten victories at the Dortmund super-tournament standing out. For almost a decade he was World Champion or playing for the crown. Special mention needs to be made of course of his world championship match against Kasparov, which he won without losing a game.

Nevertheless, in my opinion he could have done even more to popularize chess. As a person he is absolutely above-board and very cultivated. Apart from certain happenings during the world championship matches he has neither enemies nor people who wish him ill."

♔61

Leko, Peter (Hungary)

The Hungarian super-grandmaster was born on 8th September 1979 in Subotica, Yugoslavia. At the age of 14 he was awarded the grandmaster title by FIDE, at the time the youngest ever to receive it. In 1994 in his hometown of Szeged he became U16 World Champion. Between 1999 and 2008 Leko was part of the world elite and could always be found in the Top Ten.

In 2002 he won the Candidates tournament in Dortmund and became the official challenger to World Champion Vladimir Kramnik. As we know, the course of the 2004 match beside Lago Maggiore in Switzerland was dramatic. Before the 14th and final game Leko was leading 7–6. Just a draw would have sufficed to win the title. He failed, however, and Kramnik held on to the title at the very last moment.

In 2005 he won the Corus tournament in Wijk aan Zee. At that time this made him, along with Viswanathan Anand, Garry Kasparov and Vladimir Kramnik, the only one to have been able to win at least once each of the then three super-tournaments (Wijk aan Zee, Linares, Dortmund). After being regarded together with the aforementioned three players as being at the absolute peak of world chess, he was unable to hold on to this level in the years to come.

Peter Leko:

"It is against Vladimir that I have played the most games in my professional career in chess. We had intense struggles and many theoretical duels over the chess board. During these 20 years I got to know his playing style from every angle. Like that of all great players it is universal, but the conclusion one can draw from it is that Vladimir's main goal is to achieve control in his games. It was never really important whether he had a minimal positional advantage or whether a complicated tactical battle was underway – so long as he was choosing it! His technique, for example in the conversion of the tiniest of advantages, set a totally new level. But also the ability to calculate extremely deeply and precisely made him very dangerous during complications.

It is clear that Vladimir's opening preparation has had a great influence on the whole world of chess. His incredible work ethic and the will to get the maximum out of every opening are simply astonishing. Vladimir is creative; he has many new ideas in the systems for White. I somehow have the feeling that he is always a few years ahead of present-day theory. With Black he is more conservative and mainly focussed on constructing a bulletproof repertoire. In doing so he has exerted a heap of pressure on his colleagues and at the same time forced them to work unbelievably hard if they want to be competitive. Thanks for the endless work, Vladimir!

At the board he is extremely concentrated; a hard opponent who shows no pity. In private life, on the other hand, he gives the impression of an open-minded, lovable person with a great range of interests."

♔62

Mikhalchishin, Adrian (Slovenia)

Adrian is a Slovenian chess player of Ukrainian origin. He was born on 18th November 1954 in Lviv. He has been a grandmaster since 1978 and is considered one of the most successful chess trainers world-wide. He is chairman of the trainers committee of the world federation FIDE.

Adrian Mikhalchishin:

"I would see Vladimir as a successor to a line of players such as Paul Keres and Boris Spassky. It is a rounded, universal style we are talking about here. Kramnik was always prepared to attack and developed fantastic technique. But especially positionally and strategically he is probably even stronger than his predecessors. He is really a great classical player.

A match for the world championship is also always a war between different styles and personalities. His preparation for Garry Kasparov was a masterpiece. He found the weak point in Kasparov's way of playing and decided on openings which absolutely prevented Kasparov from getting on the board the positions he favoured. That is something which all participants in world championship matches in the future must study.

Vladimir has done a great deal for the sport of chess. He found lots of new pathways in the openings. He breathed new life into the Berlin Variation in the Ruy Lopez and it became a main weapon for other top players. He found many interesting ideas in the Petroff Defence, in the Grünfeld Defence and especially in the Nimzo-Indian Defence which he favoured. Practically all of modern theory bears his stamp. Most young players try to copy him since Kramnik's games are excellent models for them. His approach to the endgame, the numerous examples of converting small advantages are shown to their students by trainers all over the world.

I have known Vladimir since Dortmund 1992 and was his team captain in 1999 during the European Cup in Belgrade. He is a sincere and friendly person. I have never heard of him insulting anybody. Mikhail Tal and Paul Keres were perhaps a little like him in that respect. Unfortunately there are hardly any personalities like Kramnik left in the world of chess. I have spoken a lot with him about his father. The latter was professor of art at the University of Lviv, my home town, before he went to Tuapse. Vladimir accompanied his father to Lviv now and then to meet friends. He never forgets old friends and colleagues. If he wanted to, after his active career he could become a really strong leader of the world of chess."

♚63

Timman, Jan (Netherlands)

Jan Timman was born on 14th December 1951 and is, after Max Euwe, the most celebrated chess player in the Netherlands, which is such an enthusiastic country about chess. He was Dutch champion nine times. His world title attempts failed, but in the 1980s and early 1990s Timman was one of a very small number of West European players able to stand up to the Soviet phalanx. Today Jan Timman is editor-in-chief of the magazine New In Chess and is considered an excellent author and analyst.

Jan Timman:

"Kramnik is an all-rounder. His play is based on deep positional understanding. He possesses a remarkable ability in the calculation of complex variations. His endgame technique is outstanding.

With his victory over Garry Kasparov in London 2000, Kramnik brought an era to an end. For over two decades he was at the absolute peak of world chess, which is really very impressive. He taught us what deep opening preparation can look like.

I have known Vladimir Kramnik for more than two decades now. He is a friendly, warm-hearted person."

♔64

Yusupov, Artur (Germany)

Artur Yusupov is a German grandmaster of Russian origin. He was born on 13th February 1960 in Moscow. A student of the legendary trainer Mark Dvoretsky, who sadly died on 26th September 2016, he took part in the national championship of the Soviet Union in Minsk in 1979 and sensationally took second place. He has been a grandmaster since 1980. He regularly played in the Candidates tournaments for the world chess championship and three times reached the semi-final.

In 1991 in the Candidates quarter-final in Brussels he played a legendary combination against the Ukrainian superstar Vassily Ivanchuk. The game received numerous prizes. Amongst others it was selected by the readers of the Chess Informant as among the best games played since 1966:

Vassily Ivanchuk – Artur Yusupov

Brussels rapid tiebreak (1) 1991

1.c4 e5 2.g3 d6 3.♗g2 g6 4.d4 ♘d7 5.♘c3 ♗g7 6.♘f3 ♘gf6 7.0–0 0–0 8.♕c2 ♖e8 9.♖d1 c6 10.b3 ♕e7 11.♗a3 e4 12.♘g5 e3 13.f4 ♘f8 14.b4 ♗f5 15.♕b3 h6 16.♘f3 ♘g4 17.b5 g5 18.bxc6 bxc6 19.♘e5!? gxf4 20.♘xc6 ♕g5 21.♗xd6 ♘g6 22.♘d5 ♕h5 23.h4 ♘xh4 24.gxh4 ♕xh4 25.♘de7† ♔h8 26.♘xf5 ♕h2† 27.♔f1 ♖e6 (Looking back, Yusupov preferred 27...♗f6!.) **28.♕b7?**

28...♖g6!! (Black threatens mate: 29...♕h1† 30.♗xh1 ♘h2† 31.♔e1 ♖g1#) **29.♕xa8† ♔h7 30.♕g8†!** (White sacrifices the queen to win the rook on g6.) **30...♔xg8 31.♘ce7† ♔h7 32.♘xg6 fxg6 33.♘xg7 ♘f2! 34.♗xf4 ♕xf4 35.♘e6 ♕h2 36.♖db1 ♘h3 37.♖b7† ♔g8 38.♖b8† ♕xb8 39.♗xh3 ♕g3 0–1**

Nowadays Yusupov is active predominantly as a chess trainer and author.

Artur Yusupov:

"Vladimir Kramnik is one of the most talented players, perhaps THE most talented player, whom I have met in my chess career. He is complete and has absolutely no chess weaknesses.

But his special strength is his deep positional understanding of chess. He is one of the few chess players who have outplayed me. Then you puzzle after a defeat: where did I even make a mistake?

I would not limit his influence on modern chess only to the openings, where he has developed many ideas, above all in the King's Indian, the Berlin Variation, the Sveshnikov, the Grünfeld Defence and the Slav Defence. There are some positions, like for example with the bishop pair or with a central passed pawn, which he played as if with divine inspiration.

I have a good relationship with Vladimir, whom I know as a polite and respectful person. But despite that he has always clearly expressed his opinion on various problems in the world of chess."

The wedding of Kramnik's parents Irina Fedorovna and Boris Petrovich in 1969

1987: Vladimir aged eleven. Mikhail Botvinnik paid attention to him.

1991: In a good mood at the board, watched by Anatoly Karpov, the 12th World Champion

1994: Bohemian and chaotic genius

2000: Tennis was part of the preparation before the Kasparov match

2000: On the way to the World Championship title

2001: Handshake with Ephraim Kishon before a simultaneous game

2000: The peace after the storm – Vladimir angling

2002: Candidates tournament in Dortmund's Westfalenhallen

Team Kramnik in Bahrain 2002 (from left): Dr Valeri Krylov (physiotherapist), GM Christopher Lutz, World Champion Vladimir Kramnik, Carsten Hensel (manager), Aziz Abu Luay (bodyguard) and GM Tigran Nalbandian

2002: Two big boys at the chess board in the Westfalenhalle in Dortmund Vitaly Klitschko and Vladimir Kramnik

2002: Vladimir teaching chess to children in Bahrain

2003: Fun during a blitz game in Dortmund
Vladimir Kramnik, Carsten Hensel and Peter Leko

2004: Kramnik announces his title defence in Switzerland

2004: Supermodel Natalia Vodianova starts the 13th game of the Kramnik – Leko world championship match, watched by Joel Lautier (ACP President)

2004: Simultaneous in front of a packed house in the Bundeskunsthalle, Bonn

2005: Announcing Man vs Machine (from left): Dr Werner Müller (RAG), Vladimir Kramnik and Peer Steinbrück

2006: Total concentration against the monster Deep Fritz in Bonn

2006: Autographs after the victory in the world championship in Elista
Vladimir Kramnik, Josef Resch and Carsten Hensel

2006: Done it! The chess world is united at last and Kramnik is its champion

2006: Team Kramnik at the world championship in Elista

2006: En route to the world championship in Russia

*2010: In private – Vladimir Kramnik with
his ex-manager in his Paris flat*

2008: The title match lost –
a pensive ex-world champion

*2007: Vladimir Kramnik und Vitaly Klitschko
in the Köln Arena*

2008: Press Conference after Game 5 in Bonn

*2006: Pure happiness –
Vladimir marries Marie-Laure in Paris*

2017: A happy family – Marie-Laure and Vladimir with their children Daria and Vadim

The other 15 Classical

Steinitz 1886-1894

Lasker 1894-1921

Capablanca 1921-1927

Botvinnik
1948-1963 (with interruptions)

Smyslov 1957-1958

Fischer 1972-1975

Karpov 1975-1985

Kasparov 1985-2000

Chess World Champions

Alekhine 1927-1946
(with an interruption)

Euwe 1935-1937

Tal 1960-1961

Petrosian 1963-1969

Spassky 1969-1972

Anand 2007-2013

Carlsen 2013-

Epilogue

The tasks of a chess manager are particularly diverse. Specifically because the financial means are limited compared to those available to the major TV sports, you have to exercise several professions at the same time. The tasks include marketing, internal and external communication, organization of events all the way up to world championship matches, management of contracts and the acquisition of specific legal knowledge. Nor should one underestimate the task of acquiring and looking after sponsors, and handling national federations and the world chess federation FIDE.

Cooperation with the professional chess player is, however, of central and decisive importance. You are in almost daily contact with him. And it is far from all about business. Private worries and feelings play a part and for this reason alone a very tight and trusting relationship is the most important precondition for doing a good job. What happens is often highly complex, but the wellbeing of the protégé should always be the top priority, although this ideal can sometimes find itself in contradiction to practical considerations such as the interests of events organizers and sponsors.

On account of the different interests and standpoints, it is possible to fall not between two stools but between all possible stools. For that reason alone, the professional sportsperson should be involved in all decisions and always have the last word. I do not think much of the tendency nowadays in high-performance sport that many players are moving away from this responsibility and hiding behind their managers and advisers. Kramnik and I discussed many things and were once of a very different opinion. But all that happened within the framework of a constructive process and in an attempt to optimize matters. In this way we made progress.

In professional chess within the orbit of the elite grandmasters there is another, less well-known, side. You are confronted with the envious, the free-loaders, the know-it-alls, right up to the deceivers. In our chaotic world full of egoism and materialistic thinking, that is not surprising. The goal is financial or sporting success and it does not matter how it is reached. Values like fairness, respect and a sense of responsibility are often considered antiquated and no longer count for much. In my career I got to know thousands of people, of whom there are only a relatively small number I could totally trust.

Over the years I was able to procure for chess millions of euros from sponsors. Many people such as the professional players, public and private organizers, federations, chess firms, commentators and even journalists profited directly or indirectly from my efforts. Gratitude, however, is not something you should expect and also the remuneration of a chess manager is low in comparison to those in the major TV sports. In no way do I regret that, because I had always wanted to travel the world and that was precisely what was enabled by my entry into the professional chess scene. In 20 years I visited more than 50 countries and in doing so got to know many interesting and famous personalities from politics, business, sport and art. High society, you see, really likes to be seen beside the World Chess Champion since this title is surrounded by a mythic aura. It is the stuff of legends and still one of the most important in all sport – at least whenever social and cultural values are used as a measure.

But before starting as a manager in the chess business, I gained my spurs in event management with special responsibility for communication. Chess was in no way central to my activities. High-profile happenings such as public events of the football club Borussia Dortmund and the organization of World and European Championships in such sports as table tennis, ice hockey, handball, figure skating, show jumping and boxing moulded me and brought me the necessary equipment.

In 1990 I became press officer for Dortmund. My brief included social, youth, education, health and sports events. In the same year I was asked to cast an eye over the Dortmund Chess Days. It was already their 18th year. The sporting city of Dortmund always made an effort not to be identified solely with football and Borussia Dortmund. At that time the process of changing structures, which went along with the decline of coal and steel, was to be linked to intellectual matters. Chess was ideally suited to this. Quite in line with the thoughts of world chess champion Max Euwe, who once suggested as an advertising slogan for chess: "An intelligent game for intelligent people from an intelligent town."

Those responsible in Dortmund, right up to the present lord mayor Ullrich Sierau, did good work in organizing chess. It was not as if the royal game was making its first appearance in the city. Back at the end of the 19th century there was evidence of a thriving club scene. Prestigious tournaments had been held in Dortmund: won in 1928 by the Berlin grandmaster Fritz Sämisch (Sämisch was one of the few players to defeat Capablanca), in 1951 by the then correspondence chess world champion Alberic O'Kelly de Galway (Belgium) and in 1961 by the Ukrainian Mark Taimanov, who, as is well known, was crushed 6–0 in 1971 by Bobby Fischer in their Candidates match.

When Fischer fought through to become the challenger to Spassky, Dortmund attempted to stage this world championship duel, which of course took place in 1972 in Reykjavík. Even though Dortmund's bid was unsuccessful, this commitment gave rise to the motivation to put on a regular international chess tournament. This was staged for the first time in 1973 and has been organized annually since then under the name of the Dortmund Chess Days and later the Sparkassen Chess Meeting.

So in 1990 I visited for the first time these Dortmund Chess Days in a dance school. Only a few local and specialist journalists were accredited; there were almost no spectators. In order to develop the event, in 1991 during the CEBIT in Hanover I met Andrew Page – the then manager of Garry Kasparov. The commitment of Kasparov for 1992 which followed signified the final international breakthrough of this event. The town, the Westfalenhallen of Dortmund and sponsors brought together a total of 1.4 million marks, a mighty sum for the conditions of the day. 10,800 spectators and 156 journalists from 18 countries showed for the first time in Germany that chess could be marketed as a media event.

A win in the final round made Garry the victor of this memorable tournament. It has gone down in chess history because of its innovations. With its perfect organization and the incredible public resonance, it sets standards to this day – even for Dortmund. Only in 1997 in the Dortmund Opera House (winner Vladimir Kramnik) and following the Candidates tournament of 2002 (again in the Westfalenhallen, winner Peter Leko) were the organizers able to boast of approximately comparable numbers. To this day the Dortmund Chess Days feed off these legendary models from 1992, 1997 and 2002.

I was a decent footballer, swimmer and table tennis player. I became interested in chess at the start of the 1970s. I learned the rules with the help of school friends. Then the hype around the Spassky – Fischer match cast a spell over me. What really captivated me, however, was a book. Right after Reykjavík 1972 I bought *Grandmasters of Chess* (*Die Großmeister des Schach*) by Harold Schonberg. I still have it and it is lying before me on my writing desk. I paid 7.80 marks for it. That was roughly equivalent to my weekly pocket money. But it was worth every pfennig to me, since I read it at least five times. The broadcasts of Dr Helmut Pfleger on WDR Television later in the 1970s and 1980s maintained my interest in chess. Whenever I could, I played a few friendly games.

This interest took on another dimension in the 1990s through my intensive contacts with professional chess and the players of the world elite. In 1998 I began to advise the Hungarian Peter Leko, in his day the youngest grandmaster in the history of chess. I had met him for the first time in 1991 when he was just twelve years old. A very special story ties me to him, and I was his manager until 2009.

In 2001 I asked Peter whether he could accept it if I also took over the responsibility for the world chess champion. He knew about my friendship with Vladimir Kramnik, which went back many years, and agreed. This circumstance, as well as my specific experiences in chess which I had gained working for Leko in the three previous years, formed ideal conditions to manage Kramnik at world championship level.

Since I had been looking after Kramnik and Leko in parallel since 2002, in 2004 the media saw me as being in a win-win situation during their world championship match. People might think that, but instead it was the most difficult and complex situation of my entire career. This match was a balancing act in many respects. It was quite a challenge to get the match on stage fair and square without personally being suspected of arranging an advantage for one or the other. All that had to be done under the pressure of public scrutiny which was focused on every weakness, every possible scandal.

My time as a chess manager could also form the basis of exciting travel reporting. Some experiences were even dangerous. I have already mentioned the conditions in Moscow in the 1990s. But the journey to Belgrade in 1995 was also not stress-free. At that time the Dayton Agreement was being negotiated. De facto the Bosnian war was present everywhere. Streets were barred and crossroads protected with heavy weapons around the Serbian capital. The mood towards strangers was in accordance with that.

Twice I found my life in direct danger. In Nanking in 2009, but first in 1996 on my return from the Chess Olympiad in Yerevan to Amsterdam. I was flying with former Dortmund tournament director, Jürgen Grastat, with Armenian Airlines. The safety standards of the airline did not meet the regulations of most European countries and consequently it rarely received permission to take off or land in the western world. The Netherlands, with their international airport Schiphol close to Amsterdam, made an exception.

We circled above the airport for almost an hour because the wheels would not come down. It was an absolutely critical situation. Some Armenians began to pray, women screamed and the faces of the stewardesses were chalk-white. As we were told later, the pilots avoided an emergency landing by letting the aircraft drop abruptly a few times. Whether this was true or not, at some point they succeeded with their efforts, and the landing gear was released and we escaped with just a fright.

The second time was a little closer. In 2009 I was in Nanking, the former Chinese imperial city. After my arrival in the late evening I was again suffering with the typical jetlag. I never feel it so much in journeys towards the east as towards the west, but nevertheless I could not sleep all night. So in the morning I went for a walk at six o'clock and discovered a park close to our hotel. A crowd of Chinese had already met there for morning sport.

This also involved long, drawn-out cries. The Chinese ladies above all were giving their best, and screaming as though for dear life. Exhausted as I was, their shrill tones finally broke my nerve. I fled from the noise along a high fence, which also had a mighty overgrown hedge. I came to a metal gate in the fence which was not shut. I went into the parkland behind it and followed a path for about 200 metres. As I turned a corner, a full-grown male lion was standing in front of me.

He was a wonderful specimen, weighing 250 to 300 kilos with a mighty black mane. To my good fortune the animal stood still, then turned to one side and let out a terrible roar. I was mortally afraid for what felt like minutes, but was probably only a few moments, when a Chinese man appeared. He went up to the lion and grabbed it by its thick mane. With hysterical movements of his arm, he signalled me to go away.

I ran back down the path and fortunately escaped through the open gate. I was so shocked and full of adrenalin that I was not aware of my fear at that moment nor that I had wet myself. When I had showered, I found someone at the hotel reception who spoke a little English. I told him my story. He glanced at me and spoke to his colleague. Both of them went into rather silly fits of laughter. I found out that the separated area of the park hosted a permanent circus, as is frequently the case in China. And that circus had a zoo attached to it. The roaring of the lion followed me for ten more days until my departure.

According to an old proverb, all's well that ends well. That is the conclusion I can draw after a fulfilling career as a chess manager. A guardian angel by my side and a slice of luck were always part of it: in ticklish situations as well as in the major matches and events to which I contributed. It was an exciting dream which became reality. A wonderful journey!

Appendices

"Mercy On My Soul"
Everlast (2000)

Portraits of the World Champions

It is impossible to establish which country chess comes from. Opinions differ greatly – China, India or Persia are mentioned in the literature. In any case chess was widespread first of all in Asia and in the Orient, before being mentioned more often in Europe in the 14th and 15th centuries. The first really well-known chess master was al-Adli in the 9th century. Al-Adli was also a writer and, like other chess masters of that era, was employed at the court of the Caliph of Baghdad.

The invention of the game is dated to some point between the 3rd and the 6th centuries. We should not conclude that chess was thought up by a single person at a specific point in time. It is much too complex for that and contains elements from different languages, cultures and eras.

In the 15th century the rules of play changed to the extent that since then we can speak of modern chess as it is played today. In Europe, chess developed slowly at first. It would take until the 16th century before there was the first encounter between leading masters from Spain and Italy. One of the players who dominated was Ruy Lopez de Segura. He was the first to analyse the Ruy Lopez, the opening which is named after him to this day. Spain in the 16th century, Italy in the 16th/17th centuries, France in the 18th/19th centuries, England and Germany in the 19th century, and the Soviet Union in the 20th century: such is the order of the leading chess nations.

The royal game has produced 16 classical world chess champions so far. This tradition started in 1886 in the USA, where Wilhelm Steinitz was the first to win the title of World Champion. The "Steinitz line" has continued until Magnus Carlsen, the present World Champion. All 16 title holders have dedicated the greater part of their lives to the royal game and will eternally occupy a place of honour in the rich history of chess.

Before Steinitz no official matches or tournaments were played as world championships. Players such as François-André Philidor (1726-1795), Louis-Charles Mahé de La Bourdonnais (1795-1840), Howard Staunton (1810-1874), Adolf Anderssen (1818-1879) or Paul Morphy (1837-1884) were all chess geniuses of their day, but they were not official world champions. So we will not be taking them into account in what follows.

Wilhelm Steinitz (14.5.1836-12.8.1900)
1st World Champion 1886-1894

Wilhelm Steinitz was born in 1836 in the Prague ghetto. As an 18-year old he set off for Vienna, where he studied at the Polytechnic. At this time, however, he was more often seen in coffee houses than in the university. There, often in the Café Rebhuhn, he earned his living at chess. Very soon he was recognised as the best player in the city. In 1861 he won the championship of Vienna in brilliant fashion with 30 wins, three draws and only one loss.

In 1862 the Wiener Schachgesellschaft (Vienna Chess Society) sent him to London, where he took a respectable sixth place in a big tournament. After that Steinitz settled in London, because he hoped to make more money there. There was a chess boom in London at that time and the Austrian rapidly improved his playing strength, so much so that in a match in 1866 he defeated Adolf Anderssen by 8–6. From then on he himself considered himself to be World Champion, a view which was not shared by the public. Simply because Paul Morphy was still alive.

He finally achieved recognition in 1886, three years after having left London for New York. Morphy had died on the 10th July 1884 at the age of only 47, after not having played chess for a long time. Steinitz and Johannes Zukertort from Poland were the greatest of rivals and agreed on a world championship match which was also recognised as such by the public. On the 11th January 1886, Zukertort played 1.d4, the first move in a world championship in the history of chess. The match started in Cartier's Academy in New York and public interest was enormous.

Steinitz won 10–5 and successfully defended the title three more times: in 1889 against Mikhail Chigorin by 10½–6½ in Havana, Cuba. In 1890 against Isidor Gunsberg by 10½–8½ in New York. And for the last time in 1892 by 12½–10½ once more against Mikhail Chigorin in Havana. He lost it in 1894 to Emanuel Lasker after a 5–10 defeat in a match played in the USA and Canada.

Steinitz is widely considered a reformer of the theory of chess, which had existed since the 15th century, and one of the first players to develop broad general principles. However, Kramnik is of a different opinion: "I think that he had weaknesses whenever the game became dynamic. In very difficult positions in his duels with Chigorin he kept on retreating with his pieces. He did have some ideas but he never really got to the heart of the matter."

Steinitz may have introduced some general principles in chess, but he hardly obeyed his own rules. Nevertheless he started to study the game, whereas most other masters of the day only played it. But Kramnik could not see him as the founder of any profound doctrine: "Steinitz experimented and emphasized certain things which happened regularly and which are in any case worth thinking about."

198

Emanuel Lasker (24.12.1868-11.1.1941)
2nd World Champion 1894-1921

Emanuel Lasker ruled the world of chess for 27 years – an all-time record. The only German world champion won the title in 1894 with a 10–5 victory over Wilhelm Steinitz, with the match ending in Montreal, Canada. The return match ended 10–2 with Steinitz outclassed, though to be fair he was well past his best. Lasker successfully fought other world championship duels against Frank Marshall (1907), Siegbert Tarrasch (1908), Carl Schlechter (1910) and Dawid Janowski (1910). For various reasons eleven years would pass before his next defence of the title against José Raúl Capablanca. In 1921 he lost the title in that match.

From Kramnik's perspective, Lasker, and not Steinitz, is the real pioneer of the modern school of chess. He was the first link in the chain of universal chess, where simultaneous consideration was given to several elements of the struggle. Steinitz had always laid the focus on one specific element of the game, for example the superior pawn structure or the chance to attack the king. Whenever he had achieved that, he believed he had obtained a decisive advantage.

Kramnik: "Lasker already understood the various elements in a game and their mutual significance. I believe that Lasker was a much more complete player than Steinitz, which can also be seen in their matches which were very one-sided. Were we to judge them by modern criteria we could say that Lasker was playing at a level of 2700 and his opponent a level of 2400 Elo. Of course I knew Steinitz to be a great chess player, but when I studied his games against Lasker I saw something like a massacre. To be honest, it was like a cultural shock for me. I have never seen such a serious difference in performance levels in the world championship duels: it was as though it was not a world championship but a simultaneous exhibition. Presumably Steinitz was already weakened, but not so greatly, as his good tournament results at that time prove."

Kramnik considers Lasker to have been a great player, who was the first to have understood certain universal things about chess. Only recently Kramnik took another look at his games: "I was surprised by what he already knew in his day. He was the first to understand the psychological aspects of the game and to begin to take them into account. He was prepared to modify his strategy accordingly and to some extent his own playing style."

At the moment when Lasker won the title from Steinitz, he was much superior to his rivals – there has never been such a difference in the history of chess. Kramnik: "Naturally only until the moment when a new generation had grown up and rivals such as Tarrasch or Rubinstein had become strong enough to stand up to him." According to Kramnik, on no account should one forget Akiba Rubinstein, who possessed incredible talent. It is hard to understand that he never became World Champion nor ever got close to the title. Rubinstein was far ahead of his time but perhaps too subject to nerves and not practical enough.

José Raúl Capablanca (19.11.1888-8.3.1942)
3rd World Champion 1921-1927

Born in Havana, the Cuban was considered a child prodigy and learned the game at the age of four. He is supposed to have defeated his father at that early age. This story, however, probably belongs in the realm of fairy tales. It is certain, however, that José Raúl became a strong player at a very early age; at the age of only twelve he defeated the Cuban national champion Juan Corzo in a match.

In his early years Capablanca achieved several big international successes: at 21 he routed the American Frank Marshall with 8–1 wins. After this match the "Cuban chess machine" was considered the natural challenger to the World Champion Emanuel Lasker. He confirmed this position and notched up further tournament results, for example, in 1911 he won a strong tournament in San Sebastián. The famous St Petersburg tournament in 1914 was won by Lasker ahead of Capablanca, though in a preliminary all-play-all tournament the latter had outpaced all of the world elite. Despite these outstanding performances it would be years before he got his chance at the world championship.

Whether Lasker wanted to avoid Capablanca is unclear, but certainly the correspondence between the two became sharper and the 17 conditions set by Lasker were not easy to fulfil. They included the demand that the challenger come up with 10,000 dollars prizemoney, which adjusted for inflation would have a present-day value of easily 130,000 dollars. Many years passed after the Marshall match before finally in 1921 there was a world championship duel between Lasker and Capablanca in Havana. The Cuban defeated the now 52-year old German by 9–5.

Vladimir Kramnik sees in Capablanca a real genius. He was an exception who fitted into no pigeonhole. Such a person crops up only rarely, like for example the American Paul Morphy in the middle of the 19th century. Kramnik: "Capablanca had a totally natural feeling for the harmony of a game." He had a sort of talent which cannot be taught. Theoretically one can suppose the hard work, such as a Lasker or an Alekhine undertook, would have made him even better. "But hard work," according to Kramnik "stands in contradiction to the nature of such a talent. It was simply something he did not need."

Kramnik compares him with Mozart, whose music sprang from him of its own accord. "On studying his games my impression was that Capablanca did not know precisely why he moved here or there, it was his hand which made the moves. If he had worked hard at chess, things would not have gone so well. Simply because he would have begun to think about it. But Capablanca did not have to think, he simply had to move the pieces."

He did not, as some people say, lose to Alekhine because he had not worked hard enough. Had he worked more, he would have lost his great ability. "To be honest, I am still surprised that Alekhine beat him." José Raúl Capablanca lost his title to Alexander Alekhine in Buenos Aires in 1927 by 15½–18½. The latter would not give him an opportunity to win back the world championship.

Alexander Alexandrovich Alekhine (31.10.1892-24.3.1946)
4th World Champion 1927-1935, 1937-1946

Alexander Alekhine is the only World Chess Champion who took the title with him to his grave. He won it in 1927 against Capablanca and defended it in 1929 and 1934 against Efim Bogoljubov. In 1935 he sensationally lost the world championship match against the Dutch player Max Euwe, but then won back the chess crown in their return match in 1937. On account of the Second World War there was no further world championship duel before his death.

Alekhine was full of contradictions. The Russian left his home country in 1921 and never saw it again. He lived in France, where in 1925 he set a record for simultaneous blindfold chess. Without sight of the pieces he played 28 boards at the same time, won 22 games, lost three and drew three games. In 1933 he did the same thing in Chicago, this time with 32 opponents (+19, =9, –4). For Alekhine chess was first and foremost art. But to this day he is criticized for his collaboration with Hitler's Nazi regime. Alekhine died in 1946 in a hotel room in Estoril in Portugal. The circumstances remain mysterious – just like his life. Was it murder? Or suicide? Or simply a heart attack?

Kramnik concedes that Alekhine had great talent. But he finds it difficult to say how he was able to defeat Capablanca. He agrees with Kasparov, who is of the opinion that Capablanca was unable to cope with the intensity of the struggle. "Quite differently from playing Lasker, he overwhelmingly had to defend against Alekhine. Alekhine was not only more able to cope with the mental exertion, but even increased the pressure at the board whenever possible. Capablanca was not used to that. The match was very long and Alekhine constantly created problems for the champion," says Vladimir.

According to Kramnik, Alekhine was a workhorse and had studied openings in a way no one had done before: "He had strategic talent; he was the first to really have a feeling for the dynamics of a game." Lasker for example had understood their importance, but they had not been a component of his playing style. In contrast, Alekhine had put the accent on dynamics. Of course Alekhine also followed positional principles, but always based on the idea of developing dynamic positions. Kramnik: "He was not on the lookout for long-term advantages, but more for threats and attack whenever the opportunity presented itself."

In a certain sense Kramnik also considered Alekhine to be ahead of his time. Kramnik: "It is absolutely certain that Alekhine was an outstanding champion. He enriched his playing style and gathered experience. But I would not say that he introduced anything which was revolutionary and new. Why, before the match against Capablanca, had he not left his rivals trailing in his wake and yet was so superior to them afterwards? Quite honestly, I cannot see any reasons for that. In any case he also had weaknesses, as is shown up to a certain point by his match against Euwe."

Machgielis (Max) Euwe (20.5.1901-26.11.1981)
5th World Champion 1935-1937

Compared to his charismatic predecessors, Max Euwe was an ascetic and showed iron discipline. He neither smoked nor drank and had no other vices. For a long time his main occupation was as a mathematics teacher. Those who were close to the tall Dutchman, however, recognized quickly that he had many talents and was in no way boring.

In 1921 he was for the first time victorious in the Dutch Championship, which he would go on to win 13 times by 1955. At the turn of the year 1923/24 he drew international attention by winning the Hastings tournament in England. At the start of 1927 in The Hague there was a first warning sign of his potential in a match against Alexander Alekhine, who was preparing for his match against Capablanca: Euwe only narrowly lost by 4½–5½. In 1928 – also in The Hague – he won the Amateur World Championship of the young world federation FIDE.

At the beginning of the 1930s Euwe hesitated for a long time over whether to go for a career in science or in chess. At the urging of his friend Hans Kmoch in 1934 he challenged the World Champion Alexander Alekhine. When the latter accepted, the decision had been taken in favour of a career as a professional chess player. Machgielis Euwe, though everyone called him "Max", sensationally defeated the odds-on favourite by 15½–14½. The world championship match was played in 13 Dutch cities and unleashed in the country a powerful wave of chess euphoria.

Vladimir Kramnik judges Euwe as "a very good player". Botvinnik is reputed to have founded a basically all-embracing system of preparation. "But I believe that Euwe was the first to do this. He understood the importance of the openings and for his day and age was quite perfect in them," says Kramnik. Euwe's attitude had been very professional, his way of playing perhaps not quite brilliant, but universal. Kramnik: "Euwe had a good nervous system and was hard to play against. His style had something slippery about it, something you cannot quite grasp so as to examine it."

To this day Kramnik admits to not having really understood the central point of Euwe's game. It was possibly a combination of various factors which made him World Champion: preparation, reliable opening systems, universal understanding, a good nervous system and a healthy lifestyle. All that resulted in the title of World Champion, which he absolutely deserved to win.

However only two years later, in 1937, Euwe lost the title in a return match against Alekhine by the clear score of 9½–15½. In the middle of the 1950s he began a career as scientific director of an institute for computer technology. In 1970 Euwe was chosen as president of the world federation FIDE. He had understood better than anyone else how to accommodate the differing interests of players, federations and FIDE. His diplomatic abilities were valuable before and during the legendary and controversial duels Spassky – Fischer in Reykjavík 1972 and in Baguio 1978 between Karpov and Korchnoi.

Mikhail Moisevich Botvinnik (17.8.1911-5.5.1995)
6th World Champion 1948-1957, 1958-1960, 1961-1963

To this day Mikhail Botvinnik is considered in the world of chess as the most meticulous of all players. For him chess was above all a science. His opening preparation sometimes went deep into the middlegame. This care was unusual and enabled him to develop a much deeper positional understanding than most of his rivals. Botvinnik's first major success was taking first place in the 1931 USSR Championship, which he eventually won a total of six times. Great international tournament wins followed: in Moscow in 1935 he shared first place with Salo Flohr, just as he did in 1936 in Nottingham together with Capablanca. At this point he was already a serious pretender to the chess throne, but the Second World War would delay the hopes of all ambitious young players like him, such as Keres, Fine and Flohr: between 1937 and 1948 no world championship took place.

Only in 1948, two years after Alekhine's death, was there the opportunity: a world championship was held under the aegis of FIDE for the first time and, in another first, as a tournament not a match. During the 1947 congress in The Hague, FIDE decided the participants would be Mikhail Botvinnik, Max Euwe, Reuben Fine, Paul Keres, Samuel Reshevsky and Vassily Smyslov. Reuben Fine declined for professional reasons and the remaining players met in 1948 in The Hague. Botvinnik was the clear victor by three points, ahead of Smyslov, Keres, Reshevsky and Euwe.

The Russian thus became the first World Champion after the Second World War and the first under FIDE. He defended the title in 1951 against David Bronstein and in 1954 against Vassily Smyslov. In 1957 he lost it to Smyslov in Moscow, but regained it in the return match. In 1960 he again lost a world championship match, this time against Mikhail Tal, and again won the return match a year later, before finally losing the title in 1963 in Moscow to Tigran Petrosian 9½–12½ – he no longer had the right to a rematch. Botvinnik is the only player to have lost a world championship duel three times and to win the title back twice.

He is also the first world champion whom Vladimir Kramnik got to know personally. Very well even, since he attended Botvinnik's famous Moscow chess school. Botvinnik ushered in a new era, says Kramnik, who describes him as the first real professional who understood that a complex regime in preparation – such as thorough study of openings, a lot of sleep and physical training – made an important contribution to getting good results. "He made it abundantly clear that chess was not only about playing well over the board," said Kramnik.

Botvinnik developed some chess ideas of course, but apart from his professional preparation he did not contribute much to the development of the game. He played many games at a really high level, but from time to time for no apparent reason "he fell to pieces". Although he was nicknamed "iron man" he was not always able to endure the high level of effort. As a person, in his final years he made a positive impression on Kramnik. Botvinnik had spent a long time dealing with the ideas of communism and honestly believed in them. In this, however, Vladimir sees a total contradiction: "He had the manners of a Petersburg professor and nothing in tune with the time after the Russian Revolution. At the same time it is a riddle for me how he could combine communist points of view with the nature of an intellectual."

Vassily Vasilyevich Smyslov (24.3.1921-27.3.2010)
7th World Champion 1957-1958

Vassily Smyslov was only able to stay on the world championship throne for a year after wresting the title from Mikhail Botvinnik in 1957 with a score of 9½–12½. Previously, in 1953, he had won the Candidates tournament in Zürich with a margin of two points. The tournament is legendary and considered the strongest of that time. "It was the best result of my career," Smyslov once said, when looking back over his great successes.

In the return match in 1958 he had his chances against Botvinnik, even though after six games he was already trailing 1½–4½. After that the match was very level before Smyslov had to admit defeat by 10½–12½.

The seventh World Champion, alongside Viktor Korchnoi, is a prime example of how one can play chess at a high level even at an advanced age; he still quite often took part in tournaments in the 1990s. His strengths lay in his deep positional understanding and in outstanding endgame technique.

Vladimir Kramnik says about him: "Smyslov played 'honestly' and very naturally. Nevertheless he never achieved the aura or mystique of a Capablanca or a Tal. The reason for that is that his play was neither artistic nor particularly creative. At first sight his style was not particularly interesting, but he always really appealed to me. He played 'correctly' and sought the truth. In every position he always tried to find the strongest move."

He thinks it was entirely probable that of all the world champions Smyslov played the strongest moves. "From a professional point of view I find that very attractive. I think that Smyslov was underestimated. If you study his games, there is an easy side to them as if he really did not have to put in too much effort but was drinking coffee and reading the newspaper at the same time. There is something of the ease of Mozart," says Vladimir.

In the matches against Botvinnik the average quality of the games is very high. To a certain extent it was a pity that Smyslov did not hold onto the world title for longer, simply because he was an outstanding chess player. Kramnik: "Probably he did not hold onto the title longer because he really did not want it so much. It turned out that it was not so important for Vassily Vasilyevich. Under certain circumstances he could absolutely have remained World Champion for 15 years."

For Kramnik in any case Smyslov was a very strong world champion, who was superior to all his predecessors in positional play. He did not develop any great ideas, but his play was subtle and accurate: the first player to deal with the game with great purity. In some ways Smyslov was the founder of a playing style which was based on short variations with precise time management.

Mikhail Nekhemevich Tal (9.11.1936-28.6.1992)
8th World Champion 1960-1961

In his day Mikhail Tal was the youngest world champion in the history of chess. At the age of 23 he defeated Mikhail Botvinnik by 12½–8½. But he could not hold onto the title for even a year – also a record to this day. Tal had many gifts, not only in chess. In school he was moved up two classes right at the start, and performed particularly well in mathematics. In addition to art and music, he had a special liking for football.

Tal's chess career really got going between 1957 and 1959. Twice in a row he won the Soviet Championship, the Interzonal and after that the Candidates tournament. According to the German grandmaster Dr Helmut Pfleger, who knew Tal very well, he was a very one-sided player at first: 'attack and sacrifice at any price' was his motto. At any point he was able to conjure up fantastic fireworks on the board, but from time to time he also made hair-raising mistakes. Later he would become more mature in positional play.

Vladimir Kramnik, who played blitz games against Tal in 1990, is full of admiration: "Tal was a star, a real chess genius. The man played chess simply for pure pleasure. He enjoyed the game. That was absolutely not professional, but his talent was so great that he nonetheless became World Champion." But his meeting with Tal also made the then 15-year old Vladimir very sad: "When I saw him for the first time, his health was already very compromised. He looked really unwell."

When he was a child there were only a few chess books available to Kramnik and he studied Tal's games at a relatively late stage. Tal had been an outstanding, many-sided chess player. There were times when he played like someone from another planet. His sacrifices and combinations were incredibly attractive and had shaped his image. But at the same time he had also been a strong positional player. "His actual gift, however, was his attitude to chess, the pleasure he took from it and his great energy. Together these brought him enormous advantages," said Vladimir.

Of course Tal also had weaknesses and with his attitude it had not been possible to remain World Chess Champion for many years. Kramnik: "He rose several times, only to fall back down – quite in harmony with his being. Tal was extraordinary. A star burned within him which absorbed incredible energy. A normal person cannot sustain for long the vital energy which was required for that."

Although his heyday consequently lasted only a few years – poor health was the greatest of all his problems – he became a legend in his lifetime. For 100 years the world had not seen sacrifices and combinations like his, but in contrast to the Romantics, his were based on the foundations of modern principles. Mikhail Tal was liked by all, because to everyone he was cordial and never calculating. He lived only until the age of 55.

Tigran Vartanovich Petrosian (17.6.1929-13.8.1984)
9th World Champion 1963-1969

When Tigran Petrosian appeared for his world championship duel against Mikhail Botvinnik in Moscow, all Armenia was as if in a state of emergency. People were sitting in front of their radios and thousands stood in the capital Yerevan in what is now Republic Square. Move by move on giant demonstration boards they followed events in far-off Moscow. When after 22 games Tigran Petrosian dethroned thrice world champion Botvinnik once and for all by 12½–9½, rejoicing broke out and seemed never-ending.

Petrosian was from that moment a superstar in Armenia. Sons were named after him: names such as Tigran, Vartan or Petros were very popular at that time. Chess fans all over the world, on the other hand, were less enthusiastic. For Petrosian played in a very defensive style. All his life he was never really able to rid himself of the image of a "boring player".

There were, however, other voices. The late grandmaster and Karl-May publisher Lothar Schmid was of the opinion that Petrosian had been misunderstood. Peter Leko too, who even as a boy was a fan of Petrosian, is of the same opinion. In contrast to his image, he did possess a great capacity for tactical play as well as rapid and accurate calculation of variations. And specifically because he was strong at combinations, he could of course also see the options available to his opponent. Consequently he preferred to act according to his nature in a defensive and positional way.

"In order to recognize the creativity of Petrosian, you need to study him and his games carefully. It is, to define it more precisely, very much hidden," is how Kramnik judges him, not superficially. He was the first true defensive artist who showed that almost any position can be defended. Kramnik: "Petrosian delivered to us elements which more and more reveal that in the area of defence too, chess is a game of incredible and diverse resources."

According to Kramnik, Petrosian was a very profound chess player. Nevertheless, through the study of his games he got a clear picture of the latter's playing style. Petrosian was a brilliant tactician and strategist, though his positional play probably did not reach the level of that of a Smyslov. Nevertheless, that was precisely what the whole world considered him to have been a master of. "I do not think that positional play was his greatest strength; his defensive arts were. For that you need very strong tactical understanding," is the distinction Kramnik made. In any case it appears to him that historically Petrosian's achievements have not been well enough recognized.

Tigran Petrosian was a close friend of Mikhail Tal, whose playing style epitomized the exact opposite. Petrosian had a gentle, well-balanced character and was considered a man of undoubted integrity, which made him many friends in the world of chess.

Boris Vassilevich Spassky (30.1.1937-)
10th World Champion 1969-1972

Boris Spassky had a difficult childhood; his family was evacuated from the city where he was born, Leningrad (nowadays St Petersburg). His parents divorced. Perhaps on account of these early experiences a certain melancholy was always part of his nature. In his best years, however, he gave the impression of a carefree and approachable person.

Spassky was anything but a hard worker, not even at his peak as a chess player. He was able to permit himself this way of life because his talent was simply enormous. At 32 in 1969 he defeated Tigran Petrosian by 12½–10½ in Moscow and became the 10th World Chess Champion: a success which, when measured against his potential, was long overdue. In 1966 he had already appeared in the final against Petrosian, but lost narrowly 12½–11½.

He achieved international celebrity status in 1972 – sadly as the result of a defeat. His world championship match against Bobby Fischer is to this day the subject of numerous publications and is one of the best-known sporting events of all time. Apparently the defeat itself did not bother Spassky much. He would always emphasize that his years as world champion had been the unhappiest of his life, partly on account of the numerous obligations on the titleholder and the associated heavy workload.

Boris Spassky was a guest of honour in 2007 at Vladimir Kramnik's wedding in a Russian Orthodox church in Paris. Both world champions had lived for a time in the French capital and, despite the great difference in their ages, had got to know and to appreciate each other. Vladimir describes Spassky as the first really modern universal player: "I like his clear all-embracing style." He can absolutely be compared to Paul Keres, though there was much more fantasy in Spassky.

Of course he also played very accurately, in which he was reminiscent of Smyslov. But unlike Smyslov, Spassky was an aggressive player. "Chess reflected his nature. In every game he played his very best. It is a pleasure to study his games. He used the whole chess board, the different areas, he put pressure on many things at different times and he did things at the right time," enthused Kramnik.

Kramnik had studied the match against Bobby Fischer very closely and was able to say that in principle Spassky had been an opponent of the same strength. Yet he had made blunders in almost every other game that he lost, and practically lost each of those games with a single move. Kramnik did not understand how that could have happened to him. Otherwise the match had been very level and in the second half Spassky had exerted strong pressure. In that phase Fischer had only been able to try to escape.

Kramnik: "It was one of the few world championship matches in which the final result did not reflect the true differences in strength." For varying reasons Spassky had not been able to show his true strength over a longer period in time. And he had the bad luck to be playing in the Fischer era. Apart from that, Vladimir considers Boris Spassky in his best years to have made a significant contribution to the development of the game of chess.

Robert James Fischer (9.3.1943-17.1.2008)

11th World Champion 1972-1975

The career of Robert James Fischer, known by all as "Bobby", was practically over once he won the world title. In the "match of the century" in Reykjavik, Iceland in 1972 he defeated Boris Spassky by a clear 12½–8½, despite giving up the whole point in the second game by not playing. After the match (Fischer was just 29 years old) he completely withdrew from competitive chess (with the exception of a rematch with Spassky in 1992 where no title was at stake). Nobody knows exactly why he no longer played. A pathological fear of defeat, caused by his possession of the world championship title, was the reason, according to many in the chess world. But that is mere speculation. The fact is that the world federation FIDE took away his title in 1975 when he did not play against the official challenger Anatoly Karpov.

Bobby became known to the chess-playing public through the "game of the century" against Donald Byrne. At the time he was just 13 years old. Only a year later, in 1958, he won the US championship. He took this title on each of the eight occasions he participated from then till 1967; in 1964 he even scored eleven wins from eleven games. In 1959 he qualified for the first time for the world championship Candidates tournament and was made a grandmaster, at that time the youngest in the history of chess.

Donald Byrne – Robert James Fischer

New York 1956

1.♘f3 ♘f6 2.c4 g6 3.♘c3 ♗g7 4.d4 0–0 5.♗f4 d5 6.♕b3 dxc4 7.♕xc4 c6 8.e4 ♘bd7 9.♖d1 ♘b6 10.♕c5 ♗g4 11.♗g5 ♘a4 12.♕a3 ♘xc3 13.bxc3 ♘xe4 14.♗xe7 ♕b6 15.♗c4 ♘xc3 16.♗c5 ♖fe8† 17.♔f1 ♗e6

18.♗xb6 ♗xc4† 19.♔g1 ♘e2† 20.♔f1 ♘xd4† 21.♔g1 ♘e2† 22.♔f1 ♘c3† 23.♔g1 axb6 24.♕b4 ♖a4 25.♕xb6 ♘xd1 26.h3 ♖xa2 27.♔h2 ♘xf2 28.♖e1 ♖xe1 29.♕d8† ♗f8 30.♘xe1 ♗d5 31.♘f3 ♘e4 32.♕b8 b5 33.h4 h5 34.♘e5 ♔g7 35.♔g1 ♗c5† 36.♔f1 ♘g3† 37.♔e1 ♗b4† 38.♔d1 ♗b3† 39.♔c1 ♘e2† 40.♔b1 ♘c3† 41.♔c1 ♖c2# 0–1

His path to the world championship title was a long one. Fischer kept on failing, partly because of circumstances which he was unable to influence. For example in Curaçao, where he accused the Soviet players of agreeing draws among themselves in order to help their chances. As it later turned out, he was correct. FIDE then changed the way of deciding a challenger and, instead of all-play-all tournaments, switched to matches. In 1967, though in the lead, he quit the interzonal tournament in Sousse after an argument with the organizers which could not be settled.

In the subsequent cycle of 1970 and 1971, his time had come. Fischer won the Interzonal tournament and in the Candidates matches outclassed Mark Taimanov 6–0, Bent Larsen 6–0, and ex-World Champion Tigran Petrosian by 6½–2½. Modern chess had never experienced such domination.

"This man was simply destined to become World Champion. His opponents were run over by him as though by a tank. His energy was incredible. At that point in time any other world champion in history would have been beaten by Fischer. And not because we were any weaker in terms of chess, but because at that point Fischer had the strength to break through any obstacle," is how Kramnik evaluates the situation.

At a certain moment in their careers, all outstanding players have a period when everything works perfectly. For Fischer this was during the world championship cycle of 1970 till 1972. In principle Kramnik sees his predecessor as a precursor of modern opening preparation. "This high-tension chess," according to Kramnik, "was then continued by Kasparov, who to a certain extent has been a follower of Fischer." It didn't matter whether it was positional or tactical play, Fischer was universal and set problems from the first move till the last one. Kramnik: "It is a pity that Fischer gave up chess so soon. The match with Anatoly Karpov would have been extremely interesting."

Anatoly Yevgenevich Karpov (23.5.1951-)
12th World Champion 1975-1985

On the 3rd of April 1975 Anatoly Karpov was declared World Chess Champion by decree of FIDE, without having to play a single game in the final. Until the very last minute, millions of chess fans hoped that Bobby Fischer might still turn up at the venue in Manila. Although almost all the American's demands had been met, he let a final ultimatum pass by. Thus Karpov became the only world chess champion to this day to be awarded this title, without a game played in the final. This stain gnawed at Karpov, who went on to become a very active world champion. He was inspired by the ambition to show the whole world that he was the best, and hardly any title holder played in as many tournaments as he did; he won most of them.

Karpov had a superb career, right from the start. In 1966 he became the youngest master in the Soviet Union, in 1967 European youth champion, in 1969 World Junior Champion and 1970 he was awarded the title of grandmaster. In 1978 and 1981 he defended his world championship in each case against his former compatriot Viktor Korchnoi. Particularly the first duel in Baguio City was extremely tense and stood on a razor edge. It was only by a win in Game 32 that Karpov secured a paper-thin success by 16½–15½. The second encounter ended clearly in his favour by 11–7.

The years from 1984 to 1990 were marked by his legendary matches against Garry Kasparov. Apart from their first encounter in 1984, which was stopped under mysterious circumstances without a winner by the then FIDE President Florencio Campomanes at a score of 5–3 for Karpov (won games only), in three of the following world championship matches he was the loser (one other ended in a draw). This appears to point to a clear superiority of Kasparov. The difference, however, was in reality anything but large. In terms of won games, in all the world championship games Kasparov was in front by a nose: 21–19.

Kramnik sees something mysterious in Karpov's style. He must know something about it, because in his childhood there was no other player he studied so intensively as the twelfth World Champion. Kramnik's first and for a long time his only chess book was a collection of Karpov's best games. Later they would meet each other frequently. Karpov is a universal player – a good tactician as well as a positional player. He calculates variations brilliantly and has another excellent quality: whenever he has acquired an advantage, he is able to hang on to it passively. His advantage then grows simply because of the activity of his opponent. Kramnik: "No player before or after Karpov has displayed such a characteristic. This component of his game has always amazed me and brought me pleasure. When it was apparently time to start the attack, Karpov would play a3, h3, and it was as if his opponent's position self-destructed."

Karpov is a natural player, in the truest sense of the word. Kramnik describes certain strategic failings as his only weakness. But he knows no other person who has such a marked combative attitude as Karpov: "He plays a game in which he is under pressure for six hours. It is difficult to break through his defence. And then his opponent relaxes just a little bit and the position becomes absolutely level. Anyone in Karpov's place would now be happy to have escaped this torture. Not Karpov, who immediately launches an attempt to play for a win himself." In his best days Anatoly Karpov was able to detach himself from the course a game had taken until then, and to completely change his own mood.

Garry Kimovich Kasparov (13.4.1963-)
13th World Champion 1985-2000

Garry Kasparov is one of the best chess players of all time. At the age of only 22 he became the youngest world champion in the history of chess. He was born in the Azerbaijani capital Baku as Garik Weinstein. His father died when he was only seven and some years later his mother Klara changed the surname Weinstein into the Russian form of her maiden name Gasparian. Klara was the central person in Garry's life.

Kasparov was exceptionally talented and was already receiving instruction at only 10 years old in the famous Botvinnik school in Moscow. He was far superior to pupils of his own age and early on he had the renowned Alexander Nikitin assigned to him as his main trainer. In his early years the outstanding characteristics of the future world champion could already be recognised: talent, strength of will, a powerful memory and irrepressible ambition. Nobody before or after him trained as hard as Kasparov. He was also the first to make optimal use of chess computers and was streets ahead of his rivals in opening preparation. Kasparov himself described his playing style as a mixture of Alekhine, Tal and Fischer.

In 1980 he became World Junior Champion in Dortmund and in the same year became a grandmaster. His unstoppable march to the throne began in 1982 with victory in the Interzonal tournament. In the subsequent Candidates matches he defeated Alexander Beliavsky by 6–3 and then in 1983 Viktor Korchnoi by 7–4. In the Candidates final he did not have much trouble against the 62-year old Smyslov and won by 8½–4½.

At the age of just 20, in 1984 he faced Karpov in the world championship final and got off to a catastrophic start: 0–4 after nine games. After a series of 17 draws Garry again lost in Game 27 for a score of 0–5. It seemed to be almost over, because the match was to be played till one contestant reached six wins. But then Kasparov gave a prime example of his strength of will – he simply did not want to lose anymore. In the subsequent 21 games he won three times and had 18 draws. After the 48th game the score may still have been 5–3 for Karpov, but the trend was in Garry's favour.

In this situation FIDE President Campomanes surprisingly stopped the match. Whether this happened to protect the health of the players is something we will probably never learn. The world championship ended without a result and was rescheduled for 1985. Kasparov won by 13–11 and in the subsequent 15 years successfully defended his title five times: three times against Karpov (1986, 1987, 1990) and in 1993 against Nigel Short and in 1995 against Viswanathan Anand. He lost the title of World Champion in 2000 in London by 6½–8½ to Vladimir Kramnik.

Kramnik can hardly find any weakness in his predecessor. He has displayed an incredible work ethic, even greater than Fischer's. He can be compared with Botvinnik for willpower, but exceeds the latter by far in flexibility. Kramnik: "His adaptability was actually Garry's plus point, which distinguished him from all other chess players. He absorbed all new developments, like a sponge, and in principle was able to alter his chess philosophy within six months." Karpov had taught Kasparov a lot in their duels. Previously Garry was far from having this strength. Kramnik: "All champions had their weak points. Kasparov had hardly any. He could do more or less everything."

Although at his best Garry Kasparov had hardly any weak points, it was possible to beat him, as Vladimir Kramnik proved impressively. To do so required special strategic and psychological abilities, which Vladimir successfully incorporated into his play against Garry. It was a particular form of chess empathy. To put in simple terms: Kramnik was able to read Kasparov! Vladimir possessed the ability to guess to a certain extent how his predecessor would act under specific conditions in a game of chess. Kasparov was for Kramnik both in chess and beyond it predictable, and that was enough.

Vladimir Kramnik (25.6.1975-)

14th world chess champion 2000-2007

Viswanathan Anand (11.12.1969-)

15th world chess champion 2007-2013

Viswanathan Anand, known to his friends as "Vishy", was born on the 11th of December 1969 in India, in Madras, nowadays called Chennai. In 2007 he became the uncontested world chess champion when in a tournament in Mexico City he took first place ahead of Vladimir Kramnik. He defended the title successfully three times in final matches against Vladimir Kramnik (2008), Veselin Topalov (2010) and Boris Gelfand (2012). Then in 2013 he lost the world championship match to the present titleholder Magnus Carlsen. In a repetition of their duel in 2014 he was clearly beaten by the young Norwegian.

"Anand has outstanding natural talent. His feeling for the game is really incredible. If you just take into account pure talent, I rate him as even stronger than, for example, Kasparov," said Vladimir Kramnik. What he lacked at the start was the old Soviet chess school, which normally took over in early childhood. Later Anand worked a lot with Russian trainers and grandmasters to complete his 'basic training'. But at the beginning he lived purely off his enormous talent, without having the foundations on which to build his own game in an ideal way.

Nevertheless, from his early years Anand was considered a contender for the world title. When, however, he was clearly defeated in 1995 in New York by Garry Kasparov, there followed years of stagnation. It was only at a more mature age that his greatest successes would follow. In his homeland Vishy is a superstar. Although cricket and hockey are the most popular sports there by a long chalk, he was chosen as India's "Sportsman of the Year" in 2007 after his triumph in Mexico. On the 8th of October 2014 there was even an asteroid named after him: Vishyanand.

In Kramnik's opinion, Anand has enormous intuition. Thanks to it, Anand at first got very far without the foundations of the Russian school and without great effort. As is the case with almost every world champion, Anand has a very special characteristic which is absolutely outstanding. It is the ability to conjure up counterplay. "Not only does he master it better than anyone else, but in this area he is unique," says Kramnik with admiration. Anand understands how to create counterplay even when there is absolutely no reason to believe it is there. "His position is terribly passive, you cannot see a hint of a possibility for activity, but a few moves later he starts some from nowhere. Somehow his pieces seem to stand up and get to work; it is really magical. I studied that in many games and the preparation for our world championship match: no other player in the history of chess had this characteristic."

Anand and Kramnik started to change the mood in the world of chess. Kramnik: "He became my successor and together we held the title for 13 years. In this period the atmosphere in professional chess changed. Previously there were always conflicts; it was full of intrigues. I tried to find a consensus for solving conflicts and unifying the world of chess. Vishy continued with that and we have changed a lot. Today's generation of players deal with each other in a quite different way, more respectfully and fairly. In the past that was not always the case. I am very happy about that and I believe that in this respect Anand and I have made a great contribution."

Magnus Carlsen (30.11.1990-)
16th world chess champion since 2013

Magnus Carlsen is a chess prodigy. In 2004, at the age of only 13 he gained the title of grandmaster. In January 2010, at the age of 19, he was the youngest player so far to reach the top of the world ranking list. In doing so he broke the 14-year-old record of Vladimir Kramnik from 1996. Since July 2011 Carlsen has continually occupied the top spot in the world ranking list.

Accordingly Magnus is an extremely successful tournament player. His greatest performance to date is considered to be the success in the super-tournament in Nanking in 2009. In his victory the 18-year old Norwegian outclassed most of the world's elite. He won the tournament with 8 points from ten games (six wins and four draws), which represents an Elo performance of 3002 – one of the most impressive tournament results of all time.

Magnus succeeded in his first serious shot at the world championship throne in 2013. The Candidates tournament took place in April in London and, equal on points, he won on tiebreak ahead of Vladimir Kramnik. He became the official challenger to Anand, whom he crushingly defeated in the latter's home town Chennai in November 2013. Only ten of the twelve games arranged had to be played as he won by 6½–3½. It was after 1921 (Lasker – Capablanca 5–9) and 2000 (Kasparov – Kramnik 6½–8½) only the third time in the history of chess that the title holder was unable to win a single game. In 2014 Carlsen defended his title against Anand and won by the similarly clear score of 6½–4½.

During his latest title defence in 2016 in New York, he found things more difficult against his challenger Sergei Karjakin (Russia) who is of the same age. In the eighth game Carlsen fell behind, and in Game 9 he was also on the verge of defeat. But Karjakin overlooked the winning continuation and missed the chance to decide the match. The Norwegian saved himself with a single victory in Game 10, later tying the twelve classical games with a score of 6–6; he finally decided the tiebreak in his favour by 3–1.

Vladimir Kramnik naturally considers Magnus Carlsen an outstanding player. However, Vladimir found it a little difficult to describe the latter's unique characteristics. Every world champion has developed with his style unmistakable and unique characteristics. Not so Magnus Carlsen. For Kramnik he represents an almost 100% copy of Karpov. Their chess styles are absolutely comparable, as is the energetic play which they both epitomize. Magnus has like Karpov – and perhaps in this respect even a little more – a pronounced capacity for concentration. In recent years his opening preparation has clearly improved. "At no point in the game does Carlsen ever let up in the least. This energy, paired with outstanding endgame technique, is the main reason which makes him superior at the moment," is how Vladimir describes the strength of the Norwegian.

And he continues: "It is impossible to estimate how long he will remain on the chess throne. At the moment I can hardly see anyone who can seriously constitute a danger to him. But if at some point he really comes under pressure, such as during our Candidates tournament in London in 2013 or in his last world championship match against Karjakin, things can change quickly. In my view he did not manage such a situation very well, at least in London."

But this is not unusual for a young player; with time one learns to cope with this pressure. But the future will have to show whether London 2013 and New York 2016 were in this respect exceptions and whether in future world championship duels he can overcome similar situations without coming to harm.

World Chess Champions

1st	1886-1894:	Wilhelm Steinitz
2nd	1894-1921:	Emanuel Lasker
3rd	1921-1927:	José Raúl Capablanca
4th	1927-1935, 1937-1946:	Alexander Alekhine
5th	1935-1937:	Machgielis Euwe
6th	1948-1957, 1958-1960, 1961-1963:	Mikhail Botvinnik
7th	1957-1958:	Vassily Smyslov
8th	1960-1961:	Mikhail Tal
9th	1963-1969:	Tigran Petrosian
10th	1969-1972:	Boris Spassky
11th	1972-1975:	Robert James Fischer
12th	1975-1985:	Anatoly Karpov
13th	1985-2000:	Garry Kasparov
14th	2000-2007:	Vladimir Kramnik
15th	2007-2013:	Viswanathan Anand
16th	since 2013:	Magnus Carlsen

World Chess Championships since 1886

1st World Championship: 1886
Wilhelm Steinitz – Johannes Zukertort 12½–7½
New York, St. Louis, New Orleans (USA)
Wilhelm Steinitz becomes 1st World Chess Champion.

2nd World Championship: 1889
Wilhelm Steinitz – Mikhail Chigorin 10½–6½
Havana (Cuba)

3rd World Championship: 1890
Wilhelm Steinitz – Isidor Gunsberg 10½–8½
New York (USA)

4th World Championship: 1892
Wilhelm Steinitz – Mikhail Chigorin 12½–10½
Havana (Cuba)

5th World Championship: 1894
Wilhelm Steinitz – Emanuel Lasker 7–12
New York, Philadelphia (USA), Montreal (Canada)
Emanuel Lasker becomes 2nd World Chess Champion.

6th World Championship: 1896/97
Emanuel Lasker – Wilhelm Steinitz 12½–4½
Moscow (Russia)

7th World Championship: 1907
Emanuel Lasker – Frank Marshall 11½–3½
New York, Philadelphia, Washington, Baltimore, Chicago, Memphis (USA)

8th World Championship: 1908
Emanuel Lasker – Siegbert Tarrasch 10½–5½
Düsseldorf, Munich (Germany)

9th World Championship: 1910
Emanuel Lasker – Carl Schlechter 5–5
(In the event of a draw the title holder retained the world championship.)
Vienna (Austro-Hungarian Empire), Berlin (Germany)

10th World Championship: 1910
Emanuel Lasker – Dawid Janowski 9½–1½
Berlin (Germany)

11th World Championship: 1921
Emanuel Lasker – José Raúl Capablanca 5–9
Havana (Cuba)
José Raúl Capablanca becomes 3rd World Chess Champion.

12th World Championship: 1927
José Raúl Capablanca – Alexander Alekhine 15½–18½
Buenos Aires (Argentina)
Alexander Alekhine becomes 4th World Chess Champion.

13th World Championship: 1929
Alexander Alekhine – Efim Bogoljubov 15½–9½
Wiesbaden, Heidelberg, Berlin (Germany), The Hague (Netherlands)

14th World Championship: 1934
Alexander Alekhine – Efim Bogoljubov 15½–10½
Baden-Baden, Villingen, Freiburg, Pforzheim, Stuttgart, Munich, Bayreuth, Bad Kissingen, Mannheim, Berlin (Germany)

15th World Championship: 1935
Alexander Alekhine – Max Euwe 14½–15½
Amsterdam, Delft, Rotterdam, Utrecht, Gouda, The Hague, Groningen, Baarn, 's-Hertogenbosch, Eindhoven, Zeist, Ermelo, Zandvoort (Netherlands)
Max Euwe becomes 5th World Chess Champion.

16th World Championship: 1937
The Hague, Rotterdam, Amsterdam, Leiden, Groningen, Zwolle, Eindhoven, Delft
Max Euwe – Alexander Alekhine 9½–15½
Alexander Alekhine wins back his title.

17th World Championship: 1948
Five round tournament with five participants
The Hague (Netherlands) and Moscow (USSR)
1st place: Mikhail Botvinnik (14 points)
2nd place: Vassily Smyslov (11 points)
3rd place: Paul Keres (10½ points)
Mikhail Botvinnik becomes 6th World Chess Champion.

18th World Championship: 1951
Mikhail Botvinnik – David Bronstein 12–12
(In the event of a draw the title holder retained the world championship.)
Moscow (USSR)

19th World Championship: 1954
Mikhail Botvinnik – Vassily Smyslov 12–12
(In the event of a draw the title holder retained the world championship.)
Moscow (USSR)

20th World Championship: 1957
Mikhail Botvinnik – Vassily Smyslov 9½–12½
Moscow (USSR)
Vassily Smyslov becomes 7th World Chess Champion.

21st World Championship: 1958
Vassily Smyslov – Mikhail Botvinnik 10½–12½
Moscow (USSR)
Mikhail Botvinnik regains his title.

22nd World Championship: 1960
Mikhail Botvinnik – Mikhail Tal 8½–12½
Moscow (USSR)
Mikhail Tal becomes 8th World Chess Champion.

23rd World Championship: 1961
Mikhail Tal – Mikhail Botvinnik 8–13
Moscow (USSR)
Mikhail Botvinnik regains his title for the second time.

24th World Championship: 1963
Mikhail Botvinnik – Tigran Petrosian 9½–12½
Moscow (USSR)
Tigran Petrosian becomes 9th World Chess Champion.

25th World Championship: 1966
Tigran Petrosian – Boris Spassky 12½–11½
Moscow (USSR)

26th World Championship: 1969
Tigran Petrosian – Boris Spassky 10½–12½
Moscow (USSR)
Boris Spassky becomes 10th World Chess Champion.

27th World Championship: 1972
Boris Spassky – Robert James Fischer 8½–12½
Reykjavík (Iceland)
Robert James Fischer becomes 11th World Chess Champion.

28th World Championship: 1975
Robert James Fischer – Anatoly Karpov: Fischer did not appear.
Manila (Philippines)
Anatoly Karpov becomes 12th World Chess Champion by walkover.

29th World Championship: 1978
Anatoly Karpov – Viktor Korchnoi 16½–15½
Baguio City (Philippines)

30th World Championship: 1981
Anatoly Karpov – Viktor Korchnoi 11–7
Merano (Italy)

31st World Championship: 1984
Anatoly Karpov – Garry Kasparov 25–23
Moscow (USSR)
The match was ended without a winner.

32nd World Championship: 1985
Anatoly Karpov – Garry Kasparov 11–13
Moscow (USSR)
Garry Kasparov becomes 13th World Chess Champion.

33rd World Championship: 1986
Garry Kasparov – Anatoly Karpov 12½–11½
London (UK), Leningrad (USSR)

34th World Championship: 1987
Garry Kasparov – Anatoly Karpov 12–12
(In the event of a draw the title holder retained the world championship.)
Seville (Spain)

35th World Championship: 1990
Garry Kasparov – Anatoly Karpov 12½–11½
New York (USA), Lyon (France)

36th World Championship: 1993
Garry Kasparov – Nigel Short 12½–8½
London (UK)

37th World Championship: 1995
Garry Kasparov – Viswanathan Anand 10½–7½
New York (USA)

38th World Championship: 2000
Garry Kasparov – Vladimir Kramnik 6½–8½
London (UK)
Vladimir Kramnik becomes 14th World Chess Champion.

39th World Championship: 2004
Vladimir Kramnik – Peter Leko 7–7
(In the event of a draw the title holder retained the world championship.)
Brissago (Switzerland)

40th World Championship: 2006
Vladimir Kramnik – Veselin Topalov 8½–7½ (FIDE); 8½–6½ (Kramnik)
Elista (Russia)
Slated for twelve games. In the event of a draw extra games were to be played with shortened thinking time.
6–6 under protest (according to FIDE), 6–5 (according to Kramnik); Tiebreak: Kramnik wins by 2½–1½.
Vladimir Kramnik remains World Champion.

41st World Championship 2007
All-play-all with eight participants
Mexico City (Mexico)
1st place: Viswanathan Anand (9 points)
2nd place: Vladimir Kramnik (8 points)
3rd place: Boris Gelfand (8 points)
Viswanathan Anand becomes 15th World Chess Champion.

42nd World Championship: 2008
Viswanathan Anand – Vladimir Kramnik 6½–4½
Bonn (Germany)

43rd World Championship 2010
Viswanathan Anand – Veselin Topalov 6½–5½
Sofia (Bulgaria)

44th World Championship 2012
Viswanathan Anand – Boris Gelfand
Moscow (Russia)
Slated for twelve games. In the event of a tie, extra games were to be played with shorter time controls.
6–6 classical; Tiebreak: Anand wins by 2½–1½.
Viswanathan Anand remains World Champion.

45th World Championship 2013
Viswanathan Anand – Magnus Carlsen 3½–6½
Chennai (India)
Magnus Carlsen becomes 16th World Chess Champion.

46th World Championship 2014
Magnus Carlsen – Viswanathan Anand 6½–4½
Sochi (Russia)

47th World Championship 2016
Magnus Carlsen – Sergei Karjakin
New York (USA)
Slated for twelve games. In the event of a tie, extra games were to be played with shorter time controls.
6–6 Classical; Tiebreak: Carlsen wins by 3–1.
Magnus Carlsen remains World Champion.

48th World Championship 2018
Magnus Carlsen – Fabiano Caruana
London (UK)
The match is played right after the publication of this book...

The World Championship Games of Vladimir Kramnik

Listed below are the moves of all the world championship games which Vladimir Kramnik played between 2000 and 2008: a total of 69. At this highest level of all he had 47 draws, won 13 games and lost nine. His rating performance in these games was around 2815 Elo. A mighty playing strength which marks Kramnik as one of the best players of all time. He won the title of World Chess Champion in 2000 against Garry Kasparov and lost it seven years later in an all-play-all tournament in Mexico City.

London, UK 2000: **Garry Kasparov – Vladimir Kramnik** 6½–8½

Garry Kasparov (2849) – Vladimir Kramnik (2770)

World Championship London (1) 08.10.2000

1.e4 e5 2.♘f3 ♘c6 3.♗b5 ♘f6 4.0–0 ♘xe4 5.d4 ♘d6 6.♗xc6 dxc6 7.dxe5 ♘f5 8.♕xd8† ♔xd8 9.♘c3 ♗d7 10.b3 h6 11.♗b2 ♔c8 12.h3 b6 13.♖ad1 ♘e7 14.♘e2 ♘g6 15.♘e1 h5 16.♘d3 c5 17.c4 a5 18.a4 h4 19.♘c3 ♗e6 20.♘d5 ♔b7 21.♘e3 ♖h5 22.♗c3 ♖e8 23.♖d2 ♔c8 24.f4 ♘e7 25.♘f2 ♘f5 ½–½

Vladimir Kramnik (2770) – Garry Kasparov (2849)

World Championship London (2) 10.10.2000

1.d4 ♘f6 2.c4 g6 3.♘c3 d5 4.cxd5 ♘xd5 5.e4 ♘xc3 6.bxc3 ♗g7 7.♘f3 c5 8.♗e3 ♕a5 9.♕d2 ♗g4 10.♖b1 a6 11.♖xb7 ♗xf3 12.gxf3 ♘c6 13.♗c4 0–0 14.0–0 cxd4 15.cxd4 ♗xd4 16.♗d5 ♗c3 17.♕c1 ♘d4 18.♗xd4 ♗xd4 19.♖xe7 ♖a7 20.♖xa7 ♗xa7 21.f4 ♕d8 22.♕c3 ♖b8 23.♕f3 ♕h4 24.e5 g5 25.♖e1 ♕xf4 26.♕xf4 gxf4 27.e6 fxe6 28.♖xe6 ♔g7 29.♖xa6 ♖f5 30.♗e4 ♖e5 31.f3 ♖e7 32.a4 ♖a7 33.♖b6 ♗e5 34.♖b4 ♖d7 35.♔g2 ♖d2† 36.♔h3 h5 37.♖b5 ♔f6 38.a5 ♖a2 39.♖b6† ♔e7 40.♗d5 1–0

Garry Kasparov (2849) – Vladimir Kramnik (2770)

World Championship London (3) 12.10.2000

1.e4 e5 2.♘f3 ♘c6 3.♗b5 ♘f6 4.0–0 ♘xe4 5.d4 ♘d6 6.♗xc6 dxc6 7.dxe5 ♘f5
8.♕xd8† ♔xd8 9.♘c3 ♗d7 10.b3 h6 11.♗b2 ♔c8 12.♖ad1 b6 13.♘e2 c5 14.c4
♗c6 15.♘f4 ♔b7 16.♘d5 ♘e7 17.♖fe1 ♖g8 18.♘f4 g5 19.♘h5 ♖g6 20.♘f6
♗g7 21.♖d3 ♗xf3 22.♖xf3 ♗xf6 23.exf6 ♘c6 24.♖d3 ♖f8 25.♖e4 ♔c8 26.f4 gxf4
27.♖xf4 ♖e8 28.♗c3 ♖e2 29.♖f2 ♖e4 30.♖h3 a5 31.♖h5 a4 32.bxa4 ♖xc4 33.♗d2
♖xa4 34.♖xh6 ♖g8 35.♖h7 ♖xa2 36.♖xf7 ♘e5 37.♖g7 ♖f8 38.h3 c4 39.♖e7 ♘d3
40.f7 ♘xf2 41.♖e8† ♔d7 42.♖xf8 ♘e7 43.♖c8 ♔xf7 44.♖xc7† ♔e6 45.♗e3 ♘d1
46.♗xb6 c3 47.h4 ♖a6 48.♗d4 ♖a4 49.♗xc3 ♘xc3 50.♖xc3 ♖xh4 51.♖f3 ♖h5
52.♔f2 ♖g5 53.♖f8 ♔e5 ½–½

Vladimir Kramnik (2770) – Garry Kasparov (2849)

World Championship London (4) 14.10.2000

1.d4 d5 2.c4 dxc4 3.♘f3 e6 4.e3 c5 5.♗xc4 a6 6.0–0 ♘f6 7.dxc5 ♕xd1 8.♖xd1
♗xc5 9.♘bd2 ♘bd7 10.♗e2 b6 11.♘b3 ♗e7 12.♘fd4 ♗b7 13.f3! 0–0 14.e4 ♖fc8
15.♗e3 ♔f8 16.♘d2 ♘e5 17.♘4b3 ♖c6 18.♖ac1 ♖ac8 19.♖xc6 ♖xc6 20.g4 h6
21.h4 ♗c8! 22.g5 hxg5 23.hxg5 ♘fd7 24.f4 ♘g6 25.♘f3 ♖c2 26.♗xa6 ♗xa6
27.♖xd7 ♖xb2 28.♖a7 ♗b5 29.f5 exf5 30.exf5 ♖e2 31.♘fd4 ♖e1† 32.♔f2 ♖f1†
33.♔g2 ♘h4† 34.♔h3 ♖h1† 35.♔g4 ♗e8 36.♗f2 ♘g2 37.♖a8 ♖f1 38.♔f3 ♘h4†
39.♔e2 ♖h1 40.♘b5 ♗xg5 41.♘c7 ♔e7 42.♘xe8 ♘xf5 43.♗xb6 ♔d7! 44.a4 ♖h3
45.♘c5† ♔c6 46.a5 ♖e3† 47.♔d1 ♖e7? 48.♖c8† ♔b5 49.♘e4?! ♖xe4 50.♖c5†
♔a6 51.♘c7† ♔b7 52.♖xf5 ♗e3! 53.♗xe3 ♖xe3 54.♖xf7 ♖e5! 55.a6†? ♔b6
56.♖xg7 ♖a5 57.♔d2 ♖a1 58.♔c2 ♖h1? 59.♔b2? ♖h8! 60.♔b3 ♖c8 61.a7 ♔xa7
62.♔b4 ♔b6 63.♘d5† ♔a6 64.♖g6† ♔b7 65.♔b5 ♖c1 66.♖g2 ♔c8 67.♖g7 ♔d8
68.♘f6 ♖c7 69.♖g5 ♖f7 70.♘d5 ♔d7 71.♖g6 ♖f1 72.♔c5 ♖c1† 73.♔d4 ♖d1†
74.♔e5 ½–½

Garry Kasparov (2849) – Vladimir Kramnik (2770)

World Championship London (5) 15.10.2000

1.c4 c5 2.♘f3 ♘f6 3.g3 d5 4.cxd5 ♘xd5 5.♗g2 ♘c6 6.♘c3 g6 7.0–0 ♗g7 8.♕a4
♘b6 9.♕b5 ♘d7 10.d3 0–0 11.♗e3 ♘d4 12.♗xd4 cxd4 13.♘e4 ♕b6 14.a4 a6
15.♕xb6 ♘xb6 16.a5 ♘d5 17.♘c5 ♖d8 18.♘d2 ♖b8 19.♘c4 e6 20.♖fc1 ♗h6
21.♖cb1 ♗f8 22.♘b3 ♗g7 23.♗xd5 ♖xd5 24.♘bd2 e5 ½–½

222

Vladimir Kramnik (2770) – Garry Kasparov (2849)

World Championship London (6) 17.10.2000

1.d4 d5 2.c4 dxc4 3.♘f3 e6 4.e3 c5 5.♗xc4 a6 6.0–0 ♘f6 7.a4 ♘c6 8.♕e2 cxd4 9.♖d1 ♗e7 10.exd4 0–0 11.♘c3 ♘d5 12.♗b3 ♖e8 13.h4 ♘cb4 14.h5 b6 15.♘e5 ♗b7 16.a5 b5 17.h6 g6 18.♘e4 ♘c7 19.♘c5 ♗d5 20.♖a3 ♘c6 21.♗xd5 ♕xd5 22.♘cd7 ♖ad8 23.♘xc6 ♖xd7 24.♘xe7† ♖exe7 25.♖c3 f6 26.♗e3 ♔f7 27.♖dc1 ♕b7 28.♖c5 ♘d5 29.♕f3 ♘b4 30.♕e2 ♖c7 31.♗f4 ♖xc5 32.dxc5 e5 33.♕d2 ♘c6 34.♕d5† ♔f8 35.♗e3 ♕d7 36.♕f3 ♔f7 37.♖d1 e4 38.♕e2 ♕f5 39.♖d6 ♖e6 40.♖d7† ♖e7 41.♖d6 ♖e6 42.♕d1 g5 43.♕h5† ♔e7 44.♕d1 ♔f7 45.♖d7† ♔g6 46.♖g7† ♔xh6 47.♕d7 ♖e5 48.♕f7 ♖d5 49.♔h1 ♘d8 50.♖xh7† ♕xh7 51.♕xd5 ♔g6† 52.♔g1 ♕c7 53.♕g8† ♔f5 54.♕d5† ♔g6 55.♕xe4† ♔g7 56.♕a8 ♕d7 57.♔h2 ♕d3 58.g3 ♘f7 59.♕b7 ♔g6 60.♕xa6 ♘e5 61.♕a8 ♘g4† 62.♔h3 ♕f5! 63.♕g8† ♔h6 64.♕h8† ♔g6 65.♕e8† ♔h6 66.♕h8† ½–½

Garry Kasparov (2849) – Vladimir Kramnik (2770)

World Championship London (7) 19.10.2000

1.c4 c5 2.♘f3 ♘f6 3.d4 cxd4 4.♘xd4 a6 5.♘c3 e6 6.g3 ♕c7 7.♕d3 ♘c6 8.♘xc6 dxc6 9.♗g2 e5 10.0–0 ♗e6 11.♘a4 ½–½

Vladimir Kramnik (2770) – Garry Kasparov (2849)

World Championship London (8) 21.10.2000

1.d4 ♘f6 2.c4 e6 3.♘c3 ♗b4 4.♕c2 0–0 5.a3 ♗xc3† 6.♕xc3 b6 7.♗g5 ♗b7 8.f3 h6 9.♗h4 d5 10.e3 ♘bd7 11.cxd5 ♘xd5 12.♗xd8 ♘xc3 13.♗h4 ♘d5 14.♗f2 c5 15.♗b5 ♖fd8 16.e4 ♘c7 17.♗xd7 ♖xd7 18.dxc5 f5 19.cxb6 axb6 20.♘e2 fxe4 21.fxe4 ♗xe4 22.0–0 ♖d2 23.♘c3 ♗b7 24.b4 ♖f8 25.♖a2 ♖xa2 26.♘xa2 ♘d5 27.♗d4 ♖a8 28.♘c3 ♘xc3 29.♗xc3 ♖xa3 30.♗d4 b5 31.♖f4 ♖d3 32.♖g4 g5 33.h4 ♔f7 34.hxg5 hxg5 35.♔f2 ♖d2† 36.♔e3 ♖xg2 37.♖xg2 ♗xg2 38.♗e5 ½–½

Garry Kasparov (2849) – Vladimir Kramnik (2770)

World Championship London (9) 22.10.2000

1.e4 e5 2.♘f3 ♘c6 3.♗b5 ♘f6 4.0–0 ♘xe4 5.d4 ♘d6 6.♗xc6 dxc6 7.dxe5 ♘f5 8.♕xd8† ♔xd8 9.♘c3 h6 10.♖d1† ♔e8 11.h3 a5 12.♗f4 ♗e6 13.g4 ♘e7 14.♘d4 ♘d5 15.♘ce2 ♗c5 16.♘xe6 fxe6 17.c4 ♘b6 18.b3 a4 19.♗d2 ♔f7 20.♗c3 ♖hd8 21.♖xd8 ♖xd8 22.♔g2 ♖d3 23.♖c1 g5 24.♖c2 axb3 25.axb3 ♘d7 26.♖a2 ♗e7

27.♖a7 ♘c5 28.f3 ♘xb3 29.♖xb7 ♘c1 30.♘xc1 ♖xc3 31.♘e2 ♖c2 32.♔f1 ♖xc4 33.♖xc7 ½–½

Vladimir Kramnik (2770) – Garry Kasparov (2849)

World Championship London (10) 24.10.2000

1.d4 ♘f6 2.c4 e6 3.♘c3 ♗b4 4.e3 0–0 5.♗d3 d5 6.♘f3 c5 7.0–0 cxd4 8.exd4 dxc4 9.♗xc4 b6 10.♗g5 ♗b7 11.♖e1 ♘bd7 12.♖c1 ♖c8 13.♕b3 ♗e7 14.♗xf6 ♘xf6 15.♗xe6 fxe6 16.♕xe6† ♔h8 17.♕xe7 ♗xf3 18.gxf3 ♕xd4 19.♘b5 ♕xb2 20.♖xc8 ♖xc8 21.♘d6 ♖b8 22.♘f7† ♔g8 23.♕e6 ♖f8 24.♘d8† ♔h8 25.♕e7 1–0

Garry Kasparov (2849) – Vladimir Kramnik (2770)

World Championship London (11) 26.10.2000

1.e4 e5 2.♘f3 ♘c6 3.♗b5 a6 4.♗a4 ♘f6 5.0–0 b5 6.♗b3 ♗c5 7.a4 ♗b7 8.d3 0–0 9.♘c3 ♘a5 10.axb5 ♘xb3 11.cxb3 axb5 12.♖xa8 ♗xa8 13.♘xe5 d5 14.♗g5 dxe4 15.dxe4 ♕xd1 16.♖xd1 b4 17.♗xf6 bxc3 18.bxc3 gxf6 19.♘d7 ♗d6 20.♘xf8 ♔xf8 21.f3 h5 22.h4 ♔e7 23.♔f2 ♗b7 24.c4 ♗e5 25.♖d2 ♗c8 26.♖d5 ♗e6 27.♖a5 c5 28.♔e3 ♗d4† 29.♔d3 f5 30.b4 fxe4† 31.♔xe4 ♗f2 32.bxc5 ♗xh4 33.c6 ♗d6 34.♖xh5 ♗f2 35.g4 ♔xc6 36.♖h2 ♗c5 37.♖c2 f6 38.♖h2 ♗xc4 39.♖h6 ♗d5† 40.♔f5 ♗xf3 41.g5 ♔d5 ½–½

Vladimir Kramnik (2770) – Garry Kasparov (2849)

World Championship London (12) 28.10.2000

1.d4 ♘f6 2.c4 e6 3.♘c3 ♗b4 4.e3 0–0 5.♗d3 d5 6.♘f3 c5 7.0–0 dxc4 8.♗xc4 ♘bd7 9.a3 cxd4 10.axb4 dxc3 11.bxc3 ♕c7 12.♗e2 ♕xc3 13.♗a3 ♘d5 14.♕b1 ♕f6 15.♗d3 h6 16.b5 ♖d8 17.♗b2 ♕e7 18.♖a4 ♘c5 19.♗h7† ♔h8 20.♖h4 f6 21.♖c4 ♗d7 22.♗a3 b6 23.♗e4 a6 24.bxa6 ♖xa6 25.♗xc5 bxc5 26.♖fc1 ♖a5 27.♕b2 ♖b5 28.♕a3 ♘b6 29.♖4c3 ♖b4 30.♘d2 f5 31.♗f3 ♘a4 32.♖xc5 ♖b2 33.♘c4 ♕xc5 ½–½

Garry Kasparov (2849) – Vladimir Kramnik (2770)

World Championship London (13) 29.10.2000

1.e4 e5 2.♘f3 ♘c6 3.♗b5 ♘f6 4.0–0 ♘xe4 5.d4 ♘d6 6.♗xc6 dxc6 7.dxe5 ♘f5 8.♕xd8† ♔xd8 9.♘c3 h6 10.h3 ♔e8 11.♘e4 c5 12.c3 b6 13.♖e1 ♗e6 14.g4 ½–½

Vladimir Kramnik (2770) – Garry Kasparov (2849)

World Championship London (14) 31.10.2000

1.♘f3 ♘f6 2.c4 b6 3.g3 c5 4.♗g2 ♗b7 5.0–0 g6 6.♘c3 ♗g7 7.d4 cxd4 8.♕xd4 d6 9.♖d1 ♘bd7 10.♗e3 ♖c8 11.♖ac1 0–0 12.♕h4 a6 13.♘e1 ♗xg2 14.♘xg2 ♖e8 15.b3 ♕c7 16.♗g5 ♕b7 17.♘e3 b5 18.♘ed5 bxc4 19.bxc4 h5 20.♕f4 ♕c6 21.♗xf6 ♘xf6 22.♘xf6† ♗xf6 23.♘d5 ♗b2 24.♖b1 ♗g7 25.♕g5 ♔f8 26.♖dc1 e6 27.♘f6 ♖ed8 28.h4 ♕a8 29.c5 ♖xc5 30.♖xc5 ♗xf6 31.♕xf6 dxc5 32.♔h2 ♔g8 33.♖b6 ♖e8 34.♕f3 ♕xf3 35.exf3 ♖c8 36.♖xa6 c4 37.♖d6 c3 38.♖d1 ♖a8 39.♖c1 ♖xa2 40.♖xc3 ♖xf2† 41.♔g1 ♖a2 42.♖c7 ♔f8 43.♖b7 ♔e8 44.♖b8† ♔e7 45.♖b7† ♔f6 46.♔f1 e5 47.♖b6† ♔f5 48.♖b7 ♔e6 49.♖b6† ♔f5 50.♖b7 f6 51.♖g7 g5 52.hxg5 fxg5 53.♖g8 g4 54.♖f8† ♔e6 55.♖e8† ♔f5 56.♖f8† ♔g6 57.♖g8† ♔f5 ½–½

Garry Kasparov (2849) – Vladimir Kramnik (2770)

World Championship London (15) 02.11.2000

1.d4 ♘f6 2.c4 e6 3.g3 d5 4.♗g2 ♗e7 5.♘f3 0–0 6.0–0 dxc4 7.♕c2 a6 8.♕xc4 b5 9.♕c2 ♗b7 10.♗d2 ♗e4 11.♕c1 ♗b7 12.♗f4 ♗d6 13.♘bd2 ♘bd7 14.♘b3 ♗d5 15.♖d1 ♕e7 16.♘e5 ♗xg2 17.♔xg2 ♘d5 18.♘c6 ♘xf4† 19.♕xf4 ♕e8 20.♕f3 e5 21.dxe5 ♘xe5 22.♘xe5 ♕xe5 23.♖d2 ♖ae8 24.e3 ♖e6 25.♖ad1 ♖f6 26.♕d5 ♕e8 27.♖c1 g6 28.♖dc2 h5 29.♘d2 ♖f5 30.♕e4 c5 31.♕xe8 ♖xe8 32.e4 ♖fe5 33.f4 ♖5e6 34.e5 ♗e7 35.b3 f6 36.♘f3 fxe5 37.♘xe5 ♖d8 38.h4 ♖d5 ½–½

Brissago, Switzerland 2004: **Vladimir Kramnik – Peter Leko** 7–7

Peter Leko (2741) – Vladimir Kramnik (2770)

World Championship Brissago (1) 25.09.2004

1.e4 e5 2.♘f3 ♘f6 3.♘xe5 d6 4.♘f3 ♘xe4 5.d4 d5 6.♗d3 ♘c6 7.0–0 ♗e7 8.c4 ♘b4 9.♗e2 0–0 10.♘c3 ♗f5 11.a3 ♘xc3 12.bxc3 ♘c6 13.♖e1 ♖e8 14.cxd5 ♕xd5 15.♗f4 ♖ac8 16.h3 ♗e4 17.♗e3 ♘a5 18.c4 ♘xc4 19.♗xc4 ♕xc4 20.♘d2 ♕d5 21.♘xe4 ♕xe4 22.♗g5 ♕xe1† 23.♕xe1 ♗xg5 24.♕a5 ♗f6 25.♕xa7 c5 26.♕xb7 ♗xd4 27.♖a2 c4 28.♖e2 ♖ed8 29.a4 c3 30.♕e4 ♗b6 31.♕c2 g6 32.♕b3 ♖d6 33.♖c2 ♗a5 34.g4 ♖d2 35.♔g2 ♖cd8 36.♖xc3 ♗xc3 37.♕xc3 ♖2d5 38.♕c6 ♖a5 39.♔g3 ♖da8 40.h4 ♖5a6 41.♕c1 ♖a5 42.♕h6 ♖xa4 43.h5 ♖4a5 44.♕f4 g5 45.♕f6 h6 46.f3 ♖5a6 47.♕c3 ♖a4 48.♕c6 ♖8a6 49.♕e8† ♔g7 50.♕b5 ♖4a5 51.♕b4 ♖d5 52.♕b3 ♖ad6 53.♕c4 ♖d3 54.♔f2 ♖a3 55.♕c5 ♖a2† 56.♔g3 ♖f6 57.♕b4 ♖aa6 58.♔g2 ♖f4 59.♕b2† ♖af6 60.♕e5 ♖xf3 61.♕a1 ♖f1 62.♕c3 ♖1f2† 63.♔g3 ♖2f3† 64.♕xf3 ♖xf3† 65.♔xf3 ♔f6 0–1

Vladimir Kramnik (2770) – Peter Leko (2741)

World Championship Brissago (2) 26.09.2004

1.e4 e5 2.♘f3 ♘c6 3.♗b5 a6 4.♗a4 ♘f6 5.0–0 ♗e7 6.♖e1 b5 7.♗b3 0–0 8.h3 ♗b7 9.d3 ♖e8 10.♘c3 ♗b4 11.♘g5 ♖f8 12.a3 ♗xc3 13.bxc3 ♘a5 14.♗a2 c5 15.f4 exf4 16.e5 ♘d5 17.♗xd5 ♕xg5 18.♗xb7 ½–½

Peter Leko (2741) – Vladimir Kramnik (2770)

World Championship Brissago (3) 28.09.2004

1.e4 e5 2.♘f3 ♘f6 3.♘xe5 d6 4.♘f3 ♘xe4 5.d4 d5 6.♗d3 ♘c6 7.0–0 ♗e7 8.c4 ♘b4 9.♗e2 0–0 10.♘c3 ♗f5 11.a3 ♘xc3 12.bxc3 ♘c6 13.♖e1 ♖e8 14.cxd5 ♕xd5 15.♗f4 ♖ac8 16.c4 ♕e4 17.♗e3 ♕c2 18.d5 ♘a5 19.♘d4 ♕xd1 20.♖exd1 ♗d7 21.♗d2 ♗f6 22.♗xa5 ♗xd4 23.♖xd4 ♖xe2 ½–½

Vladimir Kramnik (2770) – Peter Leko (2741)

World Championship Brissago (4) 30.09.2004

1.e4 e5 2.♘f3 ♘c6 3.♗b5 a6 4.♗a4 ♘f6 5.0–0 ♗e7 6.♖e1 b5 7.♗b3 0–0 8.h3 ♗b7 9.d3 d6 10.a3 ♘d7 11.♘c3 ♘d4 12.♗a2 ♘xf3† 13.♕xf3 ♗g5 14.♗xg5 ♕xg5 15.♘d5 c6 16.♘e3 g6 17.♖ad1 ♖ad8 18.c3 c5 19.♗d5 ♗c8 20.b4 ♘b6 21.c4 ♘xd5 22.♘xd5 ♗e6 23.bxc5 dxc5 24.♖b1 ♖b8 25.cxb5 ♗xd5 26.exd5 axb5 27.d6 b4 28.a4 ♖fd8 29.♕d5 ♕f6 30.♕xc5 ♕xd6 31.♕xd6 ♖xd6 32.♖xe5 b3 33.♖b5 ♖a8 34.♖1xb3 ♖xa4 35.♖b6 ♖d7 36.♖f6 ♖a1† 37.♔h2 ♖d1 38.♖f3 h5 39.h4 ♖d2 40.g3 ♔g7 41.♔g2 ♖d1 42.♖e3 ♔h7 43.♔f3 ♖d2 ½–½

Peter Leko (2741) – Vladimir Kramnik (2770)

World Championship Brissago (5) 02.10.2004

1.d4 ♘f6 2.c4 e6 3.♘f3 d5 4.♘c3 ♗e7 5.♗f4 0–0 6.e3 c5 7.dxc5 ♗xc5 8.cxd5 ♘xd5 9.♘xd5 exd5 10.a3 ♘c6 11.♗d3 ♗b6 12.0–0 ♗g4 13.h3 ♗h5 14.b4 ♖e8 15.♖c1 a6 16.♗xa6 ♖xa6 17.b5 ♖xa3 18.bxc6 bxc6 19.♖xc6 ♖a7 20.♖d6 ♖d7 21.♕xd5 ♖xd6 22.♕xd6 ♕xd6 23.♗xd6 ♗xf3 24.gxf3 ♖d8 25.♖b1 ♗f6 26.♔g2 g6 27.f4 ♔g7 28.♖b7 ♖e6 29.♖d7 ♖e8 30.♖a7 ♖e6 31.♗c5 ♖c6 32.♖a5 ♗c3 33.♖b5 ♖a6 34.♖b3 ♗f6 35.♖b8 h5 36.♖b5 ♗c3 37.♖b3 ♗f6 38.e4 ♖a5 39.♗e3 ♖a4 40.e5 ♗e7 41.♖b7 ♔f8 42.♖b8† ♔g7 43.♔f3 ♖c4 44.♔e2 ♖a4 45.♔d3 ♗h4 46.♗d4 ♖a3† 47.♔c2 ♖a2† 48.♔d3 ♖a3† 49.♔c4 ♖a4† 50.♔d5 ♖a5† 51.♔c6 ♖a4 52.♔c5 ♗e7† 53.♔d5 ♖a5† 54.♔e4 ♖a4 55.♖c8 ♗h4 56.e6† ♗f6 57.e7 ♖xd4† 58.♔e3 ♗xe7 59.♔xd4 ♗h4 60.f3 f5 61.♖c7† ♗f6 62.♔d5 ♗g3 63.♖c6† ♔g7 64.♔e5 h4 65.♖c7† ♔h6 66.♖c4 ♔g7 67.♔e6 ♗h2 68.♖c7† ♔h6 69.♔f7 1–0

Vladimir Kramnik (2770) – Peter Leko (2741)

World Championship Brissago (6) 03.10.2004

1.e4 e5 2.♘f3 ♘c6 3.♗b5 a6 4.♗a4 ♘f6 5.0–0 ♗e7 6.♖e1 b5 7.♗b3 0–0 8.h3 ♗b7 9.d3 d6 10.a3 ♘a5 11.♗a2 c5 12.♘bd2 ♘c6 13.c3 ♕d7 14.♘f1 d5 15.♗g5 dxe4 16.dxe4 c4 17.♘e3 ♖fd8 18.♘f5 ♕e6 19.♕e2 ♗f8 20.♗b1 h6 ½–½

Peter Leko (2741) – Vladimir Kramnik (2770)

World Championship Brissago (7) 05.10.2004

1.d4 d5 2.c4 c6 3.♘c3 ♘f6 4.♘f3 dxc4 5.a4 e6 6.e3 c5 7.♗xc4 ♘c6 8.0–0 cxd4 9.exd4 ♗e7 10.♗e3 0–0 11.♘e5 ♘b4 12.a5 ♗d7 13.d5 exd5 14.♘xd5 ♘bxd5 15.♗xd5 ♘xd5 16.♕xd5 ♗c8 17.♖fd1 ♕xd5 18.♖xd5 ♗e6 19.♖b5 ♗f6 20.♘f3 b6 21.axb6 ½–½

Vladimir Kramnik (2770) – Peter Leko (2741)

World Championship Brissago (8) 07.10.2004

1.e4 e5 2.♘f3 ♘c6 3.♗b5 a6 4.♗a4 ♘f6 5.0–0 ♗e7 6.♖e1 b5 7.♗b3 0–0 8.c3 d5 9.exd5 ♘xd5 10.♘xe5 ♘xe5 11.♖xe5 c6 12.d4 ♗d6 13.♖e1 ♕h4 14.g3 ♕h3 15.♖e4 g5 16.♕f1 ♕h5 17.♘d2 ♗f5 18.f3 ♘f6 19.♖e1 ♖ae8 20.♖xe8 ♖xe8 21.a4 ♕g6 22.axb5 ♗d3 23.♕f2 ♖e2 24.♕xe2 ♗xe2 25.bxa6 ♕d3 26.♔f2 ♗xf3 27.♘xf3 ♘e4† 28.♔e1 ♘xc3 29.bxc3 ♕xc3† 30.♔f2 ♕xa1 31.a7 h6 32.h4 g4 0–1

Peter Leko (2741) – Vladimir Kramnik (2770)

World Championship Brissago (9) 09.10.2004

1.d4 ♘f6 2.c4 e6 3.♘f3 b6 4.g3 ♗a6 5.b3 ♗b4† 6.♗d2 ♗e7 7.♘c3 ♗b7 8.♗g2 d5 9.cxd5 exd5 10.0–0 0–0 11.♗f4 ♘a6 12.♕c2 ♖e8 13.♖fd1 c6 14.♘e5 h6 15.a3 ♘c7 16.e4 ♘e6 ½–½

Vladimir Kramnik (2770) – Peter Leko (2741)

World Championship Brissago (10) 10.10.2004

1.e4 e5 2.♘f3 ♘c6 3.♗b5 a6 4.♗a4 ♘f6 5.0–0 ♗c5 6.c3 b5 7.♗c2 d5 8.exd5 ♕xd5 9.a4 b4 10.d4 exd4 11.♗b3 ♕d8 12.♖e1† ♗e7 13.♘xd4 ♘xd4 14.♕xd4 ♕xd4 15.cxd4 ♗b7 16.♗g5 h6 17.♗xf6 gxf6 18.♘d2 ♖g8 19.g3 ♖d8 20.♖ac1 ♖d7 21.♘c4 ♖g5 22.♘e3 ♔f8 23.h4 ♖a5 24.d5 ♗c5 25.♖cd1 c6 26.♘f5 cxd5 27.♖d4 ♖dc7 28.♖ed1 ♖c1 29.♗xd5 ♖xd1† 30.♖xd1 ♗c8 31.♗e4 ♗xf5 32.♗xf5 b3 33.♖d3 ♖c4 34.♗d7 ♖b4 35.♗c6 ½–½

Peter Leko (2741) – Vladimir Kramnik (2770)

World Championship Brissago (11) 12.10.2004

1.d4 ♘f6 2.c4 e6 3.♘f3 b6 4.g3 ♗a6 5.♕a4 ♗b7 6.♗g2 c5 7.dxc5 ♗xc5 8.0–0 0–0 9.♘c3 ♗e7 10.♗f4 a6 11.♖fd1 d6 12.♕c2 ♕c7 13.♖ac1 ♖d8 14.♕d2 ♘h5 15.♗g5 ♘f6 16.♗f4 ♘h5 17.♗g5 ♘f6 ½–½

Vladimir Kramnik (2770) – Peter Leko (2741)

World Championship Brissago (12) 14.10.2004

1.e4 c6 2.d4 d5 3.♘d2 dxe4 4.♘xe4 ♗f5 5.♘g3 ♗g6 6.h4 h6 7.♘f3 ♘d7 8.h5 ♗h7 9.♗d3 ♗xd3 10.♕xd3 e6 11.♗f4 ♕a5† 12.♗d2 ♕c7 13.0–0–0 ♘gf6 14.♘e4 0–0–0 15.g3 ♘xe4 16.♕xe4 ♗d6 17.♔b1 ♖he8 18.♕h7 ♖g8 19.c4 c5 20.d5 ♘f6 21.♕c2 exd5 22.cxd5 ♕d7 23.♗c3 ♖de8 24.♗xf6 gxf6 25.♕d3 f5 26.♘d2 b5 27.♖he1 ♔b8 28.♕c3 ♖xe1 29.♖xe1 c4 30.♘f3 f4 31.g4 ♗c7 32.♕d4 ♕xg4 33.♕e4 ♕xh5 34.♘d4 ♕g6 ½–½

Peter Leko (2741) – Vladimir Kramnik (2770)

World Championship Brissago (13) 16.10.2004

1.d4 ♘f6 2.c4 e6 3.♘f3 c5 4.d5 d6 5.♘c3 exd5 6.cxd5 g6 7.♘d2 ♗g7 8.e4 0–0 9.♗e2 ♘a6 10.0–0 ♘e8 11.♘c4 ♘ac7 12.a4 f5 13.exf5 ♖xf5 14.♗g4 ♖f8 15.♗xc8 ♖xc8 16.♕b3 b6 17.♘b5 ♘xb5 18.axb5 ♖c7 19.♗d2 ♖cf7 20.♗c3 ♕d7 21.f3 g5 22.♘e3 ♖f4 23.♖fe1 h5 24.♕c2 ♕f7 25.h3 ♗d4 26.♖xd4 ♖xd4 27.♘f5 ♕xf5 28.♕xf5 ♖xf5 29.♖e8† ♔f7 30.♖b8 ♖dxd5 31.♖xa7† ♔e6 32.♖e8† ♔f6 33.g4 hxg4 34.hxg4 ♖d1† 35.♔f2 ♖e5 36.♖h8 ♖d2† 37.♔g3 ♖ee2 38.♖f8† ♔g6 39.♖g8† ♔f6 40.♖f8† ♔e6 41.♖e8† ♔d5 42.♖xe2 ♖xe2 43.♖g7 ♖e5 44.♖b7 c4 45.♖xb6 ♖e2 46.f4 ♖e3† 47.♔f2 gxf4 48.♖b8 ♖b3 49.b6 ♔e4 50.♖e8† ♔d3 51.♖e2 d5 52.♔f3 d4 53.g5 c3 54.bxc3 dxc3 55.♖g2 ♖b2 56.b7 ♖xb7 57.♔xf4 ♖b2 58.♖g1 c2 59.♖c1 ♖b1 60.♖xc2 ♔xc2 61.g6 ♔d3 62.♔f5 ♖b5† 63.♔f6 ♖b6† 64.♔f7 ♖xg6 65.♔xg6 ½–½

Vladimir Kramnik (2770) – Peter Leko (2741)

World Championship Brissago (14) 18.10.2004

1.e4 c6 2.d4 d5 3.e5 ♗f5 4.h4 h6 5.g4 ♗d7 6.♘d2 c5 7.dxc5 e6 8.♘b3 ♗xc5 9.♘xc5 ♕a5† 10.c3 ♕xc5 11.♘f3 ♘e7 12.♗d3 ♘bc6 13.♗e3 ♕a5 14.♕d2 ♘g6 15.♗d4 ♘xd4 16.cxd4 ♕xd2† 17.♔xd2 ♘f4 18.♖ac1 h5 19.♖hg1 ♗c6 20.gxh5 ♘xh5 21.b4 a6 22.a4 ♔d8 23.♘g5 ♗e8 24.b5 ♘f4 25.b6 ♘xd3 26.♔xd3 ♖c8

27.♖xc8† ♔xc8 28.♖c1† ♗c6 29.♘xf7 ♖xh4 30.♘d6† ♔d8 31.♖g1 ♖h3† 32.♔e2 ♖a3 33.♖xg7 ♖xa4 34.f4 ♖a2† 35.♔f3 ♖a3† 36.♔g4 ♖d3 37.f5 ♖xd4† 38.♔g5 exf5 39.♔f6 ♖g4 40.♖c7 ♖h4 41.♘f7† 1–0

Elista, Russia 2006: **Vladimir Kramnik – Veselin Topalov**
8½–6½ (8½–7½ FIDE)

Vladimir Kramnik (2743) – Veselin Topalov (2813)

World Championship Elista (1) 23.09.2006

1.d4 ♘f6 2.c4 e6 3.♘f3 d5 4.g3 dxc4 5.♗g2 ♗b4† 6.♗d2 a5 7.♕c2 ♗xd2† 8.♕xd2 c6 9.a4 b5 10.axb5 cxb5 11.♕g5 0–0 12.♕xb5 ♗a6 13.♕a4 ♕b6 14.0–0 ♕xb2 15.♘bd2 ♗b5 16.♘xc4 ♗xa4 17.♘xb2 ♗b5 18.♘e5 ♖a7 19.♗f3 ♘bd7 20.♘ec4 ♖b8 21.♖fb1 g5 22.e3 g4 23.♗d1 ♗c6 24.♖c1 ♗e4 25.♘a4 ♖b4 26.♘d6 ♗f3 27.♗xf3 gxf3 28.♘c8 ♖a8 29.♘e7† ♔g7 30.♘c6 ♖b3 31.♘c5 ♖b5 32.h3 ♘xc5 33.♖xc5 ♖b2 34.♖g5† ♔h6 35.♖gxa5 ♖xa5 36.♘xa5 ♘e4 37.♖f1 ♘d2 38.♖c1 ♘e4 39.♖f1 f6 40.♘c6 ♘d2 41.♖d1 ♘e4 42.♖f1 ♔g6 43.♘d8 ♖b6 44.♖c1 h5 45.♖a1 h4 46.gxh4 ♔h5 47.♖a2 ♔xh4 48.♔h2 ♔h5 49.♖c2 ♔h6 50.♖a2 ♔g6 51.♖c2 ♔f5 52.♖a2 ♖b5 53.♘c6 ♖b7 54.♖a5† ♔g6 55.♖a2 ♔h5 56.d5 e5 57.♖a4 f5 58.♘xe5 ♖b2 59.♘d3 ♖b7 60.♖d4 ♖b6 61.d6 ♘xd6 62.♔g3 ♘e4† 63.♔xf3 ♔g5 64.h4† ♔f6 65.♖d5 ♘c3 66.♖d8 ♖b1 67.♖f8† ♔e6 68.♘f4† ♔e5 69.♖e8† ♔f6 70.♘h5† ♔g6 71.♘g3 ♖b2 72.h5† ♔f7 73.♖e5 ♘d1 74.♘e2 ♔f6 75.♖d5 1–0

Veselin Topalov (2813) – Vladimir Kramnik (2743)

World Championship Elista (2) 24.09.2006

1.d4 d5 2.c4 c6 3.♘c3 ♘f6 4.♘f3 dxc4 5.a4 ♗f5 6.e3 e6 7.♗xc4 ♗b4 8.0–0 ♘bd7 9.♕e2 ♗g6 10.e4 0–0 11.♗d3 ♗h5 12.e5 ♘d5 13.♘xd5 cxd5 14.♕e3 ♗g6 15.♘g5 ♖e8 16.f4 ♗xd3 17.♕xd3 f5 18.♗e3 ♘f8 19.♔h1 ♖c8 20.g4 ♕d7 21.♖g1 ♗e7 22.♘f3 ♖c4 23.♖g2 fxg4 24.♖xg4 ♖xa4 25.♖ag1 g6 26.h4 ♖b4 27.h5 ♕b5 28.♕c2 ♖xb2 29.hxg6 h5 30.g7 hxg4 31.gxf8=♕† ♗xf8 32.♕g6† ♗g7 33.f5 ♖e7 34.f6 ♕e2 35.♕xg4 ♗f7 36.♖c1 ♖c2 37.♖xc2 ♕d1† 38.♔g2 ♕xc2† 39.♔g3 ♕e4 40.♗f4 ♕f5 41.♕xf5 exf5 42.♗g5 a5 43.♔f4 a4 44.♔xf5 a3 45.♗c1 ♗f8 46.e6 ♖c7 47.♗xa3 ♗xa3 48.♔e5 ♖c1 49.♘g5 ♖f1 50.e7 ♖e1† 51.♔xd5 ♗xe7 52.fxe7 ♖xe7 53.♔d6 ♖e1 54.d5 ♔f8 55.♘e6† ♔e8 56.♘c7† ♔d8 57.♘e6† ♔c8 58.♔e7 ♖h1 59.♘g5 b5 60.d6 ♖d1 61.♘e6 b4 62.♘c5 ♖e1† 63.♔f6 ♖e3 0–1

Vladimir Kramnik (2743) – Veselin Topalov (2813)

World Championship Elista (3) 26.09.2006

1.d4 ♘f6 2.c4 e6 3.♘f3 d5 4.g3 dxc4 5.♗g2 ♘c6 6.♕a4 ♗d7 7.♕xc4 ♘a5 8.♕d3 c5 9.0–0 ♗c6 10.♘c3 cxd4 11.♘xd4 ♗c5 12.♖d1 ♗xg2 13.♕b5† ♘d7 14.♔xg2 a6 15.♕d3 ♖c8 16.♗g5 ♗e7 17.♗xe7 ♕xe7 18.♖ac1 ♘c4 19.♘a4 b5 20.b3 0–0 21.bxc4 bxa4 22.♘c6 ♖xc6 23.♕xd7 ♕c5 24.♖c3 g6 25.♖b1 h5 26.♖b7 e5 27.e4 ♖f6 28.♖c2 ♕a3 29.♕d1 ♖d6 30.♖d2 ♖fd8 31.♖d5 ♖xd5 32.cxd5 ♕xa2 33.♕f3 ♖f8 34.♕d3 a3 35.♖b3 f5 36.♕xa6 ♕xb3 37.♕xg6† ♔h8 38.♕h6† ♔g8 ½–½

Veselin Topalov (2813) – Vladimir Kramnik (2743)

World Championship Elista (4) 27.09.2006

1.d4 d5 2.c4 c6 3.♘c3 ♘f6 4.e3 e6 5.♘f3 ♘bd7 6.♗d3 dxc4 7.♗xc4 b5 8.♗d3 ♗b7 9.a3 b4 10.♘e4 ♘xe4 11.♗xe4 bxa3 12.0–0 ♗d6 13.b3 ♘f6 14.♘d2 ♕c7 15.♗f3 ♗xh2† 16.♔h1 ♗d6 17.♘c4 ♗e7 18.♗xa3 0–0 19.♗xe7 ♕xe7 20.♖a5 ♖fd8 21.♔g1 c5 22.♖xc5 ♘e4 23.♗xe4 ♗xe4 24.♕g4 ♗d3 25.♖a1 ♖ac8 26.♖aa5 ♖b8 27.♕d1 ♗e4 28.♕a1 ♖b7 29.♘d2 ♗g6 30.♕c3 h6 31.♖a6 ♔h7 32.♘c4 ♗e4 33.f3 ♗d5 34.♘d2 ♖db8 35.♕d3† f5 36.♖c3 ♕h4 37.♖a1 ♕g3 38.♕c2 ♗f7 39.♖f1 ♕g6 40.♕d3 ♕g3 41.♖fc1 ♖fb7 42.♕c2 ♕g5 43.♖a1 ♕f6 44.♕d3 ♖d7 45.♖a4 ♖bd8 46.♖c5 ♔g8 47.♘c4 ♗xc4 48.♖axc4 f4 49.♖c6 fxe3 50.♕xe3 ♖xd4 51.♖xe6 ♕h4 52.♖xd4 ♕xd4 53.♖e8† ♔h7 54.♕xd4 ½–½

Veselin Topalov (2813) – Vladimir Kramnik (2743)

World Championship Elista (6) 02.10.2006

1.d4 d5 2.c4 c6 3.♘f3 ♘f6 4.♘c3 dxc4 5.a4 ♗f5 6.♘e5 e6 7.f3 c5 8.e4 ♗g6 9.♗e3 cxd4 10.♕xd4 ♕xd4 11.♗xd4 ♘fd7 12.♘xd7 ♘xd7 13.♗xc4 a6 14.♔e2 ♖g8 15.♖hd1 ♖c8 16.b3 ♗c5 17.a5 ♔e7 18.♘a4 ♗b4 19.♘b6 ♘xb6 20.♗xb6 f6 21.♖d3 ♖c6 22.h4 ♖gc8 23.g4 ♗c5 24.♖ad1 ♗xb6 25.♖d7† ♔f8 26.axb6 ♖xb6 27.♖1d6 ♖xd6 28.♖xd6 ♖c6 29.♖xc6 bxc6 30.b4 e5 31.♗xa6 ½–½

Veselin Topalov (2813) – Vladimir Kramnik (2743)

World Championship Elista (7) 04.10.2006

1.d4 d5 2.c4 c6 3.♘f3 ♘f6 4.e3 e6 5.♗d3 dxc4 6.♗xc4 c5 7.0–0 a6 8.♗b3 cxd4 9.exd4 ♘c6 10.♘c3 ♗e7 11.♖e1 0–0 12.a4 ♗d7 13.♘e5 ♗e8 14.♗e3 ♖c8 15.♖c1 ♘b4 16.♕f3 ♗c6 17.♕h3 ♗d5 18.♘xd5 ♘bxd5 19.♖cd1 ♖c7 20.♗g5 ♕c8 21.♕f3 ♖d8 22.h4 h6 23.♗c1 ♗b4 24.♖f1 ♗d6 25.g3 b6 26.♕e2 ♘e7 27.♖fe1 ♗xe5

28.dxe5 ♖xd1 29.♕xd1 ♘fd5 30.♗d2 ♖c5 31.♕g4 ♘f5 32.♕e4 b5 33.h5 bxa4
34.♕xa4 ♖b5 35.♖c1 ♕b7 36.♗c2 ♘b6 37.♕g4 ♖xb2 38.♗e4 ♕d7 39.♗e1 ♘d5
40.♗d3 ♘b4 41.♗f1 ♘d3 42.♕d1 ♘xe5 43.♕xd7 ♘xd7 44.♖c8† ♔h7 45.♖c7
♖b1 46.♖xd7 ♖xe1 47.♖xf7 a5 48.♔g2 ♔g8 49.♖a7 ♖e5 50.g4 ♘d6 51.♗d3 ♔f8
52.♗g6 ♖d5 53.f3 e5 54.♔f2 ♖d2† 55.♔e1 ♖d5 56.♔e2 ♖b5 57.♖d7 ♖d5 58.♖a7
♖b5 59.♗d3 ♖d5 60.♗g6 ½–½

Vladimir Kramnik (2743) – Veselin Topalov (2813)

World Championship Elista (8) 05.10.2006

1.d4 d5 2.c4 c6 3.♘f3 ♘f6 4.♘c3 e6 5.e3 ♘bd7 6.♗d3 dxc4 7.♗xc4 b5 8.♗e2
♗b7 9.0–0 b4 10.♘a4 c5 11.dxc5 ♘xc5 12.♗b5† ♘cd7 13.♘e5 ♕c7 14.♕d4 ♖d8
15.♗d2 ♕a5 16.♗c6 ♗e7 17.♖fc1 ♗xc6 18.♘xc6 ♕xa4 19.♘xd8 ♗xd8 20.♕xb4
♕xb4 21.♗xb4 ♘d5 22.♗d6 f5 23.♖c8 ♘5b6 24.♖c6 ♗e7 25.♖d1 ♔f7 26.♖c7 ♖a8
27.♖b7 ♔e8 28.♗xe7 ♔xe7 29.♖c1 a5 30.♖c6 ♘d5 31.h4 h6 32.a4 g5 33.hxg5
hxg5 34.♔f1 g4 35.♔e2 ♘5f6 36.b3 ♘e8 37.f3 g3 38.♖c1 ♘ef6 39.f4 ♔d6 40.♔f3
♘d5 41.♔xg3 ♘c5 42.♖g7 ♖b8 43.♖a7 ♖g8† 44.♔f3 ♘e4 45.♖a6† ♔e7 46.♖xa5
♖g3† 47.♔e2 ♖xe3† 48.♔f1 ♖xb3 49.♖a7† ♔f6 50.♖a8 ♘xf4 51.♖a1 ♖b2 52.a5
♖f2† 0–1

Veselin Topalov (2813) – Vladimir Kramnik (2743)

World Championship Elista (9) 07.10.2006

1.d4 d5 2.c4 c6 3.♘f3 ♘f6 4.e3 ♗f5 5.♘c3 e6 6.♘h4 ♗g6 7.♘xg6 hxg6 8.a3
♘bd7 9.g3 ♗e7 10.f4 dxc4 11.♗xc4 0–0 12.e4 b5 13.♗e2 b4 14.axb4 ♗xb4 15.♗f3
♕b6 16.0–0 e5 17.♗e3 ♖ad8 18.♘a4 ♕b8 19.♕c2 exf4 20.♗xf4 ♕b7 21.♖ad1
♖fe8 22.♗g5 ♗e7 23.♔h1 ♘h7 24.♗e3 ♗g5 25.♗g1 ♘hf8 26.h4 ♗e7 27.e5 ♘b8
28.♘c3 ♗b4 29.♕g2 ♕c8 30.♖c1 ♗xc3 31.bxc3 ♘e6 32.♗g4 ♕c7 33.♖cd1 ♘d7
34.♕a2 ♘b6 35.♖f3 ♘f8 36.♖df1 ♖e7 37.♗e3 ♘h7 38.♖xf7 ♘d5 39.♖7f3 1–0

Vladimir Kramnik (2743) – Veselin Topalov (2813)

World Championship Elista (10) 08.10.2006

1.d4 ♘f6 2.c4 e6 3.♘f3 d5 4.g3 ♗b4† 5.♗d2 ♗e7 6.♗g2 0–0 7.0–0 c6 8.♗f4 ♘bd7
9.♕c2 a5 10.♖d1 ♘h5 11.♗c1 b5 12.cxd5 cxd5 13.e4 dxe4 14.♕xe4 ♖b8 15.♕e2
♘hf6 16.♗f4 ♖b6 17.♘e5 ♘d5 18.♗xd5 exd5 19.♘c3 ♘f6 20.♘xb5 ♗a6 21.a4
♘e4 22.♖dc1 ♕e8 23.♖c7 ♗d8 24.♖a7 f6 25.♘d7 ♖f7 26.♘xb6 ♖xa7 27.♘xd5
♖d7 28.♘dc3 ♖xd4 29.♖e1 f5 30.♕c2 ♖b4 31.♘d5 ♖xb5 32.axb5 ♕xb5 33.♘c7
♕c4 34.♕d1 ♗xc7 35.♕d7 h6 36.♕xc7 ♕b4 37.♕b8† ♕xb8 38.♗xb8 ♘d2 39.♖a1
g5 40.f4 ♘b3 41.♖a3 ♗c4 42.♗c7 g4 43.♗xa5 1–0

Veselin Topalov (2813) – Vladimir Kramnik (2743)

World Championship Elista (11) 10.10.2006

1.d4 d5 2.c4 c6 3.♘f3 ♘f6 4.e3 ♗f5 5.♘c3 e6 6.♘h4 ♗g6 7.♘xg6 hxg6 8.♖b1 ♘bd7 **9.c5 a5 10.a3 e5 11.b4 axb4 12.axb4 ♕c7 13.f4 exf4 14.exf4 ♗e7 15.♗e2** ♘f8 **16.0–0 ♘e6 17.g3 ♕d7 18.♕d3 ♘e4 19.♘xe4 dxe4 20.♕xe4 ♕xd4† 21.♕xd4** ♘xd4 **22.♗c4 0–0 23.♔g2 ♖a4 24.♖d1 ♖d8 25.♗e3 ♗f6 26.g4 ♔f8 27.♗f2 ♘e6** **28.♖xd8† ♗xd8 29.f5 gxf5 30.gxf5 ♘f4† 31.♔f3 ♘h5 32.♖b3 ♗c7 33.h4 ♘f6** **34.♗d3 ♘d7 35.♗e4 ♘e5† 36.♔g2 ♖a2 37.♗b1 ♖d2 38.♔f1 ♘g4 39.♗g1 ♗h2** **40.♔e1 ♖d5 41.♗f2 ♔e7 42.h5 ♘xf2 43.♔xf2 ♔f6 44.♔f3 ♖d4 45.b5 ♖c4 46.bxc6** bxc6 **47.♖b6 ♖xc5 48.♗e4 ♔g5 49.♖xc6 ♖a5 50.♖b6 ♖a3† 51.♔g2 ♗c7 52.♖b7** ♖c3 **53.♔f2 ♔xh5 54.♗d5 f6 55.♔e2 ♔g4 56.♗e4 ♗f4 57.♗d3 ♖c5 58.♖b4† ♔g3** **59.♖c4 ♖e5† 60.♖e4 ♖a5 61.♖e3† ♔g2 62.♗e4† ♔h2 63.♖b3 ♖a2† 64.♔d3 ♗f4** **65.♔c4 ♖e2 66.♔d5 ½–½**

Vladimir Kramnik (2743) – Veselin Topalov (2813)

World Championship Elista (12) 12.10.2006

1.d4 d5 2.c4 c6 3.♘f3 ♘f6 4.e3 ♗f5 5.♘c3 e6 6.♘h4 ♗g6 7.♘xg6 hxg6 8.g3 ♘bd7 **9.♗d2 ♗b4 10.♕b3 ♗xc3 11.♗xc3 ♘e4 12.♗g2 ♘xc3 13.♕xc3 f5 14.0–0** ♕e7 **15.cxd5 exd5 16.b4 ♘f6 17.♖fc1 ♘e4 18.♕b2 0–0 19.b5 ♖ac8 20.bxc6 bxc6** **21.♕e2 g5 22.♖ab1 ♕d7 23.♖c2 ♖f6 24.♖bc1 g4 25.♖b2 ♖h6 26.♕a6 ♖c7 27.♖b8†** ♔h7 **28.♕a3 ♖b7 29.♕f8 ♖xb8 30.♕xb8 ♕f7 31.♕c8 ♕h5 32.♔f1 ♘d2† 33.♔e1** ♘c4 **34.♗f1 ♖f6 35.♗xc4 dxc4 36.♖xc4 ♕xh2 37.♔e2 ♕h1 38.♖c5 ♕b1 39.♕a6** ♕b2† **40.♔f1 ♕b1† 41.♔e2 ♕b2† 42.♔f1 ♖h6 43.♕d3 g6 44.♕b3 ♖h1† 45.♔g2** ♖h2† **46.♔xh2 ♕xf2† 47.♔h1 ♕f1† ½–½**

Veselin Topalov (2813) – Vladimir Kramnik (2743)

World Championship Elista rapid playoff (1) 13.10.2006

1.d4 d5 2.c4 c6 3.♘f3 ♘f6 4.♘c3 dxc4 5.a4 ♗f5 6.e3 e6 7.♗xc4 ♗b4 8.0–0 ♘bd7 **9.♕e2 0–0 10.e4 ♗g6 11.♗d3 ♗h5 12.e5 ♘d5 13.♘xd5 cxd5 14.♕e3 ♖e8 15.♘e1** ♖c8 **16.f4 ♗xe1 17.♖xe1 ♗g6 18.♗f1 ♖c2 19.b3 ♕a5 20.♗b5 ♖d8 21.♖e2 ♖cc8** **22.♗d2 ♕b6 23.♖f2 a6 24.♗f1 ♖c6 25.b4 ♖c2 26.b5 a5 27.♗c3 ♖xf2 28.♕xf2** ♕a7 **29.♕d2 ♖a8 30.♖c1 ♘b6 31.♗b2 ♘xa4 32.♗a3 h6 33.h3 ♗e4 34.♔h2** ♘b6 **35.♗c5 a4 36.♖a1 ♘c4 37.♗xc4 b6 38.♕e3 ♖c8 39.♗f1 bxc5 40.dxc5 ♕xc5** **41.♕xc5 ♖xc5 42.b6 ♖c6 43.b7 ♖b6 44.♗a6 d4 45.♖xa4 ♗xb7 46.♗xb7 ♖xb7** **47.♖xd4 ½–½**

Vladimir Kramnik (2743) – Veselin Topalov (2813)

World Championship Elista rapid playoff (2) 13.10.2006

1.d4 d5 2.c4 c6 3.♘f3 ♘f6 4.♘c3 e6 5.e3 ♘bd7 6.♕c2 ♗d6 7.b3 0–0 8.♗e2 b6
9.0–0 ♗b7 10.♗b2 ♖e8 11.♖ad1 ♕e7 12.♖fe1 ♖ac8 13.♗d3 e5 14.e4 dxc4 15.♗xc4
b5 16.♗f1 g6 17.♕d2 ♖cd8 18.♕g5 a6 19.h3 exd4 20.♘xd4 ♕e5 21.♕xe5 ♘xe5
22.♘c2 g5 23.♗c1 h6 24.♗e3 c5 25.f3 ♗f8 26.♗f2 ♗c8 27.♘e3 ♗e6 28.♘ed5
♗xd5 29.exd5 ♘ed7 30.♖xe8 ♖xe8 31.a4 b4 32.♘e4 ♘xe4 33.fxe4 ♘f6 34.d6
♘xe4 35.d7 ♖d8 36.♗xa6 f5 37.a5 ♗g7 38.♗c4† ♔f8 39.a6 ♘xf2 40.♔xf2 ♗d4†
41.♖xd4 cxd4 42.a7 ♔e7 43.♗d5 ♔xd7 44.a8=♕ ♖xa8 45.♗xa8 1–0

Veselin Topalov (2813) – Vladimir Kramnik (2743)

World Championship Elista rapid playoff (3) 13.10.2006

1.d4 d5 2.c4 c6 3.♘f3 ♘f6 4.e3 ♗f5 5.♘c3 e6 6.♘h4 ♗g6 7.♗e2 ♘bd7 8.0–0 ♗d6
9.g3 dxc4 10.♗xc4 ♘b6 11.♗e2 0–0 12.♘xg6 hxg6 13.e4 e5 14.f4 exd4 15.♕xd4
♕e7 16.♔g2 ♗c5 17.♕d3 ♖ad8 18.♕c2 ♗d4 19.e5 ♘fd5 20.♖f3 ♘xc3 21.bxc3
♗c5 22.♗d2 ♖d7 23.♖e1 ♖fd8 24.♗d3 ♕e6 25.♗c1 f5 26.♕e2 ♔f8 27.♖d1 ♕e7
28.h4 ♖d5 29.♕c2 ♘c4 30.♖h1 ♘a3 31.♕e2 ♕d7 32.♖d1 b5 33.g4 fxg4 34.♖g3
♔e7 35.f5 gxf5 36.♗g5† ♔e8 37.e6 ♕d6 38.♗xf5 ♖xd1 39.♗g6† ♔f8 40.e7† ♕xe7
41.♗xe7† ♗xe7 42.♗d3 ♖a1 43.♕b2 ♖d1 44.♕e2 ♖a1 45.♕xg4 ♖xa2† 46.♔h3
♗f6 47.♕e6 ♗d2 48.♗g6 ♖2d7 49.♖f3 b4 50.h5 1–0

Vladimir Kramnik (2743) – Veselin Topalov (2813)

World Championship Elista rapid playoff (4) 13.10.2006

1.d4 d5 2.c4 c6 3.♘f3 ♘f6 4.♘c3 e6 5.e3 ♘bd7 6.♗d3 dxc4 7.♗xc4 b5 8.♗e2 ♗b7
9.0–0 ♗e7 10.e4 b4 11.e5 bxc3 12.exf6 ♗xf6 13.bxc3 c5 14.dxc5 ♘xc5 15.♗b5†
♔f8 16.♕xd8† ♖xd8 17.♗a3 ♖c8 18.♘d4 ♗e7 19.♖fd1 a6 20.♗f1 ♘a4 21.♖ab1
♗e4 22.♖b3 ♗xa3 23.♖xa3 ♘c5 24.♘b3 ♔e7 25.♖d4 ♗g6 26.c4 ♖c6 27.♘xc5
♖xc5 28.♖xa6 ♖b8 29.♖d1 ♖b2 30.♖a7† ♔f6 31.♖a1 ♖f5 32.f3 ♖e5 33.♖a3 ♖c2
34.♖b3 ♖a5 35.a4 ♔e7 36.♖b5 ♖a7 37.a5 ♔d6 38.a6 ♔c7 39.c5 ♖c3 40.♖aa5 ♖c1
41.♖b3 ♔c6 42.♖b6† ♔c7 43.♔f2 ♖c2† 44.♔e3 ♖xc5 45.♖b7† 1–0

233

Vladimir Kramnik (2769) – Peter Svidler (2735)

World Championship Mexico City (1) 13.09.2007

1.♘f3 d5 2.d4 ♘f6 3.c4 c6 4.♘c3 e6 5.♗g5 h6 6.♗xf6 ♕xf6 7.e3 ♘d7 8.♗d3 g6 9.e4 dxc4 10.e5 ♕e7 11.♗xc4 ♗g7 12.0–0 0–0 13.♖e1 ♖d8 14.♕e2 b6 15.♖ad1 a5 16.♗d3 ♗b7 17.♗e4 b5 18.h4 ♘b6 19.♗b1 c5 20.♘xb5 ♗a6 21.h5 g5 22.♘h2 ♖xd4 23.♖xd4 ½–½

Vladimir Kramnik (2769) – Alexander Morozevich (2758)

World Championship Mexico City (2) 14.09.2007

1.♘f3 ♘f6 2.c4 e6 3.g3 d5 4.d4 dxc4 5.♗g2 a6 6.♘e5 ♗b4† 7.♘c3 ♘d5 8.0–0 0–0 9.♕c2 b5 10.♘xd5 exd5 11.b3 c6 12.e4 f6 13.exd5 fxe5 14.bxc4 exd4 15.dxc6 ♗e6 16.cxb5 d3 17.c7 ♕d4 18.♕a4 ♘d7 19.♗e3 ♕d6 20.♗xa8 ♖xa8 21.♗f4 ♕f8 22.b6 ♘e5 23.♗xe5 ♕f3 24.♕d1 ♕e4 25.b7 ♖f8 26.c8=♕ ♗d5 27.f3 1–0

Viswanathan Anand (2792) – Vladimir Kramnik (2769)

World Championship Mexico City (3) 15.09.2007

1.e4 e5 2.♘f3 ♘f6 3.♘xe5 d6 4.♘f3 ♘xe4 5.d4 d5 6.♗d3 ♘c6 7.0–0 ♗e7 8.c4 ♘b4 9.♗e2 0–0 10.♘c3 ♗f5 11.a3 ♘xc3 12.bxc3 ♘c6 13.♖e1 ♖e8 14.cxd5 ♕xd5 15.♗f4 ♖ac8 16.♕a4 ♗d7 17.♕c2 ♕f5 18.♕xf5 ♗xf5 19.♗b5 ♗d7 20.d5 ♘e5 21.♗xd7 ♘xd7 22.♗xc7 ♖xc7 23.d6 ♖xc3 24.dxe7 f6 25.♖ad1 ♖c7 26.♘d4 ♘e5 27.f4 ♘c6 28.♘xc6 bxc6 29.♖d6 c5 30.♖ee6 c4 31.♖c6 ♖exe7 32.♖xc4 ♖xc4 33.♖xe7 ♖a4 34.♖b7 h6 35.f5 ♖xa3 36.♔f2 h5 37.g3 a5 38.♖a7 a4 39.h4 ♖a2† 40.♔f3 a3 41.♔e3 ♖a1 42.♔f2 ♔f8 43.♔g2 a2 44.♔h2 ♔e8 45.♔g2 ♔d8 46.♔h2 ♔c8 47.♔g2 ♔b8 48.♖a3 ♔b7 49.♖a4 ♔b6 50.♖a8 ♔c5 51.♖a7 ♔d5 52.♖a4 ♔e5 53.♖a5† ♔e4 54.♔h2 ♔f3 55.♖a3† ♔f2 56.♖a4 ♔f1 57.♔h1 ♔e1 58.♔g2 ♔d1 59.♖a7 ♖c1 60.♖xa2 ♖c2† 61.♖xc2 ♔xc2 62.♔f3 ♔d3 63.g4 hxg4† 64.♔xg4 ♔e4 65.♔h5 ♔xf5 ½–½

Vladimir Kramnik (2769) – Alexander Grischuk (2726)

World Championship Mexico City (4) 16.09.2007

1.d4 ♘f6 2.c4 e6 3.g3 d5 4.♗g2 ♗e7 5.♘f3 0–0 6.0–0 dxc4 7.♕c2 a6 8.♕xc4 b5 9.♕c2 ♗b7 10.♗d2 ♖a7 11.a3 ♘bd7 12.♗a5 ♕a8 13.♕xc7 ♖c8 14.♕f4 ♖c2 15.♘bd2 ♖xb2 16.♖fc1 ♘d5 17.♕e4 b4 18.♕d3 bxa3 19.♘c4 ♗c6 20.♘xa3 ♗b5

21.♘c4 ♗b4 22.♕d1 ♗xc4 23.♖xc4 ♗xa5 24.♖xa5 ♕b8 25.♘d2 ♘5b6 26.♖c1
g6 27.♘e4 ♖b5 28.♖a2 a5 29.♘c5 ♕d6 30.♘b7 ♕b8 31.♕d3 ♖h5 32.♘c5 ♘d5
33.♕c4 ♘5b6 34.♕c3 ♘d5 35.♕a1 ♘xc5 36.♖xc5 ♘b4 37.♖axa5 ♘c2 38.♖xa7
♘xa1 39.♖a8 ♕xa8 40.♗xa8 ♖xc5 41.dxc5 ♔f8 42.c6 ♔e7 43.c7 ♔d7 44.♗c6†
♔xc7 45.♗a4 ♔b6 46.♔g2 ♘c5 47.♔f3 ♔b4 48.♗e8 f6 49.♗f7 ♘b3 50.e3 ♘c5
51.h4 ♔c3 52.♗g8 h6 53.♗f7 g5 54.♔g4 ♘e4 55.hxg5 hxg5 56.♗xe6 ♘xf2†
57.♔f5 ♘d3 58.♔xf6 ♘e4† 59.♔g6 ♘xg3 60.♔xg5 ♔xe3 ½–½

Peter Leko (2751) – Vladimir Kramnik (2769)

World Championship Mexico City (5) 18.09.2007

1.e4 e5 2.♗c4 ♘f6 3.d3 ♗c5 4.♘f3 d6 5.c3 ♘c6 6.♗b3 a6 7.0–0 ♗a7 8.♖e1 0–0
9.h3 h6 10.♘bd2 ♖e8 11.♘f1 ♗e6 12.♘3h2 ♗xb3 13.axb3 ♕d7 14.♕f3 ♕e6
15.♘g3 ♘e7 16.b4 c6 17.♘g4 ♘xg4 18.hxg4 d5 19.♘f5 ♖ad8 20.g3 f6 21.♔g2
dxe4 22.dxe4 ♘xf5 23.gxf5 ♕c4 24.♗e3 ♗xe3 ½–½

Levon Aronian (2750) – Vladimir Kramnik (2769)

World Championship Mexico City (6) 19.09.2007

1.d4 ♘f6 2.c4 e6 3.♘f3 d5 4.g3 ♗e7 5.♗g2 0–0 6.0–0 dxc4 7.♕c2 a6 8.♕xc4 b5
9.♕c2 ♗b7 10.♗d2 ♗e4 11.♕c1 ♕c8 12.♗g5 ♘bd7 13.♘bd2 ♗b7 14.♘b3 a5
15.♗xf6 ♗xf6 16.♘c5 ♗d5 17.e4 ♗c4 18.♘xd7 ♕xd7 19.♖e1 ♗xd4 20.♖d1 c5
21.♕c2 e5 22.♘xe5 ½–½

Vladimir Kramnik (2769) – Boris Gelfand (2733)

World Championship Mexico City (7) 20.09.2007

1.d4 d5 2.c4 c6 3.♘f3 ♘f6 4.♘c3 e6 5.♗g5 h6 6.♗h4 dxc4 7.e4 g5 8.♗g3 b5
9.♗e2 ♗b7 10.0–0 ♘bd7 11.♘e5 h5 12.♘xd7 ♕xd7 13.♕c1 ♖g8 14.♖d1 ♗b4
15.♕e3 ♕e7 16.h3 h4 17.♗h2 ♗xc3 18.bxc3 g4 19.♔h1 c5 20.hxg4 cxd4 21.♖xd4
e5 22.♖dd1 ♘xg4 23.♗xg4 ♖xg4 24.f3 ♖g6 25.a4 a5 26.axb5 a4 27.♕e2 ♕c5
28.♖ab1 ♖d6 29.♖xd6 ♕xd6 30.♕xc4 a3 31.♖a1 h3 32.♕e2 hxg2† 33.♕xg2 0–0–0
34.♕a2 f5 35.♕xa3 fxe4 36.♕xd6 ♖xd6 37.fxe4 ♗xe4† 38.♔g1 ♗d3 39.♗xe5
♖g6† 40.♔f2 ♗xb5 ½–½

Peter Svidler (2735) – Vladimir Kramnik (2769)

World Championship Mexico City (8) 21.09.2007

1.e4 e5 2.♘f3 ♘f6 3.♘xe5 d6 4.♘f3 ♘xe4 5.♘c3 ♘xc3 6.dxc3 ♗e7 7.♗f4 0–0 8.♕d2 ♘d7 9.0–0–0 ♘c5 10.♗e3 ♖e8 11.♗c4 ♗e6 12.♗xe6 ♘xe6 13.h4 ♕d7 14.♕d5 ♕c6 15.♕f5 ♕c4 16.♔b1 g6 17.♕h3 h5 18.♘d2 ♕e2 19.♖de1 ♕g4 20.♕h2 d5 21.f3 ♕a4 22.g4 ♗d6 23.♕f2 ♘g7 24.c4 dxc4 25.♗d4 ♕c6 26.♗c3 ♗c5 27.♕g3 ♗d6 28.♕f2 ♗c5 29.♕g3 ♗d6 ½–½

Alexander Morozevich (2758) – Vladimir Kramnik (2769)

World Championship Mexico City (9) 23.09.2007

1.c4 c5 2.♘c3 g6 3.e3 ♗g7 4.d4 ♘f6 5.d5 0–0 6.♘f3 e6 7.♗e2 exd5 8.cxd5 d6 9.0–0 ♗g4 10.h3 ♗xf3 11.♗xf3 ♘bd7 12.a4 a6 13.g4 c4 14.♗e2 ♖c8 15.g5 ♘e8 16.f4 ♕e7 17.♖a3 ♖c5 18.♗f3 ♖a5 19.♗d2 ♘c5 20.♕e2 ♘b3 21.♘e4 ♘xd2 22.♕xd2 ♕d8 23.♕b4 b5 24.axb5 ♖xb5 25.♕xc4 ♕b6 26.♕c6 ♗xb2 27.♕xb6 ♖xb6 28.♖a2 ♗g7 29.♖c1 h6 30.h4 hxg5 31.hxg5 f6 32.♖c6 ♖xc6 33.dxc6 fxg5 34.♘xg5 ♘c7 35.♖d2 ♖d8 36.♗g4 ♗c3 37.♖d3 ♗a5 38.♔g2 d5 39.e4 d4 40.e5 ♗b6 41.♖b3 ♖b8 42.♖h3 ♗a5 43.♖h6 ♖b2† 44.♔g3 ♗e1† 45.♔f3 d3 46.♖xg6† ♔f8 47.♖d6 d2 48.♔e4 1–0

Vladimir Kramnik (2769) – Viswanathan Anand (2792)

World Championship Mexico City (10) 24.09.2007

1.d4 d5 2.c4 c6 3.♘f3 ♘f6 4.♘c3 e6 5.♗g5 h6 6.♗h4 dxc4 7.e4 g5 8.♗g3 b5 9.♗e2 ♗b7 10.0–0 ♘bd7 11.♘e5 ♗g7 12.♘xd7 ♘xd7 13.♗d6 a6 14.♗h5 ♗f8 15.♗xf8 ♖xf8 16.e5 ♕b6 17.b3 0–0–0 18.bxc4 ♘xe5 19.c5 ♕a5 20.♘e4 ♕b4 21.♘d6† ♖xd6 22.cxd6 ♘d7 23.a4 ♕xd6 24.♗f3 ♘b6 25.axb5 cxb5 26.♗xb7† ♔xb7 27.♕h5 ♘d5 28.♕xh6 ♘f4 29.♔h1 ♕d5 30.f3 ♖d8 31.♕g7 ♖d7 32.♕f8 ♘e2 33.♖fe1 ♘xd4 34.♖ed1 e5 35.♖ac1 ♕d6 36.♕g8 f6 37.♖c8 a5 38.h3 a4 39.♕e8 ♔b6 40.♖b8† ♔a5 41.♖a8† ½–½

Alexander Grischuk (2726) – Vladimir Kramnik (2769)

World Championship Mexico City (11) 25.09.2007

1.e4 e5 2.♘f3 ♘f6 3.d4 ♘xe4 4.♗d3 d5 5.♘xe5 ♘d7 6.♘c3 ♘xc3 7.bxc3 ♘xe5 8.dxe5 ♗e7 9.♕h5 ♗e6 10.♖b1 ♕d7 11.♗g5 c6 12.0–0 ♗xg5 13.♕xg5 ½–½

Vladimir Kramnik (2769) – Peter Leko (2751)

World Championship Mexico City (12) 27.09.2007

1.d4 ♘f6 2.c4 e6 3.g3 d5 4.♗g2 ♗e7 5.♘f3 0–0 6.0–0 dxc4 7.♕c2 a6 8.♕xc4 b5 9.♕c2 ♗b7 10.♗d2 ♗e4 11.♕c1 ♕c8 12.♗g5 ♘bd7 13.♕f4 ♗b7 14.♖c1 ♗d6 15.♕h4 h6 16.♗xf6 ♘xf6 17.♘bd2 ♖e8 18.e4 ♘d7 19.♘b3 a5 20.♘c5 ♗e7 21.♕f4 e5 22.♘xe5 ♘xe5 23.dxe5 ♗g5 24.♕f3 ♗xc1 25.♖xc1 ♖xe5 26.♕c3 f6 27.♕b3† ♔h8 28.♕f7 ♗c6 29.♘d3 ♖e6 30.♘f4 ♖d6 31.♘g6† ♔h7 32.e5 fxe5 33.♗xc6 ♖f6 34.♕d5 ♕f5 35.♗xa8 ♕xf2† 36.♔h1 ♕xb2 37.♕c5 ♔xg6 38.♗e4† ♔h5 39.♖b1 1–0

Boris Gelfand (2733) – Vladimir Kramnik (2769)

World Championship Mexico City (13) 28.09.2007

1.d4 d5 2.c4 c6 3.♘c3 ♘f6 4.e3 e6 5.♘f3 ♘bd7 6.♗d3 dxc4 7.♗xc4 b5 8.♗d3 ♗b7 9.a3 b4 10.♘e4 ♘xe4 11.♗xe4 bxa3 12.0–0 ♘f6 13.♗d3 axb2 14.♗xb2 a5 15.♕a4 ♗b4 16.♗a3 ♘d5 17.e4 ♘b6 18.♕b3 ♕e7 19.♖ab1 ♗xa3 20.♕xb6 ♗b4 21.♘e1 0–0 22.♘c2 ♖fd8 23.♘xb4 axb4 24.♕xb4 ♕xb4 25.♖xb4 ♗a6 26.♗xa6 ½–½

Vladimir Kramnik (2769) – Levon Aronian (2750)

World Championship Mexico City (14) 29.09.2007

1.d4 ♘f6 2.c4 e6 3.♘f3 b6 4.g3 ♗a6 5.b3 ♗b4† 6.♗d2 ♗e7 7.♗g2 c6 8.♗c3 d5 9.♘e5 ♘fd7 10.♘xd7 ♘xd7 11.♘d2 0–0 12.0–0 ♖c8 13.e4 dxe4 14.♘xe4 b5 15.♖e1 bxc4 16.♗f1 ♘b6 17.♖b1 ♘d5 18.♗a1 ♗b4 19.♘c5 ♗xe1 20.♕xe1 cxb3 21.♘xa6 bxa2 22.♖b2 ♘c7 23.♖xa2 ♘xa6 24.♖xa6 ♕d7 25.♕c3 f6 26.♕c5 ♖f7 27.♗c3 ♕b7 28.♕c4 ♕d7 29.♗g2 ♔h8 30.♗xc6 ♕b7 31.♔g2 h6 32.d5 ♕b8 33.dxe6 ♖e7 34.♗b4 ♖ec7 35.e7 1–0

Bonn, Germany 2008: **Viswanathan Anand – Vladimir Kramnik** 6½–4½

Vladimir Kramnik (2772) – Viswanathan Anand (2783)

World Championship Bonn (1) 14.10.2008

1.d4 d5 2.c4 c6 3.♘c3 ♘f6 4.cxd5 cxd5 5.♗f4 ♘c6 6.e3 ♗f5 7.♘f3 e6 8.♕b3 ♗b4 9.♗b5 0–0 10.♗xc6 ♗xc3† 11.♕xc3 ♖c8 12.♘e5 ♘g4 13.♘xg4 ♗xg4 14.♕b4 ♖xc6 15.♕xb7 ♖c8 16.♕xc8 ♖fxc8 17.0–0 a5 18.f3 ♗f5 19.♖fe1 ♗g6 20.b3 f6 21.e4 dxe4 22.fxe4 ♖d8 23.♖ad1 ♖c2 24.e5 fxe5 25.♗xe5 ♖xa2 26.♖a1 ♖xa1 27.♖xa1 ♖d5 28.♖c1 ♖d7 29.♖c5 ♖a7 30.♖c7 ♖xc7 31.♗xc7 ♗c2 32.♗xa5 ♗xb3 ½–½

Viswanathan Anand (2783) – Vladimir Kramnik (2772)

World Championship Bonn (2) 15.10.2008

1.d4 ♘f6 2.c4 e6 3.♘c3 ♗b4 4.f3 d5 5.a3 ♗xc3† 6.bxc3 c5 7.cxd5 ♘xd5 8.dxc5 f5 9.♕c2 ♘d7 10.e4 fxe4 11.fxe4 ♘5f6 12.c6 bxc6 13.♘f3 ♕a5 14.♗d2 ♗a6 15.c4 ♕c5 16.♗d3 ♘g4 17.♗b4 ♕e3† 18.♕e2 0–0–0 19.♕xe3 ♘xe3 20.♔f2 ♘g4† 21.♔g3 ♘df6 22.♗b1 h5 23.h3 h4† 24.♘xh4 ♘e5 25.♘f3 ♘h5† 26.♔f2 ♘xf3 27.♔xf3 e5 28.♖c1 ♘f4 29.♗a2 ♘d3 30.♖c3 ♘f4 31.♗c2 ♘e6 32.♔g3 ♖d4 ½–½

Vladimir Kramnik (2772) – Viswanathan Anand (2783)

World Championship Bonn (3) 17.10.2008

1.d4 d5 2.c4 c6 3.♘f3 ♘f6 4.♘c3 e6 5.e3 ♘bd7 6.♗d3 dxc4 7.♗xc4 b5 8.♗d3 a6 9.e4 c5 10.e5 cxd4 11.♘xb5 axb5 12.exf6 gxf6 13.0–0 ♕b6 14.♕e2 ♗b7 15.♗xb5 ♗d6 16.♖d1 ♖g8 17.g3 ♖g4 18.♗f4 ♗xf4 19.♘xd4 h5 20.♘xe6 fxe6 21.♖xd7 ♔f8 22.♕d3 ♖g7 23.♖xg7 ♔xg7 24.gxf4 ♖d8 25.♕e2 ♔h6 26.♔f1 ♖g8 27.a4 ♗g2† 28.♔e1 ♗h3 29.♖a3 ♖g1† 30.♔d2 ♕d4† 31.♔c2 ♗g4 32.f3 ♗f5† 33.♗d3 ♗h3 34.a5 ♖g2 35.a6 ♖xe2† 36.♗xe2 ♗f5† 37.♔b3 ♕e3† 38.♔a2 ♕xe2 39.a7 ♕c4† 40.♔a1 ♕f1† 41.♔a2 ♗b1† 0–1

Viswanathan Anand (2783) – Vladimir Kramnik (2772)

World Championship Bonn (4) 18.10.2008

1.d4 ♘f6 2.c4 e6 3.♘f3 d5 4.♘c3 ♗e7 5.♗f4 0–0 6.e3 ♘bd7 7.a3 c5 8.cxd5 ♘xd5 9.♘xd5 exd5 10.dxc5 ♘xc5 11.♗e5 ♗f5 12.♗e2 ♗f6 13.♗xf6 ♕xf6 14.♘d4 ♘e6 15.♘xf5 ♕xf5 16.0–0 ♖fd8 17.♗g4 ♕e5 18.♕b3 ♘c5 19.♕b5 b6 20.♖fd1 ♖d6 21.♖d4 a6 22.♕b4 h5 23.♗h3 ♖ad8 24.g3 g5 25.♖ad1 g4 26.♗g2 ♘e6 27.♖4d3 d4 28.exd4 ♖xd4 29.♖xd4 ♖xd4 ½–½

238

Vladimir Kramnik (2772) – Viswanathan Anand (2783)

World Championship Bonn (5) 20.10.2008

1.d4 d5 2.c4 c6 3.♘f3 ♘f6 4.♘c3 e6 5.e3 ♘bd7 6.♗d3 dxc4 7.♗xc4 b5 8.♗d3 a6 9.e4 c5 10.e5 cxd4 11.♘xb5 axb5 12.exf6 gxf6 13.0–0 ♕b6 14.♕e2 ♗b7 15.♗xb5 ♖g8 16.♗f4 ♗d6 17.♗g3 f5 18.♖fc1 f4 19.♗h4 ♗e7 20.a4 ♗xh4 21.♘xh4 ♔e7 22.♖a3 ♖ac8 23.♖xc8 ♖xc8 24.♖a1 ♕c5 25.♕g4 ♕e5 26.♘f3 ♕f6 27.♖e1 ♖c5 28.b4 ♖c3 29.♘xd4 ♕xd4 30.♖d1 ♘f6 31.♖xd4 ♘xg4 32.♖d7† ♔f6 33.♖xb7 ♖c1† 34.♗f1 ♘e3 35.fxe3 fxe3 0–1

Viswanathan Anand (2783) – Vladimir Kramnik (2772)

World Championship Bonn (6) 21.10.2008

1.d4 ♘f6 2.c4 e6 3.♘c3 ♗b4 4.♕c2 d5 5.cxd5 ♕xd5 6.♘f3 ♕f5 7.♕b3 ♘c6 8.♗d2 0–0 9.h3 b6 10.g4 ♕a5 11.♖c1 ♗b7 12.a3 ♗xc3 13.♗xc3 ♕d5 14.♕xd5 ♘xd5 15.♗d2 ♘f6 16.♖g1 ♖ac8 17.♗g2 ♘e7 18.♗b4 c5 19.dxc5 ♖fd8 20.♘e5 ♗xg2 21.♖xg2 bxc5 22.♖xc5 ♘e4 23.♖xc8 ♖xc8 24.♘d3 ♘d5 25.♗d2 ♖c2 26.♗c1 f5 27.♔d1 ♖c8 28.f3 ♘d6 29.♔e1 a5 30.e3 e5 31.gxf5 e4 32.fxe4 ♘xe4 33.♗d2 a4 34.♘f2 ♘d6 35.♖g4 ♘c4 36.e4 ♘f6 37.♖g3 ♘xb2 38.e5 ♘d5 39.f6 ♔f7 40.♘e4 ♘c4 41.fxg7 ♔g8 42.♖d3 ♘db6 43.♗h6 ♘xe5 44.♘f6† ♔f7 45.♖c3 ♖xc3 46.g8=♕† ♔xf6 47.♕g7† 1–0

Viswanathan Anand (2783) – Vladimir Kramnik (2772)

World Championship Bonn (7) 23.10.2008

1.d4 d5 2.c4 c6 3.♘f3 ♘f6 4.♘c3 dxc4 5.a4 ♗f5 6.e3 e6 7.♗xc4 ♗b4 8.0–0 ♘bd7 9.♕e2 ♗g6 10.e4 0–0 11.♗d3 ♗h5 12.e5 ♘d5 13.♘xd5 cxd5 14.♕e3 ♖e8 15.♘e1 ♗g6 16.♗xg6 hxg6 17.♘d3 ♕b6 18.♘xb4 ♕xb4 19.b3 ♖ac8 20.♗a3 ♕c3 21.♖ac1 ♕xe3 22.fxe3 f6 23.♗d6 g5 24.h3 ♔f7 25.♔f2 ♔g6 26.♗e2 fxe5 27.dxe5 b6 28.b4 ♖c4 29.♖xc4 dxc4 30.♖c1 ♖c8 31.g4 a5 32.b5 c3 33.♖c2 ♔f7 34.♔d3 ♘c5† 35.♗xc5 ♖xc5 36.♖xc3 ♖xc3† 37.♔xc3 ½–½

Vladimir Kramnik (2772) – Viswanathan Anand (2783)

World Championship Bonn (8) 24.10.2008

1.d4 ♘f6 2.c4 e6 3.♘f3 d5 4.♘c3 dxc4 5.e4 ♗b4 6.♗g5 c5 7.♗xc4 cxd4 8.♘xd4 ♕a5 9.♗b5† ♗d7 10.♗xf6 ♗xb5 11.♘dxb5 gxf6 12.0–0 ♘c6 13.a3 ♗xc3 14.♘xc3 ♖g8 15.f4 ♖d8 16.♕e1 ♕b6† 17.♖f2 ♖d3 18.♕e2 ♕d4 19.♖e1 a6 20.♔h1 ♔f8

21.♖ef1 ♖g6 22.g3 ♔g7 23.♖d1 ♖xd1† 24.♘xd1 ♔h8 25.♘c3 ♖g8 26.♔g2 ♖d8
27.♕h5 ♔g7 28.♕g4† ♔h8 29.♕h5 ♔g7 30.♕g4† ♔h8 31.♕h4 ♔g7 32.e5 f5
33.♕f6† ♔g8 34.♕g5† ♔h8 35.♕f6† ♔g8 36.♖e2 ♕c4 37.♕g5† ♔h8 38.♕f6†
♔g8 39.♕g5† ♔h8 ½–½

Viswanathan Anand (2783) – Vladimir Kramnik (2772)

World Championship Bonn (9) 26.10.2008

1.d4 d5 2.c4 e6 3.♘f3 ♘f6 4.♘c3 c6 5.♗g5 h6 6.♗h4 dxc4 7.e4 g5 8.♗g3 b5 9.♗e2
♗b7 10.♕c2 ♘bd7 11.♖d1 ♗b4 12.♘e5 ♕e7 13.0–0 ♘xe5 14.♗xe5 0–0 15.♗xf6
♕xf6 16.f4 ♕g7 17.e5 c5 18.♘xb5 cxd4 19.♕xc4 a5 20.♔h1 ♖ac8 21.♕xd4 gxf4
22.♗f3 ♗a6 23.a4 ♖c5 24.♕xf4 ♖xe5 25.b3 ♗xb5 26.axb5 ♖xb5 27.♗e4 ♗c3
28.♗c2 ♗e5 29.♕f2 ♗b8 30.♕f3 ♖c5 31.♗d3 ♖c3 32.g3 ♔h8 33.♕b7 f5 34.♕b6
♕e5 35.♕b7 ♕c7 36.♕xc7 ♗xc7 37.♗c4 ♖e8 38.♖d7 a4 39.♖xc7 axb3 40.♖f2 ♖b8
41.♖b2 h5 42.♔g2 h4 43.♖c6 hxg3 44.hxg3 ♖g8 45.♖xe6 ♖xc4 ½–½

Vladimir Kramnik (2772) – Viswanathan Anand (2783)

World Championship Bonn (10) 27.10.2008

1.d4 ♘f6 2.c4 e6 3.♘c3 ♗b4 4.♘f3 c5 5.g3 cxd4 6.♘xd4 0–0 7.♗g2 d5 8.cxd5
♘xd5 9.♕b3 ♕a5 10.♗d2 ♘c6 11.♘xc6 bxc6 12.0–0 ♗xc3 13.bxc3 ♗a6 14.♖fd1
♕c5 15.e4 ♗c4 16.♕a4 ♘b6 17.♕b4 ♕h5 18.♖e1 c5 19.♕a5 ♖fc8 20.♗e3 ♗e2
21.♗f4 e5 22.♗e3 ♗g4 23.♕a6 f6 24.a4 ♕f7 25.♗f1 ♗e6 26.♖ab1 c4 27.a5 ♘a4
28.♖b7 ♕e8 29.♕d6 1–0

Viswanathan Anand (2783) – Vladimir Kramnik (2772)

World Championship Bonn (11) 29.10.2008

1.e4 c5 2.♘f3 d6 3.d4 cxd4 4.♘xd4 ♘f6 5.♘c3 a6 6.♗g5 e6 7.f4 ♕c7 8.♗xf6
gxf6 9.f5 ♕c5 10.♕d3 ♘c6 11.♘b3 ♕e5 12.0–0–0 exf5 13.♕e3 ♗g7 14.♖d5 ♕e7
15.♕g3 ♖g8 16.♕f4 fxe4 17.♘xe4 f5 18.♘xd6† ♔f8 19.♘xc8 ♖xc8 20.♔b1 ♕e1†
21.♘c1 ♘e7 22.♕d2 ♕xd2 23.♖xd2 ♗h6 24.♖f2 ♗e3 ½–½

At the website www.chessgames.com as this book went to press, there were a total of
3004 games of the 14th World Chess Champion, which are to a large extent accessible
to the public and can be played through there. Between 1984 and the 5th of October
2018 Vladimir Kramnik played 1666 tournament games. Of those he won 546, lost
166 and drew 954, for a score 61.4%.

Bibliography

Bareev, Evgeny & Levitov, Ilya: *From London To Elista*, New In Chess 2007

Breutigam, Martin: *64 Monate auf 64 Feldern*, Chessgate 2003

Breutigam, Martin: *World Chess Championship 2004*, Chessgate 2004

Breutigam, Martin: *Genies in Schwarzweiß – Die world champion im Porträt*, Verlag Die Werkstatt 2016

Damsky, Iakov: *Kramnik – My Life and Games*, Everyman Chess 2000

Davies, Nigel & Martin, Andrew: *Kasparov – Kramnik*, Batsford 2000

Hurst, Sarah: *The Curse Of Kirsan*, Russell Enterprises 2002

Keene, Raymond & Morris, Don: *The Brain Games World Chess Championship*, Everyman Chess 2000

Koblenz, Alexander: *Schach lebenslänglich*, Joachim Beyer Verlag 1997

Kohlmeyer, Dagobert & Manfred van Fondern: *Bobby Fischer: Ein Schachgenie kehrt zurück*, Joachim Beyer Verlag 1992

Krogius, Nikolai: *Psychologie im Schach*, Ullstein 1991

Linder, Isaak & Vladimir: *Das Schachgenie Alekhine*, Sportverlag Berlin 1992

Pfleger, Helmut & Behr, André: *Schach-WCh 1995*, Olms 1995

Pfleger, Helmut & Treppner, Gerd: *Brett vorm Kopf*, C.H. Beck 1994

Schonberg, Harold: *Die Großmeister des Schach*, Moewig Sachbuch 1972

Schulz, André: *Das Große Buch der Schachweltmeisterschaften*, New In Chess 2015

Suetin, Aleksei: *Das Schachgenie Botvinnik*, Sportverlag Berlin 1990

Ten Geuzendam, Dirk Jan: *The Day Kasparov Quit*, New In Chess 2005

Zweig, Stefan: *Schachnovelle*, Fischer 2000

Zweig, Stefan: *Chess Story*, English translation by Nicholas Stephens, Read More Translations 2016. More commonly known in English as *The Royal Game*.

Periodicals
64 (Moscow, Russia)
Der Spiegel (Hamburg)
British Chess Magazine (Wokingham, UK)
Karl – das kulturelle Schachmagazin (Frankfurt)
New In Chess (Alkmaar, Netherlands)
Schach (Berlin)
Schach-Magazin 64 (Bremen)

Internet sources
http://www.2700chess.com/
http://de.chessbase.com/
http://en.chessbase.com/
http://www.chessgames.com/

http://www.chesshistory.com/winter/
http://www.chessvibes.com/
http://www.claracavour.com/
http://www.e3e5.com/
http://www.gambitchess.com/
http://www.Schachwelt.de/
http://www.spiegel.de/
http://theweekinchess.com/
https://www.wikipedia.de/
https://www.wikipedia.org/
https://de.wikibooks.org/wiki/Schach:_Notation

Digital source
ChessBase Mega Database 2015

Glossary

All-play-all
Tournament with more than two players in which each player meets all of the others.

Analysis
A game which has finished is evaluated afterwards. Inaccuracies, mistakes and alternative moves are pointed out.

Appeals committee
This usually consists of three officials who decide on disputes concerning the games, according to the general laws of chess and any specific conditions agreed.

Chess clock
The chess clock measures the thinking time used by both players and consists of two linked clocks. Pressing on a button or lever starts one clock and stops the other. Time limits involving increments (extra seconds added for each move played) can be used nowadays with digital clocks.

Compensation
Specific advantages, for example space, active play or a lead in development, which make up for a material disadvantage.

Demonstration board
A large chess board on which the game is shown to the spectators during chess tournaments or matches.

Draw
The game ends in a tie, earning a half point for each player. This most frequently happens by agreement between the players. But a draw can also come about as a result of stalemate or the lack of enough pieces to deliver mate.

Elo rating
The rating of a player, which represents an objective evaluation of his or her playing strength – the higher the Elo, the stronger the player. It is based on a formula developed by the American mathematician Arpad Elo. The world ranking list is also established according to Elo ratings. As a rough guide:
Beginners are usually around 800 Elo
Hobby players around 1200 Elo
Club players around 1600 Elo
Tournament players around 2200 Elo
Grandmasters 2500 Elo and above
Super-grandmasters (top professionals) 2750 Elo and above.

Endgame
The final phase of a game, with few pieces remaining; not always but often after the exchange of queens.

FIDE

The world chess federation – pronounced 'fee-day'. It was founded as the "Fédération Internationale des Échecs" (FIDE) on 20th July 1924 in Paris. Since 1927 FIDE has organized the world team championship "Chess Olympiad", from 1948 till 1993 and then since 2006 the federation has staged the classical world chess championship continuing the line starting with the first world chess champion, Wilhelm Steinitz.

Grandmaster title

The title of International Grandmaster (IGM) is awarded for life according to specific rules of FIDE. Other titles are International Master (IM) and FIDE Master (FM). Women have their own titles: WGM and WIM.

KO tournament

Tournament in Knockout mode – a player who loses a game or a round is eliminated. The winner qualifies for the next round.

Livestream

Audio or video broadcast over the internet of a chess tournament or a match.

Manager

Person who looks after a professional chess player in all affairs away from the chess board. For example, tasks in the areas of marketing, communication, organisation of events, looking after the team and dealing with contracts.

Match

Two players meet each other over a number of games. The number of games and all other conditions are agreed beforehand. This form of encounter is the classical format for world chess championships.

Mate

The definitive end of a chess game. A king is under attack and cannot escape from the attack/check; no other piece is able to eliminate the attacker.

Middlegame

The phase of the game after the opening. The majority of the pieces are still taking part in the struggle.

Notation

The writing down of the moves of a game of chess.

Open

A chess tournament in which in principle any player may take part. Usually, however, this is limited by specific rating levels.

Opening

The start of a game during which the individual pieces are developed from their starting squares. The continuing study of opening theory, i.e. the analytical examination of main and sub-variations in the various systems, is part of the elementary armoury of every professional player.

Rest day

A day without a game. This is for the players to rest and relax during long tournaments or matches.

Second

For the most part a strong player who supports the player who is taking part in a tournament or a match with preparatory work and analyses.

Simultaneous

In a simultaneous a very strong player, usually a grandmaster, plays against several opponents at the same time.

Stalemate

One player cannot move any piece without putting his king in check, but his king is not currently in check. A stalemate means the game ends in a draw.

Strategy

The evaluation of a specific position together with the drawing up of a long-term plan. Its implementation is if possible concealed, so that the opponent only recognizes the intent when it is too late.

Tactics

Concrete, short-term combinatory elements, variations with exchanges and series of moves stand in the foreground. In contrast to the tactical player, the positional player seeks to apply long-term strategies.

Thinking time

The time available to a player to make a specific number of moves or to play the whole game. The usual classical thinking time in tournaments and world championship matches is for each player to have two hours for 40 moves, one hour for the next 20 moves and 30 minutes for the rest of the game. So the whole game could last seven hours.

For rapid chess as a rule between 15 and 30 minutes are allowed to each player for the whole game; for blitz chess only five minutes or even less. Nowadays an increment is frequently used – for every move made, a digital clock automatically adds extra seconds to the player's thinking time.

Tiebreak

A ranking tool which is used when players have the same number of points.

Tiebreak match

If in matches with classical time controls, no winner emerges, then the victor is decided by means of a tiebreak match. Before the match started, a number of rapid chess games as a tiebreak will already have been specified.

Time trouble

Time trouble arises when a player has used up almost all his thinking time and must play the remaining moves quickly. If he does not manage to do so in time, he loses by overstepping the time control.

Trainer

A teacher of chess pupils, but also of professional players.

World Championship cycle

The time after a world championship match during which qualification tournaments decide who will be the challenger of the world champion; the time includes the next world championship match.

World Championship

Deciding the best chess player in the world in the tradition founded by Steinitz and Zukertort in 1886. The classic way of deciding the world championship is by a match.

Zugzwang

The situation in which any move a player makes would decisively worsen his position and in which a player would prefer to give up the right to move. Especially in certain endgame structures, zugzwang motifs play a major part.

Diagram & Notation

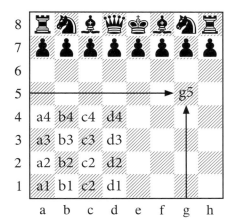

8	♜	♞	♝	♛	♚	♝	♞	♜
7	♟	♟	♟	♟	♟	♟	♟	♟
6								
5					→		g5	
4	a4	b4	c4	d4				
3	a3	b3	c3	d3				
2	a2	b2	c2	d2				
1	a1	b1	c2	d1				
	a	b	c	d	e	f	g	h

Chess Symbols

Every piece is represented by a figurine. The exception is the pawn which does not have its own symbol. Thus 1.e4 is pawn to the e4-square.

♘	knight		!	a strong move
♗	bishop		!!	an excellent move
♖	rook		?	a weak move
♕	queen		??	a blunder
♔	king		!?	an interesting move
0–0	castles kingside		?!	a dubious move
0–0–0	castles queenside		N	a novelty (a move which had not been played before)
±	White is slightly better		†	check
∓	Black is slightly better		#	checkmate
±	White is clearly better		1–0	Black resigns
∓	Black is clearly better		0–1	White resigns
+−	White has a decisive advantage		½–½	draw agreed
−+	Black has a decisive advantage			
=	the position is equal			
∞	with compensation			
⇄	with counterplay			
∞	the position is unclear			
↑	with the initiative			
→	with an attack			

247

Acknowledgements

Although during my professional career I worked as a journalist in the most varied of functions, writing a book is a very special challenge. The former German finance minister Peer Steinbrück once explained to me: "Completing a book is for me like the birth of a child. Of course, from my point of view as a man!" I did not understand him so well at first, but after completing the manuscript it became clear to me what he meant. It took me months to let go of it.

The cause for the next story is less noble. After two heart attacks at the end of 2015 and the subsequent concomitant emotional stress, my children Sarah and Sebastian kept on encouraging me to begin this project. That was a very good thing because writing was very helpful to me in many respects during difficult moments.

When I decided to compose a biographical account of the 14th World Chess Champion, it was for two important reasons: for many years a recent biography of Kramnik has been missing on the book market and at the same time the events reflect the most intense period of time in my own professional life.

Since I was personally involved in most of the important events, I at first tended to describe what I had experienced in great detail. The background of a biographical narrative combined with a lot of internal processes would make it easy to write a book three times as long. Relatively quickly, however, I noted that such attention to detail would make unreasonable demands on an outsider.

So I made an effort on one hand to portray the history of Vladimir Kramnik as briefly as possible, but on the other to do justice to the most important historical events and their interrelations. In setting priorities and wandering through the jungle of events, my wife Birgit took me by the hand and gave me valuable advice.

Of course, very special thanks are due to the main person in this story: Vladimir Kramnik! In this I would like first and foremost to mention his trust in me, because I would not even have begun the project without his agreement. I remember his words exactly: "When you write the biography, always criticize me when you think it appropriate. I have no problem with that." After that Vladimir at no point became involved in the work on the manuscript. He left me totally free to describe and judge what happened from my point of view. Over and above that he has annotated his most important games for this book and contributed to its success in other ways too, for example by making available private photos.

I am also very thankful to my editor Julia Vogt from Die Werkstatt, the biggest publisher of sports books in Germany. Months before, she had encouraged me in a first conversation to send the manuscript to that publisher. But Birgit Hildebrandt and Peter Köhler too, who checked my text for mistakes in spelling and grammar and made the necessary corrections, also deserve my thanks. Volker Kurreck and Reinhard Friemel supported me in the technical implementation. Patience and good advice were provided for me by my friends Udo Bullerdieck, Dr Michael Negele, Uwe Wolf and Ulrich Puderbach.

I am also grateful to the Glasgow-based publisher Quality Chess. Grandmasters Jacob Aagaard and John Shaw did an outstanding job on the English edition and rounded the text off by adding chess digrams where appropriate.

I had enriching conversations with the chess journalists Martin Breutigam and André Schulz. Their colleagues Dagobert Kohlmeyer and Dirk Poldauf provided important background information about the events in Berlin in the 1990s. Kohlmeyer, himself the author of several books, made some photos available to me at no cost. Thanks, Dago! The same thanks are also due to the Dutch firm DGT (www. digitalgametechnology. com) for the cover photo used in the German edition and Dr Torsten Behl, who also made his photos freely available to me. Vladimir Barsky, one of the most renowned Russian chess journalists, had some years previously done an interview with Kramnik concerning his predecessors on the chess throne. The remarks made by Vladimir in that interview were helpful when drawing up brief portraits of former world champions.

The grandmasters who cooperated in the last chapter in each case made their contribution out of respect for Vladimir Kramnik. I owe them my thanks and wish all who have cooperated much success in their future careers in chess. The present book was my first production of this sort and developed over several months. Peer Steinbrück, a great lover of chess and author of some non-fiction books, gave me important tips. I thank him and I am thankful to myself for having regularly made diary notes in my appointment books between 1999 and 2010. Additionally there are all the authors whose publications were of significant help to me. They are listed in the bibliography.

In the past 25 years I have met many famous chess players. As well as Vladimir Kramnik, the world champions Mikhail Botvinnik, Vassily Smyslov, Boris Spassky, Bobby Fischer, Anatoly Karpov, Garry Kasparov, Viswanathan Anand and the present title holder Magnus Carlsen. But it is not only the world champions, but also the meetings with numerous charismatic personalities from the world of chess which have greatly enriched my life.

It is impossible to mention individually all the chess player, reporters, organizers, chess lovers and sponsors whom Vladimir Kramnik and I have met. So as not to forget anybody, I will not even try to do so. My most heartfelt thanks are due to all of you and so are those of Vladimir Kramnik.

The Author

Carsten Hensel, born 1958, was active as a sports manager, events organizer, freelance journalist and press officer. Born in Dortmund, he was until 2009 manager of the 14th World Chess Champion Vladimir Kramnik and fulfilled the same function for the top Hungarian grandmaster Peter Leko. Hensel was a co-founder of the agency Universal Event Promotion, which in 2008 organized a world chess championship in Germany after a gap of 74 years.

Photo Credits

Photos on pages 151 and 192 by David Llada
Photos on cover and pages 164, 183 and 188 by Dr Torsten Behl
Photos on pages 175, 176, 177, 178, 179 and 189 from Vladimir Kramnik
Photos on pages 180, 181 and 183 by Dagobert Kohlmeyer
Photos on pages 181, 182, 184, 186, 187 and 188 from Carsten Hensel
Photos on page 184 and 185 by Organization Elista

Photos of the World Champions on pages 190-191:
Steinitz https://upload.wikimedia.org/wikipedia/commons/b/b2/Wilhelm_Steinitz2.jpg
Lasker https://en.wikipedia.org/wiki/Emanuel_Lasker#/media/File:Bundesarchiv_Bild_102-00457,_Emanuel_Lasker.jpg
Capablanca https://www.biography.com/people/jos%C3%A9-ra%C3%BAl-capablanca-40201
Alexander Aljechin Stockholms digitala stadsmuseum, https://arkivkopia.se/sak/digstad-SSMJDM000022S-0
Euwe http://www.gahetna.nl/en/collectie/afbeeldingen/fotocollectie/zoeken/start/201/weergave/detail/tstart/0/q/zoekterm/Max%20Euwe
Fotograaf Onbekend / Anefo
Botvinnik Image from www.diagonale.eybens.free.fr
Smyslov http://www.gahetna.nl/en/collectie/afbeeldingen/fotocollectie/zoeken/weergave/detail/start/1/tstart/0/q/zoekterm/Smyslow
Photographer Behrens, Herbert / Anefo
Tal http://www.gahetna.nl/en/collectie/afbeeldingen/fotocollectie/zoeken/weergave/detail/start/0/tstart/0/q/zoekterm/Mikhail%20Tal
Petrosian http://www.gahetna.nl/en/collectie/afbeeldingen/fotocollectie/zoeken/start/17/weergave/detail/tstart/0/q/zoekterm/petrosian%20tigran
Photographer Croes, Rob C. / Anefo
Spassky http://www.gahetna.nl/en/collectie/afbeeldingen/fotocollectie/zoeken/weergave/detail/start/3/tstart/0/q/zoekterm/Spasski
Photographer Antonisse, Marcel / Anefo
Fischer http://www.gahetna.nl/en/collectie/afbeeldingen/fotocollectie/zoeken/start/16/weergave/detail/tstart/0/q/zoekterm/fischer
Photographer Punt, […] / Anefo
Karpov, Kasparov, Anand and Carlsen Harald Fietz photos

Name Index